Good Housekeeping

Favourite
Cakes, Bakes & Cupcakes

250 Tried, tested, trusted recipes ★ Delicious results

Good Housekeeping

Favourite
Cakes, Bakes
& Cupcakes

250 Tried, tested, trusted recipes ★ Delicious results

COLLINS & BROWN

First published in the United Kingdom in 2010 by
Collins & Brown
10 Southcombe Street
London
W14 0RA

An imprint of Anova Books Company Ltd

The Good Housekeeping website is
www.allboutyou.com/goodhousekeeping

10 9 8 7 6 5 4 3 2 1

ISBN 978-1-84340-587-0

A catalogue record for this book is available from
the British Library.

Repro by Dot Gradations UK Ltd
Printed and bound by Times Offset Malaysia

This book can be ordered direct from the publisher at
www.anovabooks.com

Recipes in this book are taken from the Good Housekeeping recipe
library and may have been reproduced in previous publications.

Picture Credits:
Neil Barclay (page 50); Martin Brigdale (pages 40, 41, 53, 71, 81,
153, 155, 157, 192, 195, 221, 222 and 267); Nicki Dowey (pages
10, 11, 12, 13, 18, 21, 25, 26, 27, 29, 30, 31, 32, 34, 35, 36, 37,
38, 42, 43, 46, 47, 49, 51, 52, 54, 55, 56, 57, 58, 59, 61, 62, 64,
65, 66, 67, 68, 69, 70, 72, 73, 75, 76, 77, 79, 80, 82, 83, 84, 88,
89, 90, 91, 93, 94, 112, 134, 135, 137, 138, 139, 140, 141, 142,
143, 145, 146, 154, 156, 158, 164, 165, 166, 169, 172, 174,
175, 176, 177, 178, 179, 181, 182, 183, 184, 186, 187, 188,
189, 193, 194, 201, 203, 205, 206, 209, 211, 214, 223, 225,
226, 227, 232, 233, 237, 250, 252, 258, 262, 263 and 271); Will
Heap (page 33); Craig Robertson (pages 147, 161, 215, 236, 238,
240, 241, 244, 245, 246, 247, 248, 249, 251, 254, 255, 256,
259, 260, 261, 265, 268, 269, 270 and 272); Lucinda Symons
(pages 14, 15, 16, 17, 19, 22, 24, 48, 60, 74, 78, 85, 92, 95, 96,
97, 98, 99, 100, 101, 102, 104, 105, 106, 107, 109, 110, 111,
113, 114, 115, 116, 117, 118, 119, 120, 121, 122, 123, 124,
125, 126, 127, 128, 129, 130, 131, 144, 148, 149, 159, 160,
162, 167, 168, 197, 198, 199, 200, 207, 212, 213, 216, 217,
229, 230, 242, 243, 253, 257, 264 and 273)
Home Economists: Joanna Farrow, Emma Jane Frost,
Teresa Goldfinch, Alice Hart, Lucy McKelvie, Kim Morphew,
Bridget Sargeson and Mari Mererid Williams
Stylists: Wei Tang, Helen Trent and Fanny Ward

NOTES

★ Both metric and imperial measures are given for the
recipes. Follow either set of measures, not a mixture of
both, as they are not interchangeable.

★ All spoon measures are level.
1 tsp = 5ml spoon; 1 tbsp = 15ml spoon.

★ Ovens and grills must be preheated to the specified
temperature.

★ Medium eggs should be used except where otherwise
specified.

DIETARY GUIDELINES

★ Note that certain recipes contain raw or lightly cooked
eggs. The young, elderly, pregnant women and anyone
with immune-deficiency disease should avoid these
because of the slight risk of salmonella.

★ Note that some recipes contain alcohol. Check the
ingredients list before serving to children.

Contents

Foreword

What's your all-time favourite recipe? I have a sweet tooth, much to my dentist's eternal disappointment, so mine is most certainly sweet. But whether it would be the luxurious sweetness of home-made vanilla ice cream, the buttery sweetness of fresh croissants, or the almost tooth-aching sweetness of a treacle tart, it's hard to know – but what I do know is that it would be fun to make.

There's something deeply satisfying about baking – and it's not just licking the spoon, the wonderful aromas, or that first eagerly anticipated mouthful (although these certainly count!). It helps to understand that it's the science behind the baking that makes a recipe work. So, if a recipe hasn't turned out as you hoped, ask yourself – did I follow the recipe correctly? Are my ingredients at the right temperature? Is my tin size correct?

Baking is a precise art, and one where a small change in an ingredient can have quite an impact on the finished result. It's hard to 'wing it' when baking, as cakes might not rise, pastry can be tricky to work with, and cupcakes can stale within the hour. But fear not, baking is very simple if you follow a good recipe closely – and Good Housekeeping recipes are certainly good and have all been triple-tested, so you are sure to succeed!

Wooden spoons at the ready…

Enjoy!

Meike.

Meike Beck
Chief Home Economist

Everyday Cakes and Sponges

30-minute Fruit Cake

Preparation Time 15 minutes • **Cooking Time** 30 minutes, plus cooling • **Cuts into 18 slices** • **Per Slice** 180 calories, 9g fat (of which 5g saturates), 24g carbohydrate, 0.2g salt • **Easy**

125g (4oz) unsalted butter, softened
125g (4oz) light muscovado sugar
grated zest of 1 lemon
2 medium eggs
a few drops of vanilla extract
150g (5oz) self-raising flour, sifted
1 tsp baking powder
a little lemon juice, as needed
50g (2oz) glacé cherries, chopped
175g (6oz) mixed dried fruit
25g (1oz) desiccated coconut
25g (1oz) demerara sugar
50g (2oz) flaked almonds

1 Preheat the oven to 190°C (170°C fan oven) mark 5. Grease a 28 x 18cm (11 x 7in) shallow baking tin and baseline with baking parchment.

2 Beat the butter, muscovado sugar, lemon zest, eggs, vanilla extract, flour and baking powder together. Add a little lemon juice, if necessary, to form a soft, dropping consistency. Stir in the cherries, dried fruit and coconut.

3 Spoon the mixture into the prepared tin, level the surface and sprinkle with demerara sugar and almonds. Bake for 30 minutes or until golden.

4 Cool in the tin for a few minutes, then turn out on to a wire rack to cool completely.

★ TO STORE
Store in an airtight container. It will keep for up to one week.

Rich Fruit Cake

Preparation Time 30 minutes • **Cooking Time** 2½ hours, plus cooling • **Cuts into 16 slices** • **Per Slice** 277 calories, 11g fat (of which 6g saturates), 38g carbohydrate, 0.2g salt • **Easy**

1kg (2¼lb) mixed dried fruit
100g (3½oz) ready-to-eat dried prunes, roughly chopped
50g (2oz) ready-to-eat dried figs, roughly chopped
100g (3½oz) dried cranberries
2 balls preserved stem ginger in syrup, grated and syrup reserved
grated zest and juice of 1 orange
175ml (6fl oz) brandy
2 splashes Angostura bitters
175g (6oz) unsalted butter, cubed, plus extra to grease
175g (6oz) dark muscovado sugar
200g (7oz) self-raising flour
½ tsp ground cinnamon
½ tsp freshly grated nutmeg
½ tsp ground cloves
4 medium eggs, beaten

1 Preheat the oven to 150°C (130°C fan oven) mark 2. Grease a 20.5cm (8in) round, deep cake tin and line the base and sides with greaseproof paper.

2 Put all the dried fruit into a very large pan and add the ginger, 1 tbsp reserved ginger syrup, the orange zest and juice, brandy and Angostura bitters. Bring to the boil, then simmer for 5 minutes. Add the butter and sugar and heat gently to melt. Stir occasionally until the sugar dissolves. Take the pan off the heat and leave to cool for a couple of minutes.

3 Add the flour, spices and beaten eggs and mix well. Pour the mixture into the prepared tin and level the surface. Wrap the outside of the tin in brown paper and secure with string to protect the cake during cooking. Bake for 2–2½ hours until the cake is firm to the touch and a skewer inserted into the centre comes out clean.

4 Leave to cool in the tin for 2–3 hours, then remove from the tin, leaving the greaseproof paper on, and transfer to a wire rack to cool completely. Wrap the cake in a layer of clingfilm, then in foil. Store in an airtight container. It will keep for up to three months.

★ COOK'S TIP
If you like, after the cake has matured for two weeks, prick it all over with a metal skewer and sprinkle with 1 tbsp brandy. Leave to soak in, then rewrap and store as before.

Fruity Teacake

Preparation Time 20 minutes, plus soaking • **Cooking Time** 1 hour, plus cooling • **Cuts into 12 slices** •
Per Slice 185 calories, 1g fat (of which trace saturates), 42g carbohydrate, 0.1g salt • **Gluten Free** • **Dairy Free** • **Easy**

150ml (¼ pint) hot black tea, made
   with 2 Earl Grey tea bags
200g (7oz) sultanas
75g (3oz) ready-to-eat dried figs,
   roughly chopped
75g (3oz) ready-to-eat dried prunes,
   roughly chopped
a little vegetable oil
125g (4oz) dark muscovado sugar
2 medium eggs, beaten
225g (8oz) gluten-free flour
2 tsp wheat-free baking powder
2 tsp ground mixed spice

1 Pour the tea into a bowl and add all the dried fruit. Leave to soak for 30 minutes.

2 Preheat the oven to 190°C (170°C fan oven) mark 5. Oil a 900g (2lb) loaf tin and baseline with greaseproof paper.

3 Beat the sugar and eggs together until pale and slightly thickened. Add the flour, baking powder, mixed spice and soaked dried fruit and tea, then mix together well. Spoon the mixture into the prepared tin and level the surface.

4 Bake on the middle shelf of the oven for 45 minutes–1 hour. Leave to cool in the tin.

5 Serve sliced, with a little butter if you like.

★ TO STORE
Wrap the cake in clingfilm and store in an airtight container. It will keep for up to five days.

Fresh Cherry Cake

Preparation Time 10 minutes • **Cooking Time** 1 hour 10 minutes, plus cooling • **Cuts into 8 slices** • **Per Slice** 367 calories, 20g fat (of which 12g saturates), 44g carbohydrate, 0.8g salt • **Easy**

175g (6oz) unsalted butter, softened, plus extra to grease
175g (6oz) plain flour
2 tsp baking powder
a pinch of salt
175g (6oz) caster sugar, plus extra to dust
½ tsp vanilla extract
grated zest of 1 lemon
3 medium eggs, beaten
milk
225g (8oz) small fresh cherries, stoned

1 Preheat the oven to 190°C (170°C fan oven) mark 5. Grease a 900g (2lb) loaf tin and baseline with baking parchment.

2 Sift the flour with the baking powder and salt. In a separate bowl, cream the butter and sugar together until pale and fluffy. Gradually beat in the vanilla extract, lemon zest and eggs. Gently fold in the flour. If the mixture seems a little stiff, add a small amount of milk. Fold in the cherries.

3 Spoon the mixture into the prepared tin and level the surface. Bake for about 1 hour 10 minutes or until risen, well browned and slightly shrunk away from the sides of the tin. (After about 45 minutes, cover lightly with foil, if necessary, to prevent over-browning.)

4 Leave to cool in the tin for about 10 minutes, then turn out on to a wire rack to cool completely. Dust with caster sugar and cut into slices to serve.

 COOK'S TIP
The weight of the fruit may make it sink towards the bottom of the cake. Don't worry if this happens – it will still taste good.

 TO STORE
Store, wrapped, in the fridge. It will keep for up to two days.

Almond and Apricot Cake

Preparation Time 15 minutes, plus cooling • **Cooking Time** 15 minutes, plus cooling • **Cuts into 12 slices** •
Per Slice 325 calories, 21g fat (of which 11g saturates), 30g carbohydrate, 0.3g salt • **Easy**

175g (6oz) unsalted butter,
    softened, plus extra to grease
125g (4oz) caster sugar
4 medium eggs
175g (6oz) self-raising flour
75g (3oz) ground almonds
finely grated zest and juice of
    1 lemon

FOR THE ICING AND FILLING
250g tub mascarpone cheese
40g (1½oz) icing sugar, plus extra
    to dust
4 tbsp apricot compote

1 Preheat the oven to 200°C (180°C fan oven) mark 6. Grease two 18cm (7in) round sandwich tins and line with greaseproof paper.

2 Beat the butter and caster sugar together until fluffy. Then beat in the eggs, one at a time, until combined. Using a metal spoon, gently fold in the flour, ground almonds, lemon zest and juice and stir until smooth.

3 Divide the mixture between the tins, level the surface and bake for 15 minutes or until golden and a skewer inserted into the centre comes out clean. Cool in the tins for 5 minutes, then turn out on to a wire rack to cool completely.

4 For the icing, beat the mascarpone and icing sugar together in a bowl. Spread over one of the cakes. Spoon the apricot compote evenly over the cheese mixture and put the other cake on top. Dust with icing sugar to serve.

 TO STORE
Store the cake in an airtight container in a cool place. It will keep for up to two days.

★ FREEZING TIP
*To **freeze** Complete the recipe to the end of step 3. Wrap each cake in greaseproof paper and clingfilm. Freeze for up to one month.*
*To **use** Thaw overnight at cool room temperature and complete the recipe.*

Cherry and Lemon Curd Cake with Elderflower Cream

Preparation Time 20 minutes • **Cooking Time** 30 minutes, plus cooling • **Cuts into 12 slices** • **Per Slice** 432 calories, 34g fat (of which 20g saturates), 35g carbohydrate, 0.5g salt • **Easy**

175g (6oz) unsalted butter, at room
   temperature, plus extra to grease
175g (6oz) golden caster sugar
4 tbsp lemon curd
3 medium eggs, beaten
175g (6oz) self-raising flour
5 tbsp milk
200g (7oz) cherries, stoned and
   roughly chopped
450ml (¾ pint) double cream
5 tbsp elderflower cordial
golden icing sugar to dust

1 Preheat the oven to 180°C (160°C fan) mark 4. Line the base and sides of an 18 x 25.5cm (7 x 10in) cake tin with greaseproof paper.

2 Using a wooden spoon or a hand-held electric mixer, beat the butter, caster sugar and lemon curd together until pale and fluffy. Gradually add the eggs, alternating each addition with 1 tbsp flour Using a metal spoon, fold in the remaining flour and the milk. Gently stir in the cherries. Spoon the mixture into the prepared tin and level the surface.

3 Bake for 25–30 minutes until golden and a skewer inserted into the centre comes out clean (cover lightly with foil, if necessary, to prevent over-browning). Remove the cake from the tin, then transfer to a wire rack to cool completely.

4 Whip the cream and cordial together until softly peaking.

5 When the cake is cool, remove the greaseproof paper, then cut into 12 squares. Serve dusted with icing sugar and topped with a spoonful of elderflower cream.

Sticky Lemon Polenta Cake

Preparation Time 10 minutes • **Cooking Time** 1 hour, plus cooling • **Cuts into 12 slices** • **Per Slice** 220 calories, 7g fat (of which 3g saturates), 37g carbohydrate, 0.1g salt • **Gluten Free** • **A Little Effort**

50g (2oz) unsalted butter, softened, plus extra to grease
3 lemons
250g (9oz) golden caster sugar
250g (9oz) instant polenta
1 tsp wheat-free baking powder
2 large eggs
50ml (2fl oz) semi-skimmed milk
2 tbsp natural yogurt
2 tbsp poppy seeds

1 Preheat the oven to 180°C (160°C fan oven) mark 4. Lightly grease a 900g (2lb) loaf tin and baseline with greaseproof paper.

2 Grate the zest of 1 lemon and put into a food processor with the butter, 200g (7oz) sugar, the polenta, baking powder, eggs, milk, yogurt and poppy seeds, then whiz until smooth. Spoon the mixture into the prepared tin and level the surface. Bake for 55 minutes–1 hour until a skewer inserted into the centre comes out clean. Leave to cool in the tin for 10 minutes.

3 Next, make a syrup. Squeeze the juice from the zested lemon plus 1 more lemon. Thinly slice the third lemon. Put the lemon juice into a pan with the remaining sugar and 150ml (¼ pint) water. Add the lemon slices, bring to the boil and bubble for about 10 minutes or until syrupy. Take the pan off the heat and leave to cool for 5 minutes. Remove the lemon slices from the syrup and set aside.

4 Slide a knife around the edge of the cake and turn out on to a serving plate. Pierce the cake in several places with a skewer, spoon the syrup over it and decorate with the lemon slices.

★ TO STORE
Wrap in clingfilm and store in an airtight container. It will keep for up to three days.

Orange Syrup Cake

Preparation Time 20 minutes, plus soaking • **Cooking Time** 30–40 minutes, plus cooling • **Cuts into 10 slices** •
Per Slice 291 calories, 20g fat (of which 10g saturates), 27g carbohydrate, 0.4g salt • **Easy**

175g (6oz) unsalted butter, plus
    extra to grease
225g (8oz) caster sugar
2 medium eggs, beaten
200g (7oz) rice flour
2 tsp baking powder
75g (3oz) ground almonds
grated zest and juice of 1 large
    orange
250ml carton orange juice
2 large oranges, peeled and thickly
    sliced
2 tbsp lemon juice
blueberries to serve

1 Preheat the oven to 190°C (170°C
fan oven) mark 5. Grease a shallow
20.5cm (8in) round tin and baseline
with baking parchment.

2 Cream the butter and 75g (3oz)
sugar. Beat in the eggs gradually.
Fold in the rice flour, baking powder
and ground almonds. Stir in the zest
and juice of the orange and 8 tbsp
orange juice. The mixture should be
of a soft, dropping consistency.
Spoon the mixture into the prepared
tin and level the surface.

3 Bake for 40 minutes or until
firm. Leave to cool in the tin for
10 minutes, then turn out on to a
wire rack to cool completely.

4 Just before serving, combine the
remaining sugar and orange juice
plus the lemon juice in a small pan.
Add the orange slices, bring to the

boil and cook for 1–2 minutes.
Take the pan off the heat and leave
to cool for 5 minutes. Remove the
orange slices from the syrup and
set aside. Put the cake on a serving
plate and, with a cocktail stick,
prick the cake in a number of places.
Drizzle with the syrup and leave
to soak in for 30 minutes.

5 Serve with the orange slices
and blueberries.

★ FREEZING TIP
To freeze Complete the recipe to the end
of step 3, wrap and freeze.
To use Thaw at cool room temperature
for 2–3 hours. Complete the recipe.

Sweet Pumpkin Cake with Toffee Sauce

Preparation Time 25 minutes • **Cooking Time** 1½ hours, plus cooling • **Cuts into 16 slices** • **Per Slice** 440 calories, 24g fat (of which 9g saturates), 55g carbohydrate, 0.3g salt • **Easy**

butter to grease
225g (8oz) self-raising flour, plus
 extra to dust
550g (1¼lb) pumpkin or butternut
 squash, cut into wedges
250ml (9fl oz) sunflower oil
275g (10oz) light muscovado sugar,
 plus extra to sprinkle
3 large eggs
1 tsp bicarbonate of soda
2 tsp ground ginger
1 tsp ground cinnamon
1 tsp nutmeg
a pinch of ground cloves
a pinch of ground allspice

Toffee Sauce (see Cook's Tip)
 to serve

1 Preheat the oven to 200°C (180°C fan oven) mark 6. Grease a 23cm (9in) kugelhopf tin generously with butter and dust with flour.

2 Put the pumpkin on a baking sheet and roast for 40 minutes or until tender. Leave to cool for 15 minutes.

3 Reduce the oven temperature to 180°C (160°C fan oven) mark 4. Spoon out 250g (9oz) pumpkin flesh, put into a blender and whiz to a purée.

4 Put the oil and sugar into a freestanding mixer and whisk for 2 minutes (or use a hand-held electric whisk), then whisk in the eggs, one at a time. Sift the flour, bicarbonate of soda and spices on to the mixture and fold in. Add the pumpkin purée and stir in gently. Pour the mixture into the prepared tin.

5 Bake for 40–45 minutes until risen, springy and shrinking from the edges of the tin. Leave to cool in the tin for 10 minutes, then turn out on to a wire rack to cool completely.

6 To serve, drizzle the toffee sauce over the cake and sprinkle with muscovado sugar.

 COOK'S TIP

Toffee Sauce

Put 300g (11oz) light muscovado sugar, 300ml (½ pint) double cream and 50g (2oz) unsalted butter into a small heavy-based pan. Heat gently to dissolve the sugar, then simmer and stir for 3 minutes to thicken slightly. Pour into a jug.

Carrot Cake

Preparation Time 15 minutes • **Cooking Time** 40 minutes, plus cooling • **Cuts into 12 slices** • **Per Slice** 383 calories, 32g fat (of which 10g saturates), 24g carbohydrate, 0.3g salt • **Easy**

250ml (9fl oz) sunflower oil, plus
    extra to grease
225g (8oz) light muscovado sugar
3 large eggs
225g (8oz) self-raising flour
a large pinch of salt
½ tsp each ground mixed spice,
    ground nutmeg and ground
    cinnamon
250g (9oz) carrots, coarsely grated

FOR THE FROSTING
50g (2oz) butter, preferably
    unsalted, at room temperature
225g pack cream cheese
25g (1oz) golden icing sugar
½ tsp vanilla extract
8 pecan halves, roughly chopped

1 Preheat the oven to 180°C (160°C fan oven) mark 4. Grease two 18cm (7in) sandwich tins and baseline with greaseproof paper.

2 Using a hand-held electric whisk, whisk the oil and muscovado sugar together to combine, then whisk in the eggs, one at a time.

3 Sift the flour, salt and spices together over the mixture, then gently fold in, using a large metal spoon. Tip the carrots into the bowl and fold in.

4 Divide the cake mixture between the prepared tins and bake for 30–40 minutes until golden and a skewer inserted into the centre

comes out clean. Remove from the oven and leave in the tins for 10 minutes, then turn out on to a wire rack to cool completely.

5 To make the frosting, beat the butter and cream cheese together in a bowl until light and fluffy. Sift in the icing sugar, add the vanilla extract and beat well until smooth. Spread one-third of the frosting over one cake and sandwich together with the other cake. Spread the remaining frosting on top and sprinkle with the pecans.

★ TO STORE
Store the cake in an airtight container and eat within two days. Alternatively, the cake will keep for up to one week in an airtight container if it is stored before the frosting is applied.

Rhubarb Crumble Cake

·· ★

Preparation Time 25 minutes • **Cooking Time** 1 hour–1 hour 20 minutes • **Cuts into** 10 slices • **Per Slice** 394 calories, 25g fat (of which 11g saturates), 37g carbohydrate, 0.5g salt • **Easy**

150g (5oz) unsalted butter,
  softened, plus extra to grease
400g (14oz) rhubarb, trimmed and
  cut into 2.5cm (1in) pieces
175g (6oz) golden caster sugar
2 large eggs, beaten
100g (3½oz) ground almonds
3 tbsp milk
125g (4oz) self-raising flour
1 tsp cinnamon
½ tsp ground ginger
50g (2oz) flaked almonds
icing sugar to dust
Poached Rhubarb to serve (see
  Cook's Tip)

FOR THE CRUMBLE TOPPING
40g (1½oz) cold unsalted butter,
  diced
50g (2oz) plain flour
40g (1½oz) demerara sugar

1 Preheat the oven to 180°C (160°C fan oven) mark 4. Grease a 20.5cm (8in) springform tin and line with greaseproof paper.

2 Put the rhubarb into a pan with 25g (1oz) caster sugar and 100ml (3½fl oz) water and simmer for 5 minutes. Strain and set aside.

3 To make the topping, rub the chilled diced butter into the flour until the mixture resembles breadcrumbs. Stir in the demerara sugar and set aside.

4 Beat the softened butter and remaining caster sugar together until pale and fluffy. Gradually add the eggs, beating well after each addition. Using a large metal spoon, fold in the ground almonds, milk, flour and spices, then fold in the flaked almonds. Turn into the prepared tin, level the surface and top with rhubarb, then sprinkle with the crumble topping.

5 Bake for 1–1¼ hours until a skewer inserted into the centre comes out clean. Leave to cool in the tin for 5 minutes, then remove from the tin. Dust with icing sugar and serve warm with custard and poached rhubarb, or cool on a wire rack and serve cold.

★ COOK'S TIP
Poached Rhubarb
Chop 250g (9oz) rhubarb into 6.5cm (2½in) pieces. Put into a pan with 50g (2oz) caster sugar, 25g (1oz) stem ginger, cut into slivers, and 75ml (3fl oz) water. Cover and simmer gently for 5 minutes.

★ GET AHEAD
To prepare ahead *Complete the recipe without icing sugar up to one day in advance. Store in an airtight container.* ***To use*** *Dust with icing sugar to serve.*

Cappuccino and Walnut Cake

Preparation Time 30 minutes, plus cooling • **Cooking Time** about 45 minutes, plus cooling • **Cuts into 10 slices** •
Per Slice 449 calories, 30g fat (of which 13g saturates), 36g carbohydrate, 0.3g salt • **Easy**

65g (2½oz) unsalted butter, melted
  and cooled, plus extra to grease
100g (3½oz) plain flour
1 tsp baking powder
4 medium eggs
125g (4oz) caster sugar
1 tbsp chicory and coffee essence
75g (3oz) walnuts, toasted, cooled
  and finely chopped

FOR THE DECORATION
50g (2oz) walnuts
1 tbsp granulated sugar
¼ tsp ground cinnamon

FOR THE ICING
200g (7oz) good-quality white
  chocolate
4 tsp chicory and coffee essence
2 x 250g tubs mascarpone cheese
fresh unsprayed violets to decorate
  (optional)

1 Preheat the oven to 190°C (170°C fan oven) mark 5. Grease two 20.5 x 4cm deep (8 x 1½in deep) round cake tins and line the base of each with a circle of greased greaseproof paper. Sift the flour and baking powder together twice.

2 Using an electric mixer, whisk the eggs and caster sugar in a large heatproof bowl set over a pan of barely simmering water for 3–4 minutes until light, thick and fluffy. Remove the bowl from the heat and continue whisking until the mixture has cooled and the whisk leaves a ribbon trail for 8 seconds when lifted out of the bowl.

3 Fold in the butter, coffee essence and walnuts. Sift half the flour over the mixture, then fold in carefully but quickly with a metal spoon. Sift and fold in the rest, taking care not to knock out too much air. Pour into the tins and tap them lightly on the worktop. Bake for 20–25 minutes until the tops feel springy. Cool in the tins for 10 minutes, then turn out and transfer to a wire rack to cool completely.

4 To make the decoration, whiz the walnuts in a food processor or blender with the granulated sugar and cinnamon until finely chopped. Take care not to overprocess the nuts or they'll become oily. Set aside.

5 To make the icing, break up the chocolate and put into a heatproof bowl set over a pan of gently simmering water, making sure the base of the bowl doesn't touch the water. Allow to melt slowly without stirring. In another bowl, add the coffee essence to the mascarpone and beat until smooth, then slowly beat in the melted chocolate.

6 Spread one-third of the icing on top of one cake, then sandwich with the other half. Smooth the remaining icing over the top and sides. Lift the cake on to a large piece of greaseproof paper and scatter nuts all around it. Then lift the greaseproof up to press nuts on to the sides. Transfer to a plate and decorate with violets, if you like.

★ TO STORE
*Store in an airtight container in the
fridge. It will keep for up to two days.*

Apple and Blueberry Cake

★

Preparation Time 20 minutes, plus cooling • **Cooking Time** 1 hour, plus cooling • **Cuts into 8 slices** • **Per Slice** 396 calories, 15g fat (of which 9g saturates), 65g carbohydrate, 0.6g salt • **Easy**

125g (4oz) unsalted butter, diced, plus extra to grease
225g (8oz) self-raising flour, sifted
½ tsp salt
175g (6oz) granulated sugar, golden if possible
2 large eggs, beaten
2 large Granny Smith apples, peeled, cored and sliced
140g (4½oz) fresh blueberries
175g (6oz) apricot jam
1 tbsp lemon juice

1 Preheat the oven to 190°C (170°C fan oven) mark 5. Grease a 20.5cm (8in) springform tin with butter and baseline with baking parchment.

2 Put the flour and salt into a large mixing bowl, add the diced butter and rub in the flour until the mixture looks like fine breadcrumbs. Add 140g (4½oz) sugar and the beaten eggs and stir well.

3 Spread half the mixture in a thin layer in the tin, then layer the sliced apples and the blueberries evenly over the surface, setting aside a little of the fruit for the top of the cake. Sprinkle with the remaining sugar, then spoon in the rest of the cake mixture. Add the remaining apple slices and blueberries, pressing them down slightly into the mixture.

4 Bake for 45–55 minutes until risen and firm to the touch and a skewer inserted into the centre comes out clean. Cool in the tin for 10 minutes, then turn out on to a wire rack to cool completely.

5 Warm the jam and lemon juice in a small pan until evenly combined. Sieve the mixture and, while it's still warm, brush it over the top of the cake. Serve immediately.

★ FREEZING TIP
To freeze *Complete the recipe to the end of step 4. Wrap the cake in a freezer bag and freeze for up to one month.*
To use *Thaw for 3 hours at cool room temperature, then complete the recipe. To serve warm, heat individual cake slices in the microwave on full power for 1 minute per slice.*

Raspberry and Peach Cake

Preparation Time 15 minutes • **Cooking Time** 1–1¼ hours, plus cooling • **Cuts into 8 slices** • **Per Slice** 405 calories, 24g fat (of which 14g saturates), 44g carbohydrate, 0.8g salt • **Easy**

200g (7oz) unsalted butter, melted, plus extra to grease
250g (9oz) self-raising flour, sifted
100g (3½oz) golden caster sugar
4 medium eggs, beaten
125g (4oz) raspberries
2 large, almost-ripe peaches or nectarines, halved, stoned and sliced
4 tbsp apricot jam
juice of ½ lemon

1 Preheat the oven to 190°C (170°C fan oven) mark 5. Grease a 20.5cm (8in) springform cake tin and baseline with baking parchment.

2 Put the flour and sugar into a large bowl. Make a well in the centre and add the melted butter and the eggs. Mix well.

3 Spread half the mixture over the base of the cake tin and add half the raspberries and sliced peaches or nectarines. Spoon on the remaining cake mixture, smooth over, then add the remaining raspberries and peaches or nectarines, pressing them down into the mixture slightly.

4 Bake for 1–1¼ hours until risen and golden and a skewer inserted into the centre comes out clean. Remove from the oven and leave in the tin to cool for 10 minutes.

5 Warm the jam and the lemon juice together in a small pan and brush over the cake to glaze. Serve warm or at room temperature.

★ TO STORE
Store in an airtight container. It will keep for up to one week.

Lemon and Berry Crunch Cake

Preparation Time 40 minutes, plus setting • **Cooking Time** 1 hour, plus cooling and steeping • **Cuts into 8 slices** •
Per Slice 428 calories, 18g fat (of which 10g saturates), 67g carbohydrate, 0.5g salt • **Easy**

150g (5oz) unsalted butter,
    softened, plus extra to grease
2 medium eggs, plus 1 egg yolk
a pinch of salt
150g (5oz) caster sugar
150g (5oz) self-raising flour, sifted
grated zest and juice of 1 lemon
125g (4oz) raspberries and
    blueberries

**FOR THE LEMON CRUNCH
    TOPPING**
25ml (1fl oz) bottled lemon juice
    (see Cook's Tips)
225g (8oz) caster sugar
25g (1oz) rough white sugar cubes,
    lightly crushed
white currants, blackcurrants, wild
    strawberries and crème fraîche
    or Greek yogurt to serve

1 Preheat the oven to 170°C (150°C fan oven) mark 3. Grease a 1.1 litre (2 pint) loaf tin and baseline with baking parchment.

2 Lightly beat the eggs and egg yolk with the salt. Put the butter and sugar into a bowl and beat until light and fluffy. Gradually beat in the eggs, beating for about 10 minutes.

3 Fold in the flour with the lemon zest and 2 tbsp of the juice (put the rest to one side). Fold in the raspberries and blueberries. Spoon the mixture into the prepared tin, level the surface and bake for 50 minutes–1 hour. Leave to cool in the tin for 5 minutes, then turn out on to a wire rack to cool completely.

4 To make the topping, mix the reserved fresh lemon juice with the bottled lemon juice and caster sugar. Spoon over the cake and sprinkle the top with crushed sugar. Set aside for 1 hour. Slice and serve with berries and crème fraîche or yogurt.

⭐ COOK'S TIPS
● *Bottled lemon juice gives a more intense lemony flavour than fresh juice.*
● *The weight of the fruit may make it sink towards the bottom of the cake. Don't worry if this happens – it will still taste just as wonderful.*
● *Other summer berries such as blackberries, loganberries and blackcurrants can be used if you like.*

Cardamom and Mango Cake

Preparation Time 45 minutes • **Cooking Time** 25–30 minutes, plus cooling • **Cuts into 10 slices** • **Per Slice** 274 calories, 16g fat (of which 9g saturates), 31g carbohydrate, 0.2g salt • **A Little Effort**

50g (2oz) unsalted butter, plus extra
   to grease
4 green cardamom pods
a good pinch of saffron strands
4 large eggs
125g (4oz) caster sugar
100g (3½oz) plain flour

**FOR THE FILLING, MANGO
   SAUCE AND DECORATION**
150ml (¼ pint) double cream
150g (5oz) Greek yogurt
3 tbsp icing sugar, plus extra
   to dust
2 large, ripe mangoes
4 tbsp orange juice
orange segments

1 Preheat the oven to 180°C (160°C fan oven) mark 4. Grease two 18cm (7in) sandwich tins, or one deep 18cm (7in) round cake tin, and baseline with baking parchment.

2 Split the cardamom pods and remove the black seeds. Crush the seeds to a powder together with the saffron. Put the butter into a pan and heat gently until melted, then remove from the heat and leave to cool for a few minutes until beginning to thicken.

3 Put the eggs and caster sugar into a large heatproof bowl. Using a hand-held electric whisk, whisk until evenly blended. Put the bowl over a pan of hot water and whisk until pale and thick enough to leave a trail on the surface when the whisk is lifted. Remove the bowl from the pan and whisk until cool and thick.

4 Sift the spices and flour together. Using a large metal spoon or plastic spatula, fold half into the whisked mixture. Pour the cooled butter around the edge of the mixture, leaving the sediment behind. Gradually fold it in very lightly, cutting through the mixture until it is all incorporated. Carefully fold in the remaining flour as lightly as possible. Pour into the prepared tins.

5 Bake for 25–30 minutes until well risen and the cakes spring back when lightly pressed. Run a small knife around the cake edge to loosen and leave in the tins for 5 minutes. Turn out on to a wire rack to cool completely.

6 To make the filling, whip the cream until it holds its shape. Stir in the yogurt with 2 tbsp icing sugar. Sandwich the cakes with the cream mixture and one sliced mango. Chill for 2–3 hours.

7 To make the mango sauce, put the remaining mango flesh, 1 tbsp icing sugar and the orange juice into a blender and whiz to a purée. Pass the purée through a nylon sieve to remove all the fibres. Cover and chill.

8 Just before serving, decorate the cake with orange segments and dust with icing sugar. Serve with the mango sauce.

Warm Lemon Syrup Cake

★

Preparation Time 15 minutes • **Cooking Time** 1 hour, plus cooling and soaking • **Cuts into 12 slices** •
Per Slice 360 calories, 18g fat (of which 10g saturates), 49g carbohydrate, 0.5g salt • **Easy**

225g (8oz) unsalted butter,
    softened, plus extra to grease
grated zest of 2 lemons and 2 tbsp
    lemon juice
225g (8oz) caster sugar
4 large eggs, beaten
225g (8oz) self-raising flour, sifted
75g (3oz) candied lemon peel, finely
    chopped (optional)

**FOR THE SYRUP AND
    DECORATION**
175g (6oz) caster sugar
finely sliced zest and strained juice
    of 3 lemons
75ml (2½ fl oz) water

1 Preheat the oven to 180°C (160°C fan oven) mark 4. Grease a 20.5cm (8in) round deep cake tin and baseline with baking parchment.

2 Cream the butter and lemon zest together. Gradually beat in the sugar, followed by the eggs; the mixture should be stiff. Fold in the flour, candied peel, if using, and lemon juice. Spoon the mixture into the prepared tin, level the surface and bake for about 1 hour or until golden.

3 Meanwhile, prepare the syrup and topping. Put the sugar, lemon juice and water into a pan. Warm gently until the sugar dissolves, then bring to the boil and bubble for 1 minute. Leave to cool.

4 As soon as the cake is cooked, turn out into a shallow dish and immediately spoon the syrup over it. Leave for about 30 minutes for the syrup to soak in. Serve warm, topped with the sliced lemon zest.

Sweet Cherry Bread

Preparation Time 40 minutes, plus rising • **Cooking Time** 40 minutes, plus cooling • **Cuts into 8 slices** •
Per Slice 310 calories, 4g fat (of which trace saturates), 66g carbohydrate, 0.4g salt • **A Little Effort**

oil to grease
**350g (12oz) strong white bread
   flour, plus extra to dust**
½ tsp salt
2 tsp ground mixed spice
1 tsp ground cinnamon
25g (1oz) caster sugar
15g (½oz) fast-action dried yeast
75g (3oz) unsalted butter, diced
200ml (7fl oz) milk, warmed
**125g (4oz) white almond paste,
   roughly chopped**
125g (4oz) glacé cherries
3 tbsp honey, warmed
75g (3oz) icing sugar, sifted

1 Grease a 20.5cm (8in) round
deep cake tin and baseline with
greaseproof paper.

2 Sift the flour, salt, spices and
caster sugar into a bowl. Add the
yeast, then rub in the butter. Add
the milk to make a dough (if the
dough is too dry, add a little more
milk). Turn out on to a lightly floured
surface and knead for 10 minutes.
Put the dough into a lightly oiled
bowl, cover with oiled clingfilm and
leave in a warm place for 2 hours or
until doubled in size.

3 Turn out the dough on to a lightly
floured surface and knead lightly.
Shape into an oval, 60cm (24in)
long. Scatter the almond paste
and cherries over the surface and
roll up the dough lengthways, then
form it into a tight coil. Put in the

cake tin, cover and leave in a warm
place for 30 minutes or until
doubled in size. Preheat the oven to
180°C (160°C fan oven) mark 4.

4 Bake for 40 minutes or until
golden; it should sound hollow
when tapped underneath. Turn out
of the tin on to a wire rack to cool.
When cool, brush with honey. Mix
the icing sugar with a few drops of
water and drizzle over the bread.

★ TO STORE
*Store in an airtight container. It will keep
for up to two days.*

Apricot and Hazelnut Bread

Preparation Time 25 minutes, plus rising • **Cooking Time** 30–35 minutes, plus cooling • **Makes 2 loaves** •
Per Serving 94 calories, 3g fat (of which 1g saturates), 14g carbohydrate, 0g salt • **Easy**

75g (3oz) hazelnuts
450g (1lb) strong Granary bread
   flour, plus extra to dust
1 tsp salt
25g (1oz) unsalted butter, diced,
   plus extra to grease
75g (3oz) ready-to-eat dried
   apricots, chopped
2 tsp fast-action dried yeast
2 tbsp molasses
milk to glaze

1 Spread the hazelnuts on a baking sheet. Toast under a hot grill until golden brown, turning frequently. Put the hazelnuts in a clean teatowel and rub off the skins. Leave to cool. Chop and put to one side.

2 Put the flour into a large bowl. Add the salt, then rub in the butter. Stir in the hazelnuts, apricots and yeast. Make a well in the middle and gradually work in the molasses and about 225ml (8fl oz) hand-hot water to form a soft dough, adding a little more water if the dough feels dry. Knead for 8–10 minutes until smooth, then transfer the dough to a greased bowl. Cover and leave to rise in a warm place for 1–1¼ hours until doubled in size.

3 Punch the dough to knock back, then divide in half. Shape each portion into a small, flattish round and put on a well-floured baking sheet. Cover loosely and leave to rise for a further 30 minutes.

4 Preheat the oven to 220°C (200°C fan oven) mark 7 and put a large baking sheet on the top shelf to heat up.

5 Using a sharp knife, cut several slashes on each round, brush with a little milk and transfer to the heated baking sheet. Bake for 15 minutes, then reduce the oven temperature to 190°C (170°C fan oven) mark 5 and bake for a further 15–20 minutes until the bread is risen and sounds hollow when tapped underneath. Turn out of the tin on to a wire rack to cool.

★ TO STORE
Store in an airtight container. It will keep for up to two days.

★ TRY SOMETHING DIFFERENT
Replace the hazelnuts with walnuts or pecan nuts and use sultanas instead of apricots.

Ginger and Fruit Teabread

Preparation Time 15 minutes, plus soaking • **Cooking Time** 1 hour, plus cooling • **Cuts into 12 slices** •
Per Slice 145 calories, 1g fat (of which trace saturates), 33g carbohydrate, 0g salt • **Easy**

125g (4oz) each dried apricots,
    apples and pitted prunes,
    chopped
300ml (½ pint) strong fruit tea
a little butter to grease
25g (1oz) stem ginger in syrup,
    chopped
225g (8oz) wholemeal flour
2 tsp baking powder
125g (4oz) dark muscovado sugar
1 medium egg, beaten

1 Put the dried fruit into a large bowl, add the tea and leave to soak for 2 hours.

2 Preheat the oven to 180°C (160°C fan oven) mark 4. Grease a 900g (2lb) loaf tin and baseline with baking parchment.

3 Add the remaining ingredients to the soaked fruit and mix thoroughly. Spoon into the prepared tin and brush with 2 tbsp cold water. Bake for 1 hour or until cooked through.

4 Cool in the tin for 10–15 minutes, then turn out on to a wire rack to cool completely.

★ TO STORE
Wrap the teabread in clingfilm and store in an airtight container. It will keep for up to three days.

Banana and Butterscotch Loaf

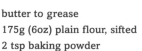

Preparation Time 20 minutes • **Cooking Time** 1 hour, plus cooling • **Makes 1 loaf (15 slices)** • **Per Slice** 221 calories, 9g fat (of which 2g saturates), 34g carbohydrate, 0.2g salt • **Easy**

butter to grease
175g (6oz) plain flour, sifted
2 tsp baking powder
½ tsp bicarbonate of soda
½ tsp salt
175g (6oz) light muscovado sugar
2 large eggs
3 medium-size ripe bananas,
    mashed
150g carton natural yogurt
150g bar butterscotch chocolate,
    roughly chopped
100g (3½oz) pecan nuts, chopped
1–2 tbsp demerara sugar

1 Preheat the oven to 170°C (150°C fan oven) mark 3. Grease a 1.4kg (3lb) loaf tin and line with greaseproof paper.

2 Put the flour, baking powder, bicarbonate of soda and salt into a large bowl and mix together.

3 In a separate bowl, beat the muscovado sugar and eggs together with a hand-held electric whisk until pale and fluffy. Carefully stir in the bananas, yogurt, chocolate and 50g (2oz) pecan nuts, followed by the flour mixture.

4 Spoon the mixture into the prepared tin and level the surface. Sprinkle with the remaining chopped pecan nuts and the demerara sugar. Bake for 1 hour or until a skewer inserted into the centre comes out clean. Leave to cool in the tin on a wire rack, then turn out and slice.

★ TRY SOMETHING DIFFERENT
If you can't find butterscotch chocolate, use a bar of plain dark chocolate instead.

★ TO STORE
Store in an airtight container. It will keep for up to two days.

Blackberry and Cinnamon Yogurt Loaf

Preparation Time 15 minutes • **Cooking Time** 55 minutes, plus cooling • **Cuts into 8 slices** • **Per Slice** 287 calories, 15g fat (of which 3g saturates), 35g carbohydrate, 0.1g salt • **Easy**

125ml (4fl oz) sunflower oil, plus
    extra to grease
175g (6oz) plain flour
1½ tsp baking powder
1½ tsp ground cinnamon
200g (7oz) frozen blackberries
125g (4oz) golden caster sugar
grated zest and juice of 1 lemon
125g (4oz) Greek yogurt
3 medium eggs, beaten
icing sugar to dust

1 Preheat the oven to 190°C (170°C fan oven) mark 5. Grease a 900g (2lb) loaf tin and baseline with baking parchment.

2 Sift the flour, baking powder and cinnamon into a bowl, add the frozen berries and toss to coat. Make a well in the centre.

3 In another bowl, whisk the caster sugar, oil, lemon zest and juice, yogurt and eggs together. Pour into the well in the flour mixture and stir.

4 Spoon the mixture into the prepared tin, level the surface and bake for 55 minutes or until a skewer inserted into the centre comes out clean (cover lightly with foil, if necessary, to prevent over-browning). Leave to cool in the tin. Remove from the tin and dust with icing sugar to serve.

 **TO STORE**
Store in an airtight container. It will keep for up to two days.

 TRY SOMETHING
DIFFERENT
Apple and Cinnamon Yogurt Loaf
Replace the blackberries with 2 small Cox's or Braeburn apples, peeled, cored and chopped.
Raspberry and White Chocolate Yogurt Loaf
Omit the ground cinnamon. Replace the blackberries with 125g (4oz) frozen raspberries and 75g (3oz) chopped white chocolate, and use orange zest and juice instead of lemon.

Pineapple and Coconut Loaf

Preparation Time 20 minutes • **Cooking Time** 50 minutes, plus cooling • **Cuts into 10 slices** • **Per Slice** 254 calories, 15g fat (of which 10g saturates), 28g carbohydrate, 0.2g salt • **Easy**

150g (5oz) wholemeal flour, sifted
125g (4oz) dark muscovado sugar
2 medium eggs
2 tsp baking powder
¼ tsp mixed spice
50g (2oz) desiccated coconut, plus
**   extra to decorate (optional)**
400g can pineapple in natural juice,
**   drained and roughly chopped**
icing sugar to decorate (optional)

1 Preheat the oven to 180°C (160°C fan oven) mark 4. Grease a 450g (1lb) loaf tin and baseline with baking parchment.

2 Put the flour and muscovado sugar into a food processor and whiz for 1–2 minutes until well mixed. (Alternatively, put into a bowl and stir until the sugar is well combined with the flour, breaking down any lumps with a wooden spoon.) Add all the remaining ingredients except the icing sugar and mix until smooth.

3 Turn the mixture into the prepared tin, level the surface and brush lightly with 2 tbsp cold water. Bake for 50 minutes or until a skewer inserted into the centre comes out clean (after 40 minutes cover lightly with foil, if necessary, to prevent over-browning).

4 Leave to cool in the tin for 10 minutes, then turn out on to a wire rack to cool completely. Decorate with a little desiccated coconut and icing sugar, if you like, to serve.

★ TO STORE
Store in an airtight container. It will keep for up to two days.

Lime Drizzle Loaf

Preparation Time 15 minutes • **Cooking Time** 45–55 minutes, plus cooling • **Cuts into 12 slices** • **Per Slice** 260 calories, 16g fat (of which 11g saturates), 27g carbohydrate, 0.5g salt • **Easy**

175g (6oz) self-raising flour, sifted
　　with a pinch of salt
175g (6oz) unsalted butter, diced
175g (6oz) golden caster sugar
3 medium eggs, beaten
50g (2oz) sweetened desiccated
　　coconut
zest and juice of 2 limes
1 tsp baking powder

FOR THE DECORATION
1 lime
125g (4oz) golden icing sugar, sifted
1 tbsp sweetened desiccated
　　coconut to decorate

1 Preheat the oven to 180°C (160°C fan oven) mark 4. Line a 900g (2lb) loaf tin with a greaseproof loaf liner.

2 Put the flour, salt, butter, caster sugar, eggs, coconut, lime zest and juice and baking powder into the bowl of a freestanding mixer, fitted with a K-beater. Mix together slowly, gradually increasing the speed and mixing for 2 minutes. (Alternatively, use a hand-held electric mixer.)

3 Pour the mixture (it will be quite runny) into the tin and bake for 45–55 minutes until golden, well

risen and cooked through and a skewer inserted into the centre comes out clean. Leave to cool in the tin for 10 minutes, then lift out, keeping the cake in the liner, and leave to cool completely.

4 To make the icing, finely grate the zest from the lime. Cut away the white pith. Chop the lime flesh, put into a mini processor or blender with the zest and whiz for 1–2 minutes until finely chopped. Add the icing sugar and blend until smooth. Pour over the top of the cake. Sprinkle the coconut on top to decorate.

 TO STORE
Store in an airtight container. It will keep for up to two days.

Victoria Sponge

Preparation Time 30 minutes • **Cooking Time** 25–30 minutes, plus cooling • **Cuts into 12 slices** • **Per Slice** 471 calories, 22g fat (of which 13g saturates), 66g carbohydrate, 0.6g salt • **Easy**

250g (9oz) unsalted butter, softened, plus extra to grease
250g (9oz) golden caster sugar
5 medium eggs
250g (9oz) self-raising flour

FOR THE FILLING
200g (7oz) mascarpone cheese
7 tbsp strawberry conserve

FOR THE DECORATION
250g (9oz) icing sugar
1 tsp rosewater
a few drops of pink food colouring

1 Preheat the oven to 190°C (170°C fan oven) mark 5. Grease two 20.5cm (8in) sandwich tins and baseline with baking parchment.

2 Put the butter and caster sugar into a large bowl and cream together using a hand-held electric whisk until the mixture is pale and fluffy. Add three of the eggs, one at a time, whisking well between each addition.

3 Add 4 tbsp of the flour (to stop the mixture curdling), then whisk in the remaining eggs, one at a time, and continue to whisk. Sift the remaining flour into the bowl and fold gently into the mixture using a large spoon. The mixture should be smooth and have a dropping consistency.

4 Divide the mixture between the prepared tins and level the surface. Bake for 25–30 minutes until golden, springy to the touch and shrinking away from the sides of the tins.

5 Leave to cool in the tins for 5 minutes, then turn out on to a wire rack, remove the lining paper and leave to cool completely.

6 When cold, spread one cake with mascarpone. Spoon on the jam and spread to the edges. Top with the other cake and press down lightly.

7 To decorate, sift the icing sugar into a bowl, then add the rosewater, pink food colouring and 2–2½ tbsp hot water to create a smooth dropping consistency. Pour the icing on top of the cake, spreading it to the edge so that it dribbles down the sides. Leave to set.

★ **TO STORE**
Store in an airtight container. It will keep for up to three days. If stored in the fridge it will keep for up to one week.

★ **TRY SOMETHING DIFFERENT**
Orange Victoria Sponge
Fill with orange buttercream and top with orange icing. For the buttercream, cream together 75g (3oz) softened unsalted butter, 175g (6oz) sifted icing sugar, a little grated orange zest and 1–2 tbsp orange juice. For the icing, replace the rosewater with orange juice and omit the food colouring.

Chocolate Swiss Roll

Preparation Time 25 minutes • **Cooking Time** 10–12 minutes, plus cooling • **Cuts into 8 slices** • **Per Slice** 197 calories, 8g fat (of which 4g saturates), 29g carbohydrate, 0.1g salt • **Easy**

3 large eggs
125g (4oz) golden caster sugar
125g (4oz) plain flour, less 1½ tbsp, sifted
1½ tbsp cocoa powder, sifted
golden caster sugar to sprinkle
chocolate buttercream (see page 282) or whipped cream
icing sugar to dust

1 Preheat the oven to 200°C (180°C fan oven) mark 6. Line a 33 x 23cm (13 x 9in) Swiss roll tin with baking parchment.

2 Whisk the eggs and caster sugar in a heatproof bowl until well blended. Stand the bowl over a pan of hot water and whisk until light and creamy. Off the heat, whisk for 5 minutes or until the mixture is cool and thick. Fold in half the flour and cocoa powder, then fold in the remaining flour and cocoa powder. Lightly fold in 1 tbsp hot water. Pour into the prepared Swiss roll tin. Bake for 10–12 minutes until well risen and the cake springs back when lightly pressed.

3 Sprinkle a sheet of greaseproof paper generously with caster sugar. Turn out the cake on to the paper and remove the lining paper. Trim off the crusty edges and cover the sponge with greaseproof paper. Roll up from a short side, with the covering paper inside, then leave to cool.

4 Unroll and remove the paper. Spread the sponge with buttercream or cream. Re-roll: make the first turn firmly, but roll more lightly after this turn. Put the rolled sponge, seam side down, on to a wire rack and dust with icing sugar. Serve cut into slices.

★ TO STORE
Store, covered, in the fridge. It will keep for up to three days.

Chocolate Victoria Sandwich

Preparation Time 20 minutes • **Cooking Time** 20 minutes, plus cooling • **Cuts into 8 slices** • **Per Slice** 520 calories, 30g fat (of which 19g saturates), 62g carbohydrate, 1g salt • **Easy**

175g (6oz) unsalted butter,
  softened, plus extra to grease
3 tbsp cocoa powder
175g (6oz) golden caster sugar
3 medium eggs, beaten
160g (5½oz) self-raising flour, sifted
golden caster sugar to dredge

**FOR THE CHOCOLATE
  BUTTERCREAM**
1 tbsp cocoa powder
75g (3oz) unsalted butter, softened
175g (6oz) icing sugar, sifted
a few drops of vanilla extract
1–2 tbsp milk or water

1 Preheat the oven to 190°C (170°C fan oven) mark 5. Grease two 18cm (7in) sandwich tins and baseline with baking parchment. Blend the cocoa powder with 3 tbsp hot water to a smooth paste, then allow to cool.

2 Using a free-standing mixer or hand-held electric whisk, cream the butter and sugar together, until pale and fluffy. Add the cooled cocoa mixture and beat until evenly blended.

3 Add the beaten eggs, a little at a time, beating well after each addition. Using a metal spoon or large spatula, fold in half the flour, then carefully fold in the rest. Divide the mixture evenly between the tins and level the surface.

4 Bake both cakes on the middle shelf of the oven for about 20 minutes or until well risen, springy to the touch and beginning to shrink away from the sides of the tins. Leave to cool in the tins for 5 minutes, then turn out on to a wire rack to cool completely.

5 To make the chocolate buttercream, blend the cocoa powder with 3 tbsp boiling water and set aside to cool. Put the butter into a bowl and beat with a wooden spoon until light and fluffy. Gradually stir in the icing sugar. Add the blended cocoa, vanilla extract and milk or water and beat well until light and smooth.

6 When the cakes are cool, sandwich them together with the chocolate buttercream and sprinkle the top with caster sugar.

⭐ TO STORE
Store in an airtight container in a cool place. It will keep well for up to one week.

Genoese Sponge

Preparation Time 25 minutes • Cooking Time 20–40 minutes, plus cooling • Cuts into 6 slices • Per Slice 433 calories, 34g fat (of which 20g saturates), 28g carbohydrate, 0.2g salt • Easy

40g (1½ oz) unsalted butter, plus extra to grease
75g (3oz) plain flour, plus extra to dust
75g (3oz) golden caster sugar, plus extra to dust
3 large eggs
1 tbsp cornflour

FOR THE FILLING AND DECORATION
300ml (½ pint) double cream, lightly whipped
350g (12oz) fresh summer berries
icing sugar, to dust

1 Preheat the oven to 180°C (160°C fan oven) mark 4. Grease two 18cm (7in) sandwich tins, or one deep 18cm (7in) round cake tin, and baseline with baking parchment, then dust with a little flour and caster sugar.

2 Put the butter into a pan and heat gently until melted, then remove from the heat and leave to cool slightly for a few minutes until beginning to thicken.

3 Put the eggs and caster sugar into a large heatproof bowl and, using a hand-held electric whisk, whisk until evenly blended. Put the bowl over a pan of hot water and whisk until pale and thick enough to leave a trail when the whisk is lifted. Remove the bowl from the pan and continue whisking until cool and thick.

4 Sift the flour and cornflour together. Using a large metal spoon, fold half into the whisked mixture. Pour the cooled butter around the edge of the mixture, leaving the sediment behind. Gradually fold it in very lightly, until it is all incorporated. Carefully fold in the remaining flour as lightly as possible. Pour into the prepared tin(s).

5 Bake for 20–25 minutes, or the deep cake for 35–40 minutes, until well risen and the sponge springs back when lightly pressed. Loosen the cake edge and leave in the tins for 5 minutes. Turn out on to a wire rack, remove the lining paper and leave to cool. Mix the cream with the fruit and use to sandwich the cakes together. Dust with icing sugar.

★ TRY SOMETHING DIFFERENT
Coffee Sponge
Dissolve 1 tbsp espresso coffee powder in 2 tsp boiling water, mix with the melted butter and fold in at step 4. Dissolve 1 tbsp espresso coffee powder in 1 tbsp boiling water, then beat with 250g (9oz) mascarpone cheese and 125g (4oz) sifted icing sugar until smooth. Fill as in step 5.

Sticky Ginger Ring

★

Preparation Time 15 minutes, plus cooling • **Cooking Time** 1 hour, plus cooling and setting • **Cuts into 8 slices** •
Per Slice 375 calories, 12g fat (of which 7g saturates), 64g carbohydrate, 0.3g salt • **Easy**

100g (3½oz) unsalted butter, diced,
   plus extra to grease
100g (3½oz) light brown soft sugar
3 tbsp black treacle
100ml (3½fl oz) milk
2 tbsp brandy
1 large egg, beaten
150g (5oz) plain flour
2 tsp ground ginger
2 tsp ground cinnamon
1 tsp bicarbonate of soda
75g (3oz) ready-to-eat dried prunes,
   chopped coarsely

FOR THE DECORATION
225g (8oz) icing sugar, sifted
2 pieces stem ginger, drained (2–3
   tbsp syrup reserved) of syrup
   and roughly chopped

1 Preheat the oven to 150°C (130°C
fan oven) mark 2. Generously grease
a 21cm (8½in), 600ml (1 pint) round
ring mould with butter.

2 Put the butter, brown sugar and
treacle into a pan and heat gently
until melted, stirring all the time.
Add the milk and brandy and leave
to cool, then beat in the egg.

3 Sift the flour, spices and
bicarbonate of soda into a mixing
bowl. Make a well in the centre,
pour in the treacle mixture and stir
until all the flour has been combined
– it should have a soft, dropping
consistency. Stir in the prunes. Pour
the mixture into the prepared ring
mould and level the surface.

4 Bake for 1 hour or until the cake
is firm to the touch and a skewer
inserted in the centre comes out
clean. Leave to cool in the tin for
10 minutes, then loosen the sides of
the cake and turn out on to a wire
rack to cool completely.

5 To make the icing, mix the icing
sugar with enough of the reserved
ginger syrup to create a coating
consistency. Drizzle over the cake
and down the sides, then decorate
with the stem ginger. Leave to set.

★ FREEZING TIP
To freeze Complete the recipe to the
end of step 4, then wrap the cake in
clingfilm and foil. Freeze for up to one
month.
To use Thaw for 3 hours and complete
the recipe.

Brownies, Traybakes, Cookies and Biscuits

Figgy Fruit Slice

Preparation Time 30 minutes, plus chilling • **Cooking Time** 10 minutes • **Cuts into 4 slices** • **Per Slice** 577 calories, 20g fat (of which 4g saturates), 86g carbohydrate, 0.4g salt • **Gluten Free** • **Dairy Free** • **Easy**

500g (1lb 2oz) ready-to-eat dried
   figs, hard stalks removed
50g (2oz) candied orange peel,
   finely chopped
75g (3oz) hazelnuts, toasted
50g (2oz) shelled pistachio nuts
50g (2oz) plain chocolate, broken
   into pieces
50g (2oz) ready-to-eat pitted dates
¼ tsp ground cinnamon
a pinch of freshly grated nutmeg
4 tbsp brandy, plus extra to drizzle
rice paper

1 Put the figs and candied orange peel into a food processor and whiz for 1 minute to mince the fruit finely. Tip into a large bowl.

2 Put the hazelnuts, pistachio nuts, chocolate and dates into the food processor with the spices and 4 tbsp brandy and pulse to chop roughly. Add to the fig mixture and mix, using your hands.

3 Put a sheet of rice paper on a baking sheet. Spoon the fig mixture evenly on top, then press down with the back of a wet spoon to form an

even layer about 2cm (¾in) thick. Put another sheet of rice paper on top and press down well. Chill for 1 hour.

4 Cut the slice into four rectangles to serve.

★ TO STORE
If not serving straight away, wrap in baking parchment, tie up with string and store in the fridge. It will keep for up to four weeks – unwrap and drizzle with 1 tsp brandy every week.

Apricot and Almond Traybake

Preparation Time 20 minutes • **Cooking Time** 30–40 minutes, plus cooling • **Cuts into 18 bars** • **Per Bar** 277 calories, 16g fat (of which 8g saturates), 30g carbohydrate, 0.4g salt • **Easy**

250g (9oz) unsalted butter, softened, plus extra to grease
225g (8oz) golden caster sugar
275g (10oz) self-raising flour, sifted
2 tsp baking powder
finely grated zest of 1 orange and 2 tbsp orange juice
75g (3oz) ground almonds
5 medium eggs, lightly beaten
225g (8oz) ready-to-eat dried apricots, roughly chopped
25g (1oz) flaked almonds
icing sugar to dust (optional)

1 Preheat the oven to 180°C (160°C fan oven) mark 4. Grease a 33 x 20.5cm (13 x 8in) baking tin and baseline with baking parchment.

2 Put the butter, caster sugar, flour, baking powder, orange zest, ground almonds and eggs into the bowl of a large freestanding mixer. Mix on a low setting for 30 seconds, then increase the speed and mix for 1 minute or until thoroughly combined. (Alternatively, mix well using a wooden spoon.)

3 Remove the bowl from the mixer. Using a large metal spoon, fold in the apricots. Spoon the mixture into the prepared tin, level the surface and sprinkle the flaked almonds over the top.

4 Bake for 30–40 minutes until risen and golden brown and a skewer inserted into the centre comes out clean. Leave to cool in the tin.

5 Cut into 18 bars. Dust with icing sugar, if you like.

 TO STORE
Wrap in clingfilm and store in an airtight container. They will keep for up to three days.

Blackberry Traybake

★

Preparation Time 20 minutes • **Cooking Time** about 45 minutes, plus cooling and setting • **Cuts into 24 squares** •
Per Square 239 calories, 12g fat (of which 7g saturates), 32g carbohydrate, 0.4g salt • **Easy**

275g (10oz) unsalted butter,
    softened, plus extra to grease
275g (10oz) golden caster sugar
400g (14oz) self-raising flour
1½ tsp baking powder
5 medium eggs
finely grated zest of 1 large orange
1 tbsp vanilla extract
4–5 tbsp milk
250g (9oz) blackberries
40g (1½oz) flaked almonds

FOR THE ICING
150g (5oz) icing sugar
1 tsp vanilla extract
about 2 tbsp orange juice

1 Preheat the oven to 190°C (170°C fan oven) mark 5. Grease a shallow 30.5 x 20.5cm (12 x 8in) baking tin and line with greaseproof paper.

2 Put the butter and caster sugar into a large bowl. Sift in the flour and baking powder, then add the eggs, orange zest, vanilla and milk and beat together until light and fluffy.

3 Using a metal spoon, fold in half the blackberries. Spoon into the tin and dot with the remaining blackberries, then the almonds.

4 Bake for 40–45 minutes until springy to the touch. Cool in the tin for 5 minutes, then turn out on to a wire rack to cool completely.

5 When the cake is cool, make the icing. Sift the icing sugar into a bowl, then add the vanilla and orange juice, mixing as you go, until smooth and runny. Drizzle over the cake and leave for 30 minutes to set. Cut into 24 squares to serve.

★TO STORE
Wrap in clingfilm and store in an airtight container. It will keep for up to four days.

★FREEZING TIP
To freeze Complete the recipe to the end of step 4. Cool completely, keeping the cake in its greaseproof paper, then wrap in clingfilm. Freeze for up to one month. To use Thaw overnight at cool room temperature. Complete the recipe.

Carrot Traybake

⭐

Preparation Time 30 minutes • **Cooking Time** 50 minutes–1 hour 5 minutes • **Cuts into 15 squares** •
Per Square 399 calories, 25g fat (of which 13g saturates), 41g carbohydrate, 0.4g salt • **Easy**

100g (3½oz) unsalted butter,
    chopped, plus extra to grease
140g (4½oz) carrots, grated
100g (3½oz) sultanas
100g (3½oz) chopped dried dates
50g (2oz) tenderised coconut
1 tsp ground cinnamon
½ tsp freshly grated nutmeg
330g bottle maple syrup
150ml (¼ pint) apple juice
zest and juice of 2 oranges
225g (8oz) wholemeal self-raising
    flour, sifted
2 tsp bicarbonate of soda
125g (4oz) walnut pieces

FOR THE TOPPING
pared zest from ½–1 orange
200g (7oz) cream cheese
200g (7oz) crème fraîche
2 tbsp icing sugar
1 tsp vanilla extract

1 Preheat the oven to 190°C (170°C fan oven) mark 5. Grease a 23 × 23cm (9 × 9in) cake tin and line with greaseproof paper.

2 Put the butter, carrots, sultanas, dates, coconut, spices, syrup, apple juice and orange zest and juice into a large pan. Cover and bring to the boil, then cook for 5 minutes. Tip into a bowl and leave to cool.

3 Put the flour, bicarbonate of soda and walnuts into a large bowl and stir together. Add the cooled carrot mixture and stir well. Spoon the mixture into the prepared tin and level the surface.

4 Bake for 45 minutes–1 hour until firm. Leave to cool in the tin for 10 minutes, then turn out on to a wire rack to cool completely.

5 To make the topping, finely slice the orange zest. Put the cream cheese, crème fraîche, icing sugar and vanilla into a bowl and stir with a spatula. Spread over the cake and top with the zest. Cut into 15 squares to serve.

Quick Chocolate Slices

Preparation Time 10 minutes • **Cooking Time** 2 minutes, plus chilling • **Cuts into 40 slices** • **Per Slice** 137 calories, 9g fat (of which 6g saturates), 13g carbohydrate, 0.3g salt • **Easy**

225g (8oz) unsalted butter or olive oil spread

50g (2oz) cocoa, sifted

3 tbsp golden syrup

300g pack digestive biscuits, crushed

400g (14oz) plain chocolate (at least 70 per cent cocoa solids), broken into pieces

1 Put the butter or olive oil spread into a heatproof bowl, add the cocoa and syrup and melt over a pan of gently simmering water. Mix everything together.

2 Remove from the heat and stir in the biscuits. Mix well until thoroughly coated in chocolate, crushing any large pieces of biscuit. Turn into a greased 25.5 x 16.5cm (10 x 6½in) tin and leave to cool, then cover and chill for 20 minutes.

3 Melt the chocolate in a heatproof bowl in a 900W microwave oven on full power for 1 minute 40 seconds, stirring twice. Alternatively, put into a heatproof bowl set over a pan of gently simmering water (making sure the base of the bowl doesn't touch the water). Stir once more and pour over the chocolate biscuit base, then chill for 20 minutes.

4 Cut in half lengthways. Cut each half into 20 rectangular slices.

★ TO STORE

Store in an airtight container. They will keep for up to one week.

Hazelnut and Chocolate Flapjacks

Preparation Time 10 minutes • **Cooking Time** 30 minutes, plus cooling • **Cuts into 12 flapjacks** •
Per Flapjack 229 calories, 14g fat (of which 6g saturates), 26g carbohydrate, 0.2g salt • **Easy**

125g (4oz) unsalted butter, plus
   extra to grease
125g (4oz) light muscovado sugar
1 tbsp golden syrup
50g (2oz) hazelnuts, roughly
   chopped
175g (6oz) jumbo or porridge oats
50g (2oz) plain chocolate such as
   Bournville, roughly chopped

1 Preheat the oven to 180°C
(160°C fan oven) mark 4. Lightly
grease a shallow 28 x 18cm
(11 x 7in) baking tin.

2 Put the butter, sugar and syrup
into a pan and melt together over
a low heat. Stir in the hazelnuts
and oats. Leave the mixture to cool
slightly, then stir in the chocolate.

3 Spoon the mixture into the
prepared tin, level the surface and
bake for about 30 minutes or until
golden and firm.

4 Leave to cool in the tin for a few
minutes, then cut into 12 pieces.
Turn out on to a wire rack and leave
to cool completely.

★TO STORE
*Store in an airtight container. They will
keep for up to one week.*

★TRY SOMETHING
DIFFERENT
**Tropical Fruit and Coconut
Flapjacks**
*Replace the hazelnuts and chocolate with
mixed dried tropical fruits, chopped into
pieces. Replace 50g (2oz) of the oats
with desiccated coconut.*
Apricot and Mixed Seed Flapjacks
*Replace the hazelnuts with 50g (2oz)
mixed seeds (such as pumpkin,
sunflower, linseed and sesame).
Reduce the oats to 125g (4oz) and
replace the chocolate with 100g (3½oz)
chopped dried apricots.*

Nutty Fudge Shortbread

Preparation Time 15 minutes, plus 3 hours chilling • **Cooking Time** 40 minutes, plus cooling, chilling and setting •
Cuts into 16 pieces • **Per Piece** 450 calories, 26g fat (of which 12g saturates), 51g carbohydrate, 0.3g salt • **Easy**

225g (8oz) unsalted butter,
  softened, plus extra to grease
300g (11oz) plain flour, sifted
a pinch of salt
125g (4oz) caster sugar
125g (4oz) light muscovado sugar,
  sifted
2 tbsp golden syrup
170g can condensed milk
300g (11oz) plain chocolate, such
  as Bournville
100g (3½oz) walnut halves
100g (3½oz) hazelnuts, lightly
  toasted

1 Preheat the oven to 180°C (160°C fan oven) mark 4. Grease a 20.5 × 30.5cm (8 × 12in) Swiss roll tin.

2 Whiz the flour, salt, caster sugar and 140g (4½oz) butter in a food processor until it begins to come together. Press the mixture into the prepared tin and smooth over with the back of a spoon. Bake for 20–30 minutes until golden. Leave to cool in the tin.

3 Put the remaining butter, the muscovado sugar, syrup and condensed milk into a pan and heat gently, but don't boil. Whisk together until combined. Pour over the shortbread, smooth the surface and chill for 3 hours.

4 Melt the chocolate in a heatproof bowl set over a pan of gently simmering water, making sure the base of the bowl doesn't touch the water. Remove the bowl from the pan, then mix the chocolate with the nuts and pour over the fudge mixture. Smooth the top and leave to set. Cut into pieces to serve.

★ TO STORE
Store in an airtight container. They will keep for up to one week.

Chocolate Fudge Shortbread

Preparation Time 30 minutes • **Cooking Time** 20 minutes, plus cooling • **Cuts into 20 squares** • **Per Square** 369 calories, 19g fat (of which 12g saturates), 48g carbohydrate, 0.4g salt • **Easy**

175g (6oz) unsalted butter, at room temperature, diced, plus extra to grease

250g (9oz) plain flour, plus extra to dust

75g (3oz) golden caster sugar

FOR THE TOPPING

2 x 397g cans sweetened condensed milk

100g (3½oz) light muscovado sugar

100g (3½oz) butter

250g (9oz) plain chocolate (at least 70% cocoa solids), broken into pieces

1 Preheat the oven to 180°C (160°C fan oven) mark 4. Grease a 33 x 23cm (13 x 9in) Swiss roll tin and line with baking parchment. Put the flour, caster sugar and butter into a food processor and blend until the mixture forms crumbs, then pulse a little more until it forms a ball. Turn out on to a lightly floured surface and knead lightly to combine.

2 Press the mixture into the prepared tin and bake for 20 minutes or until firm to the touch and a very pale brown.

3 To make the topping, put the condensed milk, muscovado sugar and butter into a non-stick pan and cook over a medium heat, stirring continuously until a fudge-like consistency. (Alternatively, put into a heatproof bowl and microwave on full power for 12 minutes – based on a 900W oven – or until the mixture is thick and fudgy, beating with a whisk every 2–3 minutes.) Spoon the caramel on to the shortbread, smooth over and allow to cool.

4 To finish, melt the chocolate in a heatproof bowl set over a pan of gently simmering water, making sure the base of the bowl doesn't touch the water, then pour over the caramel layer. Leave to set at room temperature, then cut into 20 squares to serve.

★ TO STORE

Store in an airtight container. They will keep for up to one week.

Chocolate Pecan Bars

Preparation Time 15 minutes • **Cooking Time** 1¼ hours, plus cooling • **Cuts into 25 bars** • **Per Bar** 189 calories, 13g fat (of which 6g saturates), 18g carbohydrate, 0.2g salt • **Easy**

125g (4oz) plain flour, sifted
25g (1oz) icing sugar
200g (7oz) unsalted butter, plus
   extra to grease
1 large egg yolk and 2 large eggs
125g (4oz) self-raising flour
1 tsp baking powder
125g (4oz) caster sugar
3–4 drops vanilla extract
150g (5oz) milk chocolate chips
75g (3oz) pecan nuts, chopped
6 tbsp chocolate and hazelnut
   spread

1 Preheat the oven to 200°C (180°C fan oven) mark 6. Grease a 25.5 x 15cm (10 x 6in) shallow baking tin and baseline with baking parchment.

2 Put the plain flour and icing sugar into a food processor with 75g (3oz) roughly chopped butter and whiz until crumb-like in texture. (Alternatively, rub the butter into the dry ingredients in a large bowl by hand or using a pastry cutter.) Add the egg yolk and whiz for 10–15 seconds, or add to the bowl with the dry ingredients and stir until the mixture begins to come together. Turn into the tin and press into a thin layer. Bake for 15 minutes or until golden.

3 Meanwhile, put the self-raising flour, baking powder, caster sugar, vanilla extract and the remaining eggs into the food processor with the remaining softened butter and blend for 15 seconds or until smooth (or put the ingredients into a bowl and mix well with a wooden spoon). Remove the blade and fold in the chocolate chips and pecan nuts. Set aside.

4 Spread the chocolate and hazelnut spread over the cooked base and top with the cake mixture. Reduce the oven temperature to 180°C (160°C fan oven) mark 4 and bake for 45–50 minutes until golden – cover loosely with foil if necessary. Leave to cool in the tin for about 10 minutes, then turn out on to a wire rack to cool completely. Cut into 25 pieces.

★ TO STORE
Store in an airtight container. They will keep for up to two days.

Muesli Bars

Preparation Time 10 minutes, plus cooling • **Cooking Time** 30–35 minutes, plus cooling • **Cuts into 12 bars** •
Per Bar 386 calories, 21g fat (of which 8g saturates), 48g carbohydrate, 0.3g salt • **Easy**

175g (6oz) unsalted butter, cut into
   pieces
150g (5oz) light muscovado sugar
2 tbsp golden syrup
375g (13oz) porridge oats
100g (3½oz) ready-to-eat dried
   papaya, roughly chopped
50g (2oz) sultanas
50g (2oz) pecan nuts, roughly
   chopped
25g (1oz) pinenuts
25g (1oz) pumpkin seeds
1 tbsp plain flour
1 tsp ground cinnamon

1 Preheat the oven to 180°C (160°C fan oven) mark 4. Melt the butter, sugar and syrup together in a heavy-based pan over a low heat.

2 Meanwhile, put the oats, dried fruit, nuts, seeds, flour and cinnamon into a large bowl and stir to mix. Pour in the melted mixture and mix together until combined.

3 Spoon the mixture into a 30.5 × 20.5cm (12 × 8in) non-stick baking tin and press down into the corners.

4 Bake for 25–30 minutes until golden. Press the mixture down again if necessary, then use a palette knife to mark into 12 bars. Leave in the tin to cool completely.

5 Use a palette knife to lift the bars out of the tin.

★TO STORE
Store in an airtight container. They will keep for up to one week.

Vanilla Crumble Bars

Preparation Time 15 minutes • **Cooking Time** 50–60 minutes, plus cooling • **Cuts into 25 bars** • **Per Bar** 295 calories, 10g fat (of which 5g saturates), 50g carbohydrate, 0.6g salt • **Easy**

250g (9oz) unsalted butter,
    softened, plus extra to grease
250g (9oz) caster sugar
125g (4oz) plain flour, sifted
175g (6oz) self-raising flour
grated zest of 1 lemon
3 large eggs
1½ tsp vanilla extract

1 Preheat the oven to 180°C (160°C fan oven) mark 4. Grease a 25.5 x 18cm (10 x 7in) shallow baking tin and baseline with baking parchment.

2 To make the crumble topping, put 75g (3oz) butter and 75g (3oz) sugar into a food processor and whiz until smooth. Add the plain flour and whiz for 8–10 seconds until the mixture forms very rough breadcrumbs, then put to one side.

3 Put the remaining butter and sugar, the self-raising flour, lemon zest, eggs and vanilla extract into

the food processor and whiz for about 15 seconds or until smooth. Pour the mixture into the prepared tin, sprinkle the crumble topping over the surface and press down to cover.

4 Bake for 50–60 minutes (if necessary, cover loosely with foil for the last 10 minutes if the top is browning too quickly). Leave to cool in the tin for 5 minutes. Turn out on to a wire rack and cut into 25 bars.

★TO STORE
Store in an airtight container. They will keep for up to three days.

★TRY SOMETHING DIFFERENT
Cherry and Coconut Crumble Bars
Rinse and dry 225g (8oz) glacé cherries and quarter them; fold the cherries into the crumble topping at the end of step 2. Make the sponge base as in step 3, adding 50g (2oz) desiccated coconut to the ingredients.

Sticky Ginger Flapjacks

★

Preparation Time 10 minutes • **Cooking Time** 40 minutes, plus cooling • **Cuts into 24 flapjacks** •
Per Flapjack 259 calories, 14g fat (of which 8g saturates), 33g carbohydrate, 0.3g salt • **Easy**

350g (12oz) unsalted butter, plus
   extra to grease
275g (10oz) caster sugar
225g (8oz) golden syrup
450g (1lb) rolled oats
1 tbsp ground ginger

1 Preheat the oven to 180°C (160°C fan oven) mark 4. Grease a 28 x 18cm (11 x 7in) shallow cake tin and baseline with baking parchment.

2 Put the butter, sugar and syrup into a large pan and heat gently until melted. Mix in the rolled oats and ground ginger until they are thoroughly combined.

3 Pour the mixture into the tin, level the surface and bake for 30–35 minutes until golden brown around the edges. Leave to cool in the tin for 15 minutes.

4 While still warm, score into 24 pieces with a sharp knife. Leave in the tin to cool completely, then turn out and cut out the pieces.

★ TO STORE
Store in an airtight container. They will keep for up to one week.

★ COOK'S TIP
Don't overcook the flapjacks or they will be hard and dry. When they are cooked, they should still be sticky and slightly soft when you press them in the middle.

Fruit and Nut Flapjack Bites

Preparation Time 10 minutes • **Cooking Time** 25–30 minutes, plus cooling • **Cuts into 36 squares** •
Per Square 162 calories, 8g fat (of which 4g saturates), 22g carbohydrate, 0.2g salt • **Easy**

250g (9oz) unsalted butter, cut into
   pieces, plus extra to grease
250g (9oz) caster sugar
175g (6oz) golden syrup
425g (15oz) rolled oats
125g (4oz) mixed dried fruit,
   including glacé cherries
75g (3oz) chopped nuts, toasted

1 Preheat the oven to 180°C (160°C fan oven) mark 4. Grease a shallow 28 x 20.5cm (11 x 8in) baking tin.

2 Put the butter, sugar and syrup into a large heavy-based pan. Stir over a moderate heat until the butter has melted. Remove from the heat and stir in the oats, dried fruit and nuts. Turn into the prepared tin and level the surface.

3 Bake for 25–30 minutes until deep golden around the edges; the mixture will still be very soft in the middle. Leave in the tin until almost cold. Remove from the tin and cut into 36 squares.

★**TO STORE**
Store in an airtight container. They will keep for up to one week.

★**COOK'S TIP**
Don't worry if your baking tin is not the exact size; use one of similar dimensions.

★**TRY SOMETHING DIFFERENT**
Instead of mixed dried fruit, use chopped dried apricots.

Lamingtons

★

Preparation Time 40 minutes • **Cooking Time** 30 minutes, plus cooling and setting • **Cuts into 16 squares** •
Per Square 273 calories, 17g fat (of which 12g saturates), 29g carbohydrate, 0.4g salt • **Easy**

125g (4oz) unsalted butter,
    softened, plus extra to grease
125g (4oz) golden caster sugar
2 medium eggs
125g (4oz) self-raising flour, sifted
1 tsp baking powder
2 tsp vanilla extract

FOR THE COATING
200g (7oz) icing sugar
50g (2oz) cocoa powder
25g (1oz) unsalted butter, cubed
5 tbsp milk
200g (7oz) desiccated coconut

1 Preheat the oven to 180°C (160°C fan oven) mark 4. Grease a 15cm (6in) square cake tin and baseline with baking parchment.

2 Put the butter, caster sugar, eggs, flour, baking powder and vanilla extract into a bowl and beat with a hand-held electric whisk until creamy. Turn the mixture into the prepared tin and level the surface. Bake for about 30 minutes or until just firm to the touch and a skewer inserted into the centre comes out clean. Transfer to a wire rack to cool completely. Wrap and store, preferably overnight, so that the cake is easier to slice.

3 To make the topping, sift the icing sugar and cocoa powder into a bowl. Put the butter and milk into a small pan and heat until the butter has just melted. Pour over the icing sugar and stir until smooth, adding 2–3 tbsp water if necessary, so that the icing thickly coats the back of a spoon.

4 Trim the side crusts from the cake and cut into 16 squares. Place a sheet of greaseproof paper under a wire rack to catch the drips. Scatter the coconut on to a large plate.

Pierce a piece of cake through the top crust and dip into the icing until coated, turning the cake gently. Transfer to the wire rack. Once you've coated half the pieces, roll them in the coconut and transfer to a plate. Repeat with the remainder and leave to set for a couple of hours before serving.

★ COOK'S TIP
If, towards the end of coating the cakes, the chocolate topping mixture has thickened, carefully stir in a drop of water to thin it down.

Raspberry and Cream Cheese Chocolate Brownies

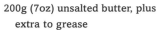

Preparation Time 20 minutes, plus cooling • **Cooking Time** around 35 minutes, plus cooling • **Cuts into 9 brownies** •
Per Brownie 465 calories, 32g fat (of which 20g saturates), 41g carbohydrate, 0.7g salt • **Easy**

200g (7oz) unsalted butter, plus
    extra to grease
150g (5oz) each dark chocolate and
    plain chocolate (at least 70%
    cocoa solids), chopped
4 medium eggs
150g (5oz) light muscovado sugar
125g (4oz) plus 1 tbsp self-raising
    flour, sifted
125g (4oz) curd cheese or cream
    cheese
2 tbsp raspberry jam
crème fraîche to serve

1 Preheat the oven to 200°C (180°C fan oven) mark 6. Grease a 23cm (9in) square tin and line with greaseproof paper. Put both chocolates and the butter into a heatproof bowl set over a pan of simmering water and stir to combine. When they have melted, take off the heat and set aside to cool.

2 Put 3 of the eggs and all but 1 tsp sugar into a bowl and whisk together with a hand-held electric whisk until thick and mousse-like. Fold in the cooled chocolate mixture and all but 1 tbsp flour, then pour into the prepared tin.

3 Put the cheese into a bowl with the remaining egg and the reserved 1 tsp sugar and 1 tbsp flour. Mix well to combine.

4 Place dollops of the cheese mixture randomly over the surface, then top each with a teaspoonful of the raspberry jam. Use a skewer to marble the cheese, jam and brownie mixture together.

5 Bake for 25–30 minutes. Remove from the oven and leave to cool in the tin for 10 minutes, then lift out the brownie and transfer to a wire rack to cool completely. Cut into 9 individual brownies and serve with a dollop of crème fraîche.

Chocolate Fudge Brownies

★

Preparation Time 20 minutes • **Cooking Time** 1 hour, plus cooling • **Cuts into 12 brownies** • **Per Brownie** 174 calories, 5g fat (of which 3g saturates), 33g carbohydrate, 0.1g salt • **Easy**

butter to grease
125g (4oz) milk chocolate
9 ready-to-eat dried prunes
200g (7oz) light muscovado sugar
3 large egg whites
1 tsp vanilla extract
75g (3oz) plain flour, sifted
50g (2oz) white chocolate, chopped
icing sugar to dust

1 Preheat the oven to 180°C (160°C fan oven) mark 4. Grease a 15cm (6in) square shallow cake tin and baseline with baking parchment.

2 Melt the milk chocolate in a heatproof bowl set over a pan of gently simmering water, making sure the base of the bowl doesn't touch the water. Remove from the heat and leave to cool slightly.

3 Put the prunes into a food processor or blender with 100ml (3½fl oz) water and whiz for 2–3 minutes to make a purée. Add the muscovado sugar and whiz briefly to mix.

4 Put the egg whites into a clean, grease-free bowl and whisk until soft peaks form.

5 Add the vanilla extract, prune mixture, flour, white chocolate and egg whites to the bowl of melted chocolate and fold everything together gently. Pour the mixture into the prepared tin and bake for 1 hour or until firm to the touch.

6 Leave to cool in the tin. Turn out, dust with icing sugar and cut into 12 individual brownies.

★ TO STORE
Store in an airtight container. They will keep for up to two days.

Double-chocolate Brownies

Preparation Time 15 minutes • **Cooking Time** 20–25 minutes, plus cooling • **Cuts into 16 brownies** •
Per Brownie 352 calories, 25g fat (of which 13g saturates), 29g carbohydrate, 0.3g salt • **Easy**

250g (9oz) butter, plus extra
 to grease
250g (9oz) plain chocolate (at least
 50% cocoa solids), broken into
 pieces
100g (3½oz) white chocolate,
 broken into pieces
4 medium eggs
175g (6oz) light muscovado sugar
1 tsp vanilla extract
75g (3oz) plain flour, sifted
¼ tsp baking powder
1 tbsp cocoa powder, sifted, plus
 extra to dust
100g (3½oz) pecan nuts, chopped
a pinch of salt
a little icing sugar to dust

1 Preheat the oven to 200°C (180°C fan oven) mark 6. Grease a 20.5cm (8in) square shallow tin and baseline with baking parchment. Melt the butter and plain chocolate in a heatproof bowl set over a pan of gently simmering water, making sure the base of the bowl doesn't touch the water. Remove the bowl from the pan and put to one side.

2 In a separate bowl, melt the white chocolate over a pan of gently simmering water, making sure the base of the bowl doesn't touch the water. Remove the bowl from the pan and put to one side.

3 Put the eggs into a separate large bowl. Add the muscovado sugar and vanilla extract and whisk together until the mixture is pale and thick.

4 Add the flour, baking powder, cocoa powder, the pecan nuts and a pinch of salt to the bowl, then carefully pour in the dark chocolate mixture. Using a large metal spoon, gently fold the ingredients together to make a smooth batter – if you fold too roughly, the chocolate will seize up and become unusable.

5 Pour the brownie mixture into the prepared tin. Spoon dollops of the white chocolate over the brownie mix, then swirl a skewer through it several times to create a marbled effect.

6 Bake for 20–25 minutes. The brownie should be fudgy inside and the top should be cracked and crispy. Leave to cool in the tin.

7 Transfer the brownies to a board and cut into 16 individual brownies. To serve, dust with a little icing sugar and cocoa powder.

★ TO STORE
Complete the recipe to the end of step 6, then store in an airtight tin. It will keep for up to one week. Complete the recipe to serve.

★ TRY SOMETHING DIFFERENT
Try making these brownies without butter – believe it or not, this recipe will still work. But you'll need to eat them within an hour of taking them out of the oven – fat is what makes cakes moist and allows them to be stored.

Low-fat Brownies

Preparation Time 10 minutes • **Cooking Time** 20 minutes, plus cooling • **Cuts into 16 brownies** •
Per Brownie 172 calories, 8g fat (of which 3g saturates), 24g carbohydrate, 0.1g salt • **Easy**

50ml (2fl oz) sunflower oil, plus
   extra to grease
250g (9oz) plain chocolate (at least
   50% cocoa solids)
4 medium eggs
150g (5oz) light muscovado sugar
1 tsp vanilla extract
75g (3oz) plain flour
¼ tsp baking powder
1 tbsp cocoa powder

1 Preheat the oven to 200°C (180°C fan oven) mark 6. Grease a 20.5cm (8in) square shallow tin and baseline with baking parchment.

2 Melt the chocolate in a heatproof bowl set over a pan of gently simmering water, making sure the base of the bowl doesn't touch the water. Remove the bowl from the pan and put to one side to cool slightly.

3 Put the eggs into a large bowl, add the oil, sugar and vanilla extract and whisk together until pale and thick. Sift the flour, baking powder and cocoa powder into the bowl, then carefully pour in the chocolate. Using a large metal spoon, gently fold all the ingredients together – if you fold too roughly, the chocolate will seize up and become unusable.

4 Carefully pour the brownie mixture into the prepared tin and bake for 20 minutes – when cooked, the brownie should be fudgy inside and the top should be cracked and crispy. Cut into 16 individual brownies immediately, then leave to cool in the tin.

TO STORE
Wrap in clingfilm and store in an airtight container. They will keep for up to three days.

Cherry Chocolate Fudge Brownies

Preparation Time 20 minutes • **Cooking Time** 50 minutes, plus cooling and 1 hour setting • **Cuts into 12 brownies** •
Per Brownie 462 calories, 24g fat (of which 14g saturates), 59g carbohydrate, 0.3g salt • **Easy**

150g (5oz) unsalted butter, plus
   extra to grease
200g (7oz) plain chocolate (at least
   70% cocoa solids)
175g (6oz) caster sugar
2 tsp vanilla extract
5 medium eggs
175g (6oz) plain flour
¾ tsp baking powder
250g (9oz) glacé cherries, halved

FOR THE ICING
150g (5oz) plain chocolate (at least
   70% cocoa solids)
2 tbsp Kirsch
4 tbsp double cream

1 Preheat the oven to 180°C (160°C fan oven) mark 4. Grease an 18cm (7in) square shallow cake tin and baseline with greaseproof paper. Put the butter and chocolate into a heatproof bowl set over a pan of gently simmering water, making sure the base of the bowl doesn't touch the water. Leave the chocolate to melt without stirring. Remove the bowl from the pan and stir until smooth. Leave to cool.

2 Whisk the sugar, vanilla extract and eggs until pale and thick. Stir the chocolate into the egg mixture. Sift the flour and baking powder together and lightly fold into the mixture with the cherries. Pour the mixture into the prepared tin and bake for 40 minutes or until just set. Cool slightly in the tin before icing.

3 To make the icing, put the chocolate and Kirsch into a heatproof bowl set over a pan of gently simmering water, making sure the base of the bowl doesn't touch the water. Once melted, add the cream and 4 tbsp water and stir well. Pour over the brownie and leave to set. Cut into 12 individual brownies.

⭐ TO STORE
Store in an airtight container. They will keep for up to one week.

⭐FREEZING TIP
To freeze Complete the recipe up to the end of step 2. Remove from the tin, wrap and freeze.
To use Thaw at cool room temperature for about 5 hours. Complete the recipe.

White Chocolate and Nut Brownies

Preparation Time 20 minutes • **Cooking Time** 30–35 minutes, plus cooling • **Cuts into 12 brownies** •
Per Brownie 502 calories, 31g fat (of which 13g saturates), 52g carbohydrate, 0.4g salt • **Easy**

75g (3oz) unsalted butter, plus extra
   to grease
500g (1lb 2oz) white chocolate,
   roughly chopped
3 large eggs
175g (6oz) golden caster sugar
175g (6oz) self-raising flour
a pinch of salt
175g (6oz) macadamia nuts,
   roughly chopped
1 tsp vanilla extract

1 Preheat the oven to 190°C (170°C fan oven) mark 5. Grease a 25.5 x 20.5cm (10 x 8in) baking tin and baseline with baking parchment.

2 Melt 125g (4oz) white chocolate with the butter in a heatproof bowl set over a pan of gently simmering water, making sure the base of the bowl doesn't touch the water, stirring occasionally. Remove the bowl from the pan and leave to cool slightly.

3 Whisk the eggs and sugar together in a large bowl until smooth, then gradually beat in the melted chocolate mixture – the consistency will become quite firm. Sift the flour and salt over the mixture, then fold in with the nuts, the remaining chopped chocolate and the vanilla extract. Turn the mixture into the prepared tin and level the surface.

4 Bake for 30–35 minutes until risen and golden and the centre is just firm to the touch – the mixture will still be soft under the crust; it firms up on cooling. Leave to cool in the tin.

5 Turn out and cut into 12 individual brownies.

★ TO STORE
Store in an airtight container. They will keep for up to one week.

The Ultimate Chocolate Brownie

Preparation Time 15 minutes, plus cooling • **Cooking Time** 1 hour 20 minutes, plus cooling • **Cuts into 16 brownies** •
Per Brownie 257 calories, 11g fat (of which 6g saturates), 38g carbohydrate, 0.2g salt • **Easy**

200g (7oz) salted butter, plus extra
    to grease
400g (14oz) good-quality plain
    chocolate
225g (8oz) light muscovado sugar
1 tsp vanilla extract
150g (5oz) pecan nuts, roughly
    chopped
25g (1oz) cocoa powder, sifted
75g (3oz) self-raising flour, sifted
3 large eggs, beaten
sifted cocoa powder to dust

1 Preheat the oven to 170°C (150°C fan oven) mark 3. Grease a 20.5cm (8in) square, 5cm (2in) deep baking tin and baseline with baking parchment.

2 Put the butter and chocolate into a heatproof bowl set over a pan of gently simmering water, making sure the base of the bowl doesn't touch the water. Stir until melted. Remove from the heat and stir in the sugar, vanilla extract, pecan nuts, cocoa, flour and eggs. Turn the mixture into the prepared tin and level the surface.

3 Bake for about 1¼ hours or until set to the centre on the surface but still soft underneath. Leave to cool in the tin for 2 hours.

4 Turn out, dust with sifted cocoa powder and cut into 16 individual brownies. Eat cold or serve warm with ice cream.

★ COOK'S TIP
The secret to really moist, squidgy brownies is all in the timing. A few minutes too long in the oven will produce a dry texture, so be careful not to bake them for too long.

Cherry Chocolate Chip Cookies

Preparation Time 20 minutes • **Cooking Time** 10–12 minutes, plus cooling • **Makes 24** • **Per Cookie** 104 calories, 5g fat (of which 3g saturates), 15g carbohydrate, 0.1g salt • **Easy**

75g (3oz) unsalted butter, softened, plus extra to grease
25g (1oz) caster sugar
50g (2oz) light muscovado sugar
a few drops of vanilla extract
1 large egg, lightly beaten
175g (6oz) self-raising flour, sifted
finely grated zest of 1 orange
125g (4oz) white chocolate, broken into pieces
125g (4oz) glacé cherries, roughly chopped

1 Preheat the oven to 180°C (160°C fan oven) mark 4 and grease several baking sheets.

2 Using a hand-held electric whisk, beat the butter, caster sugar, muscovado sugar and vanilla extract together in a large bowl until well combined. Beat in the egg.

3 Using a metal spoon, lightly fold in the flour, orange zest, chocolate and glacé cherries. Put heaped teaspoonfuls, spaced well apart, on the prepared baking sheets. Press lightly with the back of a spoon.

4 Bake for 10–12 minutes. The biscuits should be soft under a crisp crust. Transfer to a wire rack and leave to cool.

★ TO STORE
Store in an airtight container. They will keep for up to one week.

Hazelnut and Chocolate Biscotti

Preparation Time 10 minutes • **Cooking Time** 35–40 minutes, plus cooling • **Makes about 28** • **Per Biscuit** 50 calories, 1g fat (of which trace saturates), 9g carbohydrate, 0g salt • **Easy**

125g (4oz) plain flour, sifted, plus
    extra to dust
75g (3oz) golden caster sugar
¼ tsp baking powder
a pinch of cinnamon
a pinch of salt
1 large egg, beaten
1 tbsp milk
¼ tsp vanilla extract
25g (1oz) hazelnuts
25g (1oz) plain chocolate chips

1 Preheat the oven to 200°C (180°C fan oven) mark 6. Put the flour into a large bowl. Stir in the sugar, baking powder, cinnamon and salt. Make a well in the centre and, using a fork, stir in the beaten egg, milk, vanilla extract, hazelnuts and chocolate chips to form a sticky dough.

2 Turn out the dough on to a lightly floured worksurface and gently knead into a ball. Roll into a 28cm (11in) log shape. Put on a non-stick baking sheet and flatten slightly. Bake for 20–25 minutes until pale golden.

3 Reduce the oven temperature to 150°C (130°C fan oven) mark 2. Transfer the biscotti log on to a chopping board and slice diagonally with a bread knife at 1cm (½in) intervals. Arrange the slices on the baking sheet and put back into the oven for 15 minutes or until golden and dry. Transfer to a wire rack to cool completely.

 TO STORE
Store in an airtight container. They will keep for up to one month.

⭐COOK'S TIPS
● *To enjoy Italian-style, dunk in coffee or dessert wine.*
● *To make as gifts, divide the biscuits among four large squares of cellophane, then draw up the edges and tie with ribbon. Label the packages with storage information and an eat-by date.*

Chocolate and Pistachio Biscotti

Preparation Time 15 minutes • **Cooking Time** about 1 hour, plus cooling • **Makes 30** • **Per Biscuit** 152 calories, 7g fat (of which 3g saturates), 20g carbohydrate, 0.2g salt • **Easy**

300g (11oz) plain flour, sifted
75g (3oz) cocoa powder, sifted
1 tsp baking powder
150g (5oz) plain chocolate chips
150g (5oz) shelled pistachio nuts
a pinch of salt
75g (3oz) unsalted butter, softened
225g (8oz) granulated sugar
2 large eggs, beaten
1 tbsp icing sugar

1 Preheat the oven to 180°C (160°C fan oven) mark 4. Line a large baking sheet with baking parchment.

2 Mix the flour with the cocoa powder, baking powder, chocolate chips, pistachio nuts and salt. Using a hand-held electric whisk, beat the butter and granulated sugar together until light and fluffy. Gradually whisk in the beaten eggs.

3 Stir the dry ingredients into the mixture until it forms a stiff dough. With floured hands, shape the dough into two slightly flattened logs, each about 30.5 x 5cm (12 x 2in). Sprinkle with icing sugar. Put the logs on to the prepared baking sheet and bake for 40–45 minutes until they are slightly firm to the touch.

4 Leave the logs on the baking sheet for 10 minutes, then cut diagonally into 15 slices, 2cm (¾in) thick. Arrange them, cut side down, on the baking sheet and bake again for 15 minutes or until crisp. Cool on a wire rack.

★ TO STORE
Store in an airtight container. They will keep for up to one month.

★ TRY SOMETHING DIFFERENT
Cranberry, Hazelnut and Orange Biscotti
Increase the flour to 375g (13oz), omit the cocoa powder and add the grated zest of 1 orange. Replace the chocolate chips with dried cranberries and the pistachios with chopped blanched hazelnuts.

Chocolate Chip Oat Cookies

Preparation Time 15 minutes • **Cooking Time** 12–15 minutes, plus cooling • **Makes 18** • **Per Cookie** 197 calories, 10g fat (of which 6g saturates), 26g carbohydrate, 0.2g salt • **Easy**

125g (4oz) unsalted butter, softened, plus extra to grease
125g (4oz) golden caster sugar
1 medium egg
1 tsp vanilla extract
125g (4oz) porridge oats
150g (5oz) plain flour
½ tsp baking powder
200g (7oz) plain chocolate (at least 70% cocoa solids), cut into 1cm (½in) chunks

1 Preheat the oven to 180°C (160°C fan oven) mark 4. Lightly grease two baking sheets.

2 Cream the butter and sugar together in a bowl until pale and creamy. Add the egg, vanilla extract and oats. Sift the flour and baking powder together over the mixture and mix until evenly combined. Stir in the chocolate chunks.

3 Put dessertspoonfuls of the mixture on to the prepared baking sheets, spacing them well apart to allow room for spreading. Flatten each one slightly with the back of a fork.

4 Bake for 12–15 minutes until risen and turning golden, but still quite soft. Leave on the baking sheet for 5 minutes, then transfer to a wire rack to cool completely.

★TO STORE
Store in an airtight tin. They will keep for up to one week.

★FREEZING TIP
To freeze Complete the recipe and allow the cookies to cool. Wrap, seal, label and freeze.
To use Thaw the cookies individually, as needed, at room temperature for 1–2 hours.

Creamed Choc-oat Cookies

Preparation Time 10 minutes • **Cooking Time** 15–20 minutes, plus cooling • **Makes 18** • **Per Cookie** 212 calories, 11g fat (of which 6g saturates), 27g carbohydrate, 0.2g salt • **Easy**

125g (4oz) white chocolate
125g (4oz) plain chocolate
125g (4oz) unsalted butter, softened
125g (4oz) caster sugar
1 medium egg
1 tsp vanilla extract
125g (4oz) porridge oats
150g (5oz) plain flour
½ tsp baking powder

1 Preheat the oven to 180°C (160°C fan oven) mark 4. Lightly grease two baking sheets. Using a sharp knife, chop the white and plain chocolate into small chunks, no larger than 1cm (½in).

2 Cream the butter and sugar together in a bowl until pale. Add the egg, vanilla extract and oats. Sift in the flour and baking powder and mix until evenly combined. Stir in the chocolate chunks.

3 Place dessertspoonfuls of the mixture on to the prepared baking sheets, spacing them well apart to allow room for spreading. Flatten each one slightly with the back of a fork.

4 Bake for 12–15 minutes until risen and turning golden. Leave on the baking sheets for 5 minutes, then transfer to a wire rack to cool completely. Biscuits and cookies made using this creaming method firm up when cool.

★ TO STORE
Store in an airtight container. They will keep for up to one week.

White and Dark Chocolate Cookies

★

Preparation Time 15 minutes, plus chilling • **Cooking Time** 10–12 minutes, plus cooling • **Makes 26** •
Per Cookie 133 calories, 7g fat (of which 4g saturates), 17g carbohydrate, 0.1g salt • **Easy**

125g (4oz) unsalted butter,
    softened, plus extra to grease
125g (4oz) golden caster sugar
2 medium eggs, beaten
2 tsp vanilla extract
250g (9oz) self-raising flour, sifted
finely grated zest of 1 orange
100g (3½oz) white chocolate,
    roughly chopped
100g (3½oz) plain chocolate (at
    least 70% cocoa solids), roughly
    chopped

1 Preheat the oven to 180°C (160°C fan oven) mark 4. Lightly grease three baking sheets.

2 Cream the butter and sugar together until the mixture is pale and fluffy. Gradually beat in the eggs and vanilla extract. Sift in the flour, then add the orange zest and sprinkle in the white and plain chocolate. Mix the dough together with your hands. Knead lightly, then wrap in clingfilm and chill for at least 30 minutes.

3 Divide the mixture into 26 pieces and roll each into a ball. Using a dampened palette knife, flatten each ball slightly to make a disc, then put on the prepared baking sheets, spaced well apart.

4 Bake for about 10–12 minutes until golden. Leave on the baking sheets for 5 minutes, then transfer to a wire rack to cool completely.

★TO STORE
Store in an airtight container. They will keep for up to one week.

Oat and Sultana Cookies

★

Preparation Time 15 minutes, plus cooling • **Cooking Time** 12–15 minutes, plus cooling • **Makes 12** •
Per Cookie 187 calories, 10g fat of which 6g saturates), 23g carbohydrate, 0.3g salt • **Easy**

125g (4oz) unsalted butter,
    softened, plus extra to grease
75g (3oz) light muscovado sugar
1 medium egg
150g (5oz) rolled oats
50g (2oz) self-raising flour, plus
    extra to dust
½ tsp baking powder
grated zest of 1 lemon
50g (2oz) sultanas
1 tbsp maple syrup

1 Preheat the oven to 190°C (170°C fan oven) mark 5. Lightly grease two baking sheets.

2 Put the butter and muscovado sugar into a large bowl and, using a hand-held electric whisk, cream together until pale and fluffy. Beat in the egg until combined, then use a wooden spoon to stir in the oats, flour, baking powder, lemon zest, sultanas and syrup.

3 Dust a worksurface with a little flour, then take spoonfuls of the mixture and roll into 12 even-sized balls. Put them on to the prepared baking sheets, spaced well apart, and bake for 12–15 minutes until golden.

4 Leave to cool on the baking sheets for 5 minutes, then transfer to a wire rack to cool completely.

★ TO STORE
Store in an airtight container. They will keep for up to three days.

★ FREEZING TIP
To freeze *Complete the recipe to the end of step 3, but don't put the cookies on the baking sheets. Instead, put into a freezerproof container lined with greaseproof paper. Seal and freeze for up to one month.*
To use *Put the cookies on baking sheets and bake from frozen for 20–25 minutes.*

Sultana and Pecan Cookies

★

Preparation Time 15 minutes • **Cooking Time** 12–15 minutes, plus cooling • **Makes 20** • **Per Cookie** 276 calories, 18g fat (of which 7g saturates), 27g carbohydrate, 0.2g salt • **Easy**

225g (8oz) unsalted butter, at room
   temperature, plus extra to grease
175g (6oz) light muscovado sugar
2 medium eggs, lightly beaten
225g (8oz) pecan nut halves
300g (11oz) self-raising flour, sifted
¼ tsp baking powder
125g (4oz) sultanas
2 tbsp maple syrup

1 Preheat the oven to 190°C (170°C fan oven) mark 5. Lightly grease four baking sheets.

2 Cream the butter and sugar together until the mixture is pale and fluffy. Gradually beat in the eggs until thoroughly combined.

3 Put 20 pecan nut halves to one side, then roughly chop the rest and fold into the mixture with the flour, baking powder, sultanas and syrup.

4 Roll the mixture into 20 balls and place them, spaced well apart, on to the prepared baking sheets. Using a dampened palette knife, flatten the cookies and top each with a piece of pecan nut.

5 Bake for 12–15 minutes until pale golden. Leave on the baking sheets for 5 minutes, then transfer to a wire rack to cool completely.

★TO STORE
Store in an airtight container. They will keep for up to one week.

FREEZING TIP
To freeze *Complete the recipe to the end of step 4, then open-freeze a tray of unbaked cookies. When frozen, pack into bags or containers.*
To use *Cook from frozen for 18–20 minutes.*

Almond Cookies

Preparation Time 15 minutes • **Cooking Time** 20 minutes, plus cooling • **Makes 12** • **Per Cookie** 204 calories, 10g fat (of which 1g saturates), 27g carbohydrate, 0g salt • **Easy**

2 medium egg whites
200g (7oz) caster sugar
200g (7oz) ground almonds
zest of 1 orange
½ tsp ground ginger
40g (1½oz) stem ginger in syrup, drained and roughly chopped
2 tbsp plain flour, sifted, to dust
12 natural glacé cherries
rice paper for lining

1 Preheat the oven to 180°C (160°C fan oven) mark 4. Line two baking sheets with rice paper. Put the egg whites into a large, clean, grease-free bowl and whisk until they form stiff peaks. In another large bowl, stir the sugar, ground almonds, orange zest, ¼ tsp ground ginger and the stem ginger together. With a wooden spoon, mix in the egg whites to form a sticky dough.

2 Roll the dough into 12 equal-sized balls. Mix the flour and remaining ground ginger together in a bowl. Lightly coat each ball in the flour and shake off the excess. Put the balls, spaced well apart, on to the prepared baking sheets. Using a dampened palette knife, flatten each one into a round.

3 Push a glacé cherry into the middle of each cookie and bake for 15–20 minutes until lightly golden. Cool on a wire rack, then trim away the excess rice paper.

★ TO STORE
Store in an airtight container. They will keep for up to three days.

★ TRY SOMETHING DIFFERENT
Instead of a glacé cherry, use whole almonds or a sprinkling of lemon zest to top each cookie.

Cherry Chip Cookies

★

Preparation Time 20 minutes • **Cooking Time** 10–12 minutes, plus cooling • **Makes 14** • **Per Cookie** 179 calories, 8g fat (of which 5g saturates), 27g carbohydrate, 0.1g salt • **Easy**

75g (3oz) unsalted butter, softened,
   plus extra to grease
25g (1oz) caster sugar
50g (2oz) light soft brown sugar
a few drops of vanilla extract
1 large egg, lightly beaten
175g (6oz) self-raising flour, sifted
finely grated zest of 1 orange
125g (4oz) white chocolate, roughly
   broken
125g (4oz) glacé cherries, roughly
   chopped
icing sugar to dust

1 Preheat the oven to 180°C (160°C fan oven) mark 4 and lightly grease two baking sheets. Using a hand-held electric whisk, beat the butter, caster sugar, light soft brown sugar and vanilla extract together until well combined. Gradually beat in the egg until the mixture is light and fluffy.

2 Using a metal spoon, lightly fold in the flour, orange zest, chocolate and glacé cherries. Put tablespoonfuls of the mixture on to the prepared baking sheets.

3 Bake for 10–12 minutes. The biscuits should be soft under a crisp crust. Leave on the baking sheets for 1 minute, then transfer to a wire rack to cool completely. Dust with icing sugar just before serving.

★TO STORE
Store in an airtight container. They will keep for up to three days.

Cinnamon Whirls

⭐

Preparation Time 20 minutes, plus cooling • **Cooking Time** 20 minutes, plus cooling • **Makes about 34** •
Per Whirl 49 calories, 3g fat (of which 0g saturates), 6g carbohydrate, 0.1g salt • **Easy**

3 tbsp golden caster sugar, plus
　extra to dust
375g pack ready-rolled puff pastry
1 tsp ground cinnamon
1 tsp ground mixed spice
1 medium egg, beaten

1 Preheat the oven to 200°C (180°C fan oven) mark 6. Sprinkle the worksurface with caster sugar in a rectangle measuring 35.5 x 23cm (14 x 9in). Unroll the pastry and lay it on top to fit the shape of the sugar rectangle. Trim the edges, then cut vertically down the middle to make two smaller rectangles.

2 Mix the cinnamon with the mixed spice and golden caster sugar in a small bowl. Sprinkle half the spice mixture evenly over the pastry rectangles. Fold the top and bottom edges of the pastry pieces into the

middle so they meet at the centre. Sprinkle the remaining spice mixture over the surface and repeat, folding the upper and lower folded edges in to meet in the centre. Finally, fold in half lengthways to make a log shape.

3 Turn each roll over so that the seam faces down, trim off the ragged ends, then cut into slices 1cm (½in) wide. Lay the slices flat, spaced well apart, on two non-stick baking sheets. Reshape them slightly if needed, but don't worry if the rolls look loose – as the pastry cooks, they'll puff up.

4 Lightly brush each pastry whirl with a little beaten egg, sprinkle with a dusting of sugar and bake for 20 minutes or until pale golden. Cool on a wire rack before serving.

⭐ TO STORE
Store in an airtight tin. They will keep for up to three days.

⭐ FREEZING TIP
To freeze *Put the whirls into a freezerproof container and freeze for up to one month.*
To use *Thaw overnight at cool room temperature.*

Almond Macaroons

Preparation Time 10 minutes • **Cooking Time** 12–15 minutes, plus cooling • **Makes 22** • **Per Macaroon** 86 calories, 6g fat (of which 1g saturates), 7g carbohydrate, 0g salt • **Vegetarian** • **Gluten free** • **Dairy free** • **Easy**

2 medium egg whites
125g (4oz) caster sugar
125g (4oz) ground almonds
¼ tsp almond extract
22 blanched almonds

1 Preheat the oven to 180°C (fan oven 160°C) mark 4. Line baking trays with baking parchment. Whisk the egg whites in a clean, grease-free bowl until stiff peaks form. Gradually whisk in the caster sugar, a little at a time, until thick and glossy. Gently stir in the ground almonds and almond extract.

2 Spoon teaspoonfuls of the mixture on to the prepared baking trays, spacing them slightly apart. Press an almond into the centre of each one and bake in the oven for 12–15 minutes until just golden and firm to the touch.

3 Leave on the baking sheets for 10 minutes, then transfer to wire racks to cool completely. On cooling, these biscuits have a soft, chewy centre; they harden up after a few days.

★ TO STORE
Store in airtight containers. They will keep for up to one week.

Cranberry Biscuits

Preparation Time 15 minutes, plus chilling • **Cooking Time** 8–10 minutes, plus cooling • **Makes 24** •
Per Biscuit 79 calories, 4g fat (of which 3g saturates), 10g carbohydrate, 0.1g salt • **Easy**

125g (4oz) unsalted butter, chilled
50g (2oz) caster sugar
25g (1oz) dried cranberries
125g (4oz) plain flour, sifted, plus
extra to dust
75g (3oz) ground rice

1 Whiz the butter and sugar in a food processor, or use a hand-held electric mixer. Add the cranberries, flour and ground rice and pulse or mix until the mixture comes together. Turn out on to a lightly floured worksurface and shape into a rectangle about 12.5 × 7.5 × 2cm (5 × 3 × ¾in). Wrap and chill for 30 minutes. Preheat the oven to 200°C (180°C fan oven) mark 6.

2 Cut the dough into 3mm (⅛in) slices and put on a non-stick baking sheet.

3 Bake for 8–10 minutes until golden. Leave to cool on the sheet.

⭐TO STORE
Store in an airtight container. They will keep for up to one week.

⭐TRY SOMETHING DIFFERENT
You can use dried cherries or dried blueberries in place of the cranberries.

Florentines

Preparation Time 15 minutes • **Cooking Time** 8–10 minutes, plus cooling • **Makes 18** • **Per Biscuit** 115 calories, 8g fat (of which 4g saturates), 11g carbohydrate, 0.1g salt • **Easy**

65g (2½oz) unsalted butter, plus extra to grease
50g (2oz) golden caster sugar
2 tbsp double cream
25g (1oz) sunflower seeds
20g (¾oz) chopped mixed candied peel
20g (¾oz) sultanas
25g (1oz) natural glacé cherries, roughly chopped
40g (1½oz) flaked almonds, lightly crushed
15g (½oz) plain flour
125g (4oz) plain chocolate (at least 70% cocoa solids), broken into pieces

1 Preheat the oven to 180°C (160°C fan oven) mark 4. Lightly grease two large baking sheets.

2 Melt the butter in a small heavy-based pan. Add the sugar and heat gently until dissolved, then bring to the boil. Take off the heat and stir in the cream, seeds, peel, sultanas, cherries, almonds and flour. Mix until evenly combined. Put heaped teaspoonfuls on to the prepared baking sheets, spaced well apart to allow for spreading.

3 Bake one sheet at a time, for 6–8 minutes, until the biscuits have spread considerably and the edges are golden brown. Using a large plain metal biscuit cutter, push the edges into the centre to create neat rounds. Bake for a further 2 minutes

or until deep golden. Leave on the baking sheet for 2 minutes, then transfer to a wire rack to cool completely.

4 Melt the chocolate in a heatproof bowl set over a pan of gently simmering water, making sure the base of the bowl doesn't touch the water, and stirring occasionally. Spread on the underside of each Florentine and mark wavy lines with a fork. Put, chocolate side up, on a sheet of baking parchment and leave to set.

Peanut and Raisin Cookies

Preparation Time 10 minutes • **Cooking Time** 15 minutes, plus cooling • **Makes 30** • **Per Cookie** 111 calories, 6g fat (of which 3g saturates), 14g carbohydrate, 0.2g salt • **Easy**

125g (4oz) unsalted butter,
    softened, plus extra to grease
150g (5oz) caster sugar
1 medium egg
150g (5oz) plain flour, sifted
½ tsp baking powder
½ tsp salt
125g (4oz) crunchy peanut butter
175g (6oz) raisins

1 Preheat the oven to 190°C (170°C fan oven) mark 5 and grease two baking sheets. Beat together all the ingredients except the raisins, until well blended. Stir in the raisins.

2 Spoon large teaspoonfuls of the mixture, spaced well apart, on to the prepared baking sheets, leaving room for the mixture to spread.

3 Bake for about 15 minutes or until golden brown around the edges. Leave to cool slightly, then transfer to a wire rack to cool completely.

⭐ TO STORE
Store in an airtight container. They will keep for up to three days.

⭐ TRY SOMETHING DIFFERENT
Chocolate Nut Cookies
Omit the peanut butter and raisins and add 1 tsp vanilla extract. Stir in 175g (6oz) roughly chopped chocolate and 75g (3oz) roughly chopped walnuts.
Coconut and Cherry Cookies
Omit the peanut butter and raisins, reduce the sugar to 75g (3oz) and stir in 50g (2oz) desiccated coconut and 125g (4oz) rinsed, roughly chopped glacé cherries.
Oat and Cinnamon Cookies
Omit the peanut butter and raisins and add 1 tsp vanilla extract. Stir in 1 tsp ground cinnamon and 75g (3oz) rolled oats.

Spiced Star Biscuits

Preparation Time 15 minutes, plus chilling • **Cooking Time** 15–20 minutes, plus cooling • **Makes 35** •
Per Biscuit 51 calories, 2g fat (of which 1g saturates), 8g carbohydrate, 0g salt • **Easy**

2 tbsp runny honey
25g (1oz) unsalted butter
50g (2oz) light muscovado sugar
finely grated zest of ½ lemon
finely grated zest of ½ orange
225g (8oz) self-raising flour, plus
    extra to roll out
1 tsp ground cinnamon
1 tsp ground ginger
½ tsp freshly grated nutmeg
a pinch of ground cloves
a pinch of salt
1 tbsp finely chopped candied peel
50g (2oz) ground almonds
1 large egg, beaten
1½ tbsp milk

FOR THE DECORATION
150g (5oz) icing sugar
silver sugar balls

1 Put the honey, butter, muscovado sugar and citrus zests into a small pan and stir over a low heat until the butter has melted and the ingredients are well combined.

2 Sift the flour, spices and salt together into a bowl, then add the chopped candied peel and ground almonds. Add the melted mixture, beaten egg and milk and mix until the dough comes together. Knead the dough briefly until smooth, then wrap in clingfilm and chill for at least 4 hours, or overnight.

3 Preheat the oven to 180°C (160°C fan oven) mark 4. Roll out the dough on a lightly floured worksurface to 5mm (¼ in) thick. Using a 5cm (2in) cutter, stamp out stars and put on baking sheets.

4 Bake for 15–20 minutes until just beginning to brown at the edges. Transfer the biscuits to a wire rack to cool completely.

5 To decorate, mix the icing sugar with 1½ tbsp warm water to make a smooth icing. Coat some of the biscuits with icing and finish with a piped edging if you like, then decorate with silver balls. Pipe dots of icing on the plain biscuits and attach silver balls, then leave to set.

★TO STORE
Store in an airtight container. They will keep for up to one week.

Orange Tuile Biscuits

Preparation Time 10 minutes, plus chilling • **Cooking Time** 12 minutes, plus cooling • **Makes 24** • **Per Biscuit** 55 calories, 3g fat (of which 2g saturates), 8g carbohydrate, 0.1g salt • **Easy**

3 large egg whites
100g (3½oz) icing sugar, sifted
100g (3½oz) plain flour
finely grated zest of 1 orange
75g (3oz) unsalted butter, melted

1 Put the egg whites into a clean, grease-free bowl and lightly whisk with the sugar. Stir in the flour, orange zest and melted butter, then cover and chill for 30 minutes.

2 Preheat the oven to 200°C (180°C fan oven) mark 6. Line a baking sheet with baking parchment.

3 Put 3 teaspoonfuls of the mixture, spaced well apart, on the prepared baking sheet and spread out into 9cm (3½in) circles.

4 Bake for 12 minutes or until just brown around the edges. Remove from the oven and, while still warm, shape each biscuit over a rolling pin to curl. Repeat with the remaining mixture. Leave on a wire rack to cool completely.

Filo Cigars

★

Preparation Time 15 minutes • **Cooking Time** 10–12 minutes • **Makes 12** • **Per Cigar** 139 calories, 5g fat (of which 2g saturates), 24g carbohydrate, 0.1g salt • **Easy**

24 sheets filo pastry, cut into 12.5cm (5in) squares
40g (1½oz) unsalted butter, melted
175g (6oz) mincemeat
icing sugar to dust

1 Preheat the oven to 200°C (180°C fan oven) mark 6. Line a baking sheet with greaseproof paper.

2 Lay out a square of filo pastry on a clean dry worksurface. Lightly brush with melted butter, then lay another square of pastry on top. Spoon a thin line of mincemeat diagonally from corner to corner across the filo square. Fold the pastry over the mincemeat to form a triangle. Starting along the long edge, roll up to make a cigar shape. Transfer carefully to the baking sheet. Repeat with the remaining filo squares and mincemeat. Brush the remaining butter over the cigars.

3 Bake for 10–12 minutes until crisp and golden. Dust with icing sugar and serve with coffee as a light alternative to mince pies.

★TO STORE
Store in an airtight container. They will keep for up to two days.

★FREEZING TIP
To freeze *Complete the recipe to the end of step 2. Leave the cigars on the baking sheet and wrap the whole sheet in clingfilm, then freeze for up to one month.*
To use *Finish and cook the filo cigars from frozen as in steps 2 and 3, but cook for slightly longer – 10–15 minutes.*

Cupcakes

Dainty Cupcakes

★

Preparation Time 15 minutes, plus drying • **Cooking Time** 15–20 minutes, plus cooling and setting • **Makes 12** •
Per Cupcake 306 calories, 14g fat (of which 8g saturates), 46g carbohydrate, 0.4g salt • **Easy**

175g (6oz) unsalted butter, softened
175g (6oz) golden caster sugar
3 medium eggs
175g (6oz) self-raising flour, sifted
finely grated zest and juice of
   1 lemon

FOR THE FROSTED FLOWERS
1 medium egg white
6 edible flowers, such as violas
caster sugar to dust

FOR THE ICING
225g (8oz) icing sugar, sifted
1 drop violet food colouring
2–3 tbsp lemon juice, strained

1 Preheat the oven to 190°C (170°C fan oven) mark 5. Line a 12-hole bun tin or muffin tin with paper muffin cases.

2 Put the butter and caster sugar into a bowl and cream together until pale, light and fluffy. Add the eggs, one at a time, and beat together, folding 1 tbsp flour into the mixture if it looks as if it is going to curdle. Fold in the flour, lemon zest and juice and mix well.

3 Spoon the mixture into the cases and bake for 15–20 minutes until pale golden, risen and springy to the touch. Transfer to a wire rack to cool completely.

4 To make the frosted flowers, whisk the egg white in a clean bowl for 30 seconds or until frothy. Brush over the flower petals and put on a wire rack resting on a piece of greaseproof paper. Dust heavily with caster sugar, then leave the flowers to dry.

5 To make the icing, put the icing sugar into a bowl with the food colouring. Mix in the lemon juice to make a smooth dropping consistency. Spoon the icing on to the cakes, then decorate with the frosted flowers. Stand the cakes upright on the wire rack and leave for about 1 hour to set.

★ **TO STORE**
Store in an airtight container. They will keep for 3–5 days. To freeze, see opposite.

★ **TRY SOMETHING DIFFERENT**
Ginger and Orange Cupcakes
Replace the lemon zest and juice with orange and add two pieces of drained and chopped preserved stem ginger. Omit the frosted flowers and make the icing with orange juice instead of lemon. Decorate with finely chopped stem ginger.

Fairy Cakes

Preparation Time 20 minutes • **Cooking Time** 10–15 minutes, plus cooling and setting • **Makes 18** • **Per Cake** 160 calories, 6g fat (of which 4g saturates), 26g carbohydrate, 0.2g salt • **Easy**

125g (4oz) self-raising flour, sifted
1 tsp baking powder
125g (4oz) caster sugar
125g (4oz) unsalted butter, very soft
 2 medium eggs
1 tbsp milk

**FOR THE ICING AND
   DECORATION**
225g (8oz) icing sugar, sifted
assorted food colourings (optional)
sweets, sprinkles or coloured sugar

1 Preheat the oven to 200°C (180°C fan oven) mark 6. Put paper cases into 18 of the holes in two bun tins.

2 Put the flour, baking powder, sugar, butter, eggs and milk into a mixing bowl and beat with a hand-held electric whisk for 2 minutes or until the mixture is pale and very soft. Half-fill each paper case with the mixture.

3 Bake for 10–15 minutes until golden brown. Transfer to a wire rack to cool completely.

4 Put the icing sugar into a bowl and gradually blend in 2–3 tbsp warm water until the icing is fairly stiff, but spreadable. Add a couple of drops of food colouring, if you like.

5 When the cakes are cold, spread the tops with the icing and decorate.

★ TO STORE
Store in an airtight container. They will keep for 3–5 days.

★ TRY SOMETHING DIFFERENT
Chocolate Fairy Cakes
Replace 2 tbsp of the flour with the same amount of cocoa powder. Stir 50g (2oz) chocolate drops, sultanas or chopped dried apricots into the mixture at the end of step 1. Complete the recipe.

★ FREEZING TIP
To freeze *Complete the recipe to the end of step 3. Open-freeze, then wrap and freeze.*
To use *Thaw for about 1 hour, then complete the recipe.*

Kitten Cupcakes

Preparation Time 25 minutes • **Cooking Time** 20 minutes, plus cooling • **Makes 12** • **Per Cupcake** 223 calories, 10g fat (of which 6g saturates), 34g carbohydrate, 0.2g salt • **Easy**

125g (4oz) unsalted butter, very soft
125g (4oz) caster sugar
grated zest of 1 lemon
2 medium eggs, beaten
125g (4oz) self-raising flour, sifted

**FOR THE ICING AND
    DECORATION**
175g (6oz) icing sugar
black and assorted writing icings
jelly diamonds and Smarties
black liquorice laces, cut into short
    lengths

1 Preheat the oven to 190°C (170°C fan oven) mark 5. Line a 12-hole bun tin with paper cases.

2 Put the butter, caster sugar and lemon zest into a mixing bowl and, using a hand-held electric whisk, beat until pale and fluffy. Add the eggs, a little at a time, beating well after each addition. Fold in the flour. Divide the mixture between the paper cases. Bake for about 20 minutes or until golden and risen. Transfer to a wire rack to cool completely.

3 Sift the icing sugar into a bowl. Stir in 1–2 tbsp warm water, a few drops at a time, until you have a smooth, spreadable icing. If necessary, slice the tops off the cooled buns to make them level. Cover the top of each cake with icing.

4 Decorate the buns to make kittens' faces. Use black writing icing for the eyes, halve the jelly diamonds for the ears, press a Smartie in the centre for a nose, and use black writing icing to draw on a mouth. Use different coloured writing icing for the pupils and markings. Press on liquorice whiskers.

 TO STORE
Store in an airtight container. They will keep for 3–5 days.

 FREEZING TIP
To freeze *Complete the recipe to the end of step 2. Open-freeze, then wrap and freeze.*
To use *Thaw for about 1 hour, then complete the recipe.*

Sour Cherry Cupcakes

Preparation Time 30 minutes • **Cooking Time** 15–20 minutes, plus cooling and setting • **Makes 12** • **Per Cupcake** 323 calories, 14g fat (of which 8g saturates), 50g carbohydrate, 0.4g salt • **Easy**

175g (6oz) unsalted butter, softened
175g (6oz) golden caster sugar
3 medium eggs
175g (6oz) self-raising flour, sifted
75g (3oz) dried cherries
2 tbsp milk

FOR THE ICING
225g (8oz) golden icing sugar, sifted
3 tbsp lemon juice, strained

1 Preheat the oven to 190°C (170°C fan oven) mark 5. Line a 12-hole bun tin or muffin tin with paper muffin cases.

2 Put the butter and caster sugar into a bowl and cream together until pale, light and fluffy. Beat in the eggs, one at a time, folding in 1 tbsp flour if the mixture looks like it is starting to curdle.

3 Put 12 dried cherries to one side. Fold the remaining flour, the cherries and milk into the creamed mixture until evenly combined.

Spoon the mixture into the paper cases and bake for 15–20 minutes until pale golden and risen. Transfer to a wire rack to cool completely.

4 Put the icing sugar into a bowl and mix with the lemon juice to make a smooth dropping consistency. Spoon a little icing on to each cake and decorate each with a cherry, then stand the cakes upright on the wire rack and leave for about 1 hour to set.

 TO STORE
Store in an airtight container. They will keep for 3–5 days.

 FREEZING TIP
To freeze *Complete the recipe to the end of step 3. Open-freeze, then wrap and freeze.*
To use *Thaw for about 1 hour, then complete the recipe.*

Orange and Poppy Seed Cupcakes

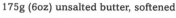

Preparation Time 30 minutes • **Cooking Time** 20 minutes, plus cooling • **Makes 12** • **Per Cupcake** 408 calories, 24g fat (of which 14g saturates), 49g carbohydrate, 0.5g salt • **Easy**

175g (6oz) unsalted butter, softened
175g (6oz) caster sugar
3 medium eggs
175g (6oz) self-raising flour, sifted
grated zest and juice of 1 large
    orange
2 tbsp poppy seeds
1 tsp baking powder

**FOR THE ICING AND
    DECORATION**
125g (4oz) unsalted butter, softened
250g (9oz) icing sugar, sifted
1 tbsp orange flower water
12 orange jelly slices and orange
    edible glitter (optional)

1 Preheat the oven to 190°C (170°C fan oven), mark 5. Line a 12-hole muffin tin with paper muffin cases.

2 Whisk the butter and caster sugar in a bowl with a hand-held electric whisk, or beat with a wooden spoon, until pale and creamy. Gradually whisk in the eggs until just combined. Using a metal spoon, fold in the flour, orange zest and juice, poppy seeds and baking powder until combined. Divide the mixture equally between the paper cases.

3 Bake for 20 minutes or until golden and risen. Leave to cool in the tin for 5 minutes, then transfer to a wire rack to cool completely.

4 For the decoration, put the butter into a bowl and whisk until fluffy. Gradually add the icing sugar and orange flower water and whisk until light and fluffy.

5 Insert a star nozzle into a piping bag, then fill the bag with the buttercream and pipe a swirl on to the top of each cake. Decorate each with an orange slice and edible glitter, if you like.

★ TO STORE
Store in an airtight container. They will keep for 3–5 days.

★ FREEZING TIP
__To freeze__ Complete the recipe to the end of step 3. Open-freeze, then wrap and freeze.
__To use__ Thaw for about 1 hour, then complete the recipe.

Vanilla and White Chocolate Cupcakes

Preparation Time 25 minutes • **Cooking Time** 15–20 minutes, plus cooling and setting • **Makes 12** •
Per Cupcake 270 calories, 15g fat (of which 9g saturates), 32g carbohydrate, 0.2g salt • **Easy**

125g (4oz) unsalted butter, at room
   temperature
125g (4oz) golden caster sugar
1 vanilla pod
2 medium eggs
125g (4oz) self-raising flour, sifted
1 tbsp vanilla extract

**FOR THE TOPPING AND
   DECORATION**
200g (7oz) white chocolate, broken
   into pieces
12 crystallised violets or frosted
   flowers (see Cook's Tip)

1 Preheat the oven to 190°C (170°C fan oven) mark 5. Line a 12-hole bun tin or muffin tin with paper muffin cases.

2 Put the butter and sugar into a bowl. Split the vanilla pod lengthways, scrape out the seeds and add to the bowl. Add the eggs, flour and vanilla extract and then, using a hand-held electric whisk, beat thoroughly until smooth and creamy. Spoon the mixture into the muffin cases.

3 Bake for 15–20 minutes until pale golden, risen and springy to the touch. Leave in the tin for 2–3 minutes, then transfer to a wire rack to cool completely.

4 Melt the chocolate in a heatproof bowl set over a pan of gently simmering water, making sure the base of the bowl doesn't touch the water. Stir until smooth and leave to cool slightly. Spoon the chocolate on to the cakes and top with a frosted flower. Stand the cakes upright on the wire rack and leave for about 1 hour to set.

 TO STORE
Store in an airtight container. They will keep for 3–5 days.

★ FREEZING TIP
To freeze Complete the recipe to the end of step 3. Open-freeze, then wrap and freeze.
To use Thaw for about 1 hour, then complete the recipe.

★COOK'S TIP
To make the frosted flowers, whisk 1 medium egg white in a clean bowl for 30 seconds or until frothy. Brush it over 12 violet petals and put on a wire rack. Lightly dust with caster sugar and leave to dry.

Chocolate Cupcakes

Preparation Time 15 minutes • **Cooking Time** 20 minutes, plus cooling and setting • **Makes 18** • **Per Cupcake** 203 calories, 14g fat (of which 8g saturates), 19g carbohydrate, 0.2g salt • **Easy**

125g (4oz) unsalted butter, softened
125g (4oz) light muscovado sugar
2 medium eggs, beaten
15g (½oz) cocoa powder
100g (3½oz) self-raising flour
100g (3½oz) plain chocolate
    (at least 70% cocoa solids),
    roughly chopped

FOR THE TOPPING
150ml (¼ pint) double cream
100g (3½oz) plain chocolate
    (at least 70% cocoa solids),
    broken up

1 Preheat the oven to 190°C (170°C fan oven) mark 5. Line a 12-hole and a 6-hole bun tin or muffin tin with paper muffin cases.

2 Beat the butter and sugar together until light and fluffy. Gradually beat in the eggs. Sift the cocoa powder with the flour and fold into the creamed mixture with the chopped chocolate. Divide the mixture among the paper cases and lightly flatten the surface with the back of a spoon.

3 Bake for 20 minutes, then transfer to a wire rack to cool completely.

4 For the topping, put the cream and chocolate into a heavy-based pan over a low heat and heat until melted, then allow to cool and thicken slightly. Spoon on to the cooled cakes, then stand the cakes upright on the wire rack and leave for 30 minutes to set.

★ TO STORE
Store in an airtight container in the fridge. They will keep for 2–3 days.

★ FREEZING TIP
__To freeze__ Complete the recipe to the end of step 3. Open-freeze, then wrap and freeze.
__To use__ Thaw for about 1 hour, then complete the recipe.

Cookies and Cream Cupcakes

Preparation Time 30 minutes • **Cooking Time** 15–20 minutes, plus cooling • **Makes 12** • **Per Cupcake** 357 calories, 21g fat (of which 13g saturates), 41g carbohydrate, 0.5g salt • **Easy**

75g (3oz) mini Oreo cookies
175g (6oz) unsalted butter, softened
150g (5oz) caster sugar
3 medium eggs
175g (6oz) self-raising flour, sifted
½ tsp baking powder
3 tbsp milk
½ tsp vanilla extract

FOR THE TOPPING
75g (3oz) unsalted butter, softened
150g (5oz) icing sugar, sifted
2 tsp vanilla extract
1 tsp cocoa powder

1 Preheat the oven to 200°C (180°C fan oven), mark 6. Line a 12-hole muffin tin with paper muffin cases. Reserve 12 mini cookies and roughly chop the remainder.

2 Using a hand-held electric whisk, whisk the butter and caster sugar in a bowl (or beat with a wooden spoon) until pale and creamy. Gradually whisk in the eggs until just combined. Using a metal spoon, fold in the flour, baking powder, milk, vanilla extract and chopped cookies until combined. Divide the mixture equally between the paper cases.

3 Bake for 15–20 minutes until golden and risen. Leave to cool in the tin for 5 minutes, then transfer to a wire rack to cool completely.

4 For the decoration, put the butter into a bowl and whisk until fluffy. Gradually add the icing sugar and vanilla extract and whisk until light and fluffy. Using a small palette knife, spread the buttercream over the top of each cake. Sift a little cocoa powder on to the top of each cake and then decorate each with a reserved Oreo cookie.

 TO STORE
Store in an airtight container. They will keep for 2–3 days.

 FREEZING TIP
To freeze *Complete the recipe to the end of step 3. Open-freeze, then wrap and freeze.*
To use *Thaw for about 1 hour, then complete the recipe.*

Coconut and Lime Cupcakes

Preparation Time 30 minutes • **Cooking Time** 18–20 minutes, plus cooling and setting • **Makes 12** •
Per Cupcake 291 calories, 13g fat (of which 6g saturates), 42g carbohydrate, 0.1g salt • **Easy**

275g (10oz) plain flour, sifted
1 tbsp baking powder
100g (3½oz) caster sugar
zest of 1 lime
50g (2oz) desiccated coconut
2 medium eggs
100ml (3½fl oz) sunflower oil
225ml (8fl oz) natural yogurt
50ml (2fl oz) milk

FOR THE TOPPING
150g (5oz) icing sugar, sifted
juice of 1 lime
1–2 tsp boiling water
50g (2oz) desiccated coconut

1 Preheat the oven to 200°C (180°C fan oven), mark 6. Line a 12-hole muffin tin with paper muffin cases.

2 Put the flour, baking powder, caster sugar, lime zest and coconut into a large bowl. Put the eggs, oil, yogurt and milk into a jug and lightly beat together until combined. Pour the yogurt mixture into the flour and stir with a spatula until just combined. Divide the mixture equally between the paper cases.

3 Bake for 18–20 minutes until lightly golden and risen. Leave to cool in the tin for 5 minutes, then transfer to a wire rack to cool completely.

4 For the decoration, mix the icing sugar with the lime juice and enough boiling water to make a thick, smooth icing. Put the coconut into a shallow bowl. Dip each cake top into the icing until coated, allowing the excess to drip off, then carefully dip into the coconut until coated. Stand the cakes upright on the wire rack and leave for about 1 hour to set.

 TO STORE
Store in an airtight container. They will keep for 3–5 days.

★ FREEZING TIP
To freeze Complete the recipe to the end of step 3. Open-freeze, then wrap and freeze.
To use Thaw for about 1 hour, then complete the recipe.

Pavlova Cupcakes

Preparation Time 30 minutes • **Cooking Time** 25 minutes, plus cooling and setting • **Makes 12** • **Per Cupcake** 226 calories, 10g fat (of which 6g saturates), 34g carbohydrate, 0.2g salt • **Easy**

125g (4oz) unsalted butter, softened
100g (3½oz) caster sugar
2 medium eggs
150g (5oz) self-raising flour, sifted
1 tbsp milk
zest of 1 lemon
50g (2oz) small fresh blueberries
12 fresh raspberries

FOR THE FROSTING
1 medium egg white
175g (6oz) caster sugar
2 tbsp water
a pinch of cream of tartar

1 Preheat the oven to 190°C (170°C fan oven), mark 5. Line a 12-hole muffin tin with paper fairy cake or bun cases.

2 Using a hand-held electric whisk, whisk the butter and sugar in a bowl, or beat with a wooden spoon, until pale and creamy. Gradually whisk in the eggs until just combined. Using a metal spoon, fold in the flour, milk, lemon zest and blueberries until combined.

3 Divide the mixture equally between the paper cases and press 1 raspberry into the centre of each cake. Bake for 15 minutes or until golden and risen. Leave to cool in the tin for 5 minutes, then transfer to a wire rack to cool completely.

4 For the frosting, put all the ingredients into a heatproof bowl and whisk lightly using a hand-held electric whisk. Put the bowl over a pan of simmering water and whisk continuously for about 7 minutes or until the mixture thickens sufficiently to stand in peaks.

5 Insert a star nozzle into a piping bag, then fill the bag with the frosting and pipe a swirl on to the top of each cake. Stand the cakes upright on the wire rack and leave for about 1 hour to set.

★ TO STORE
Store, un-iced, in an airtight container. They will keep for 3–5 days. Ice to serve.

★ FREEZING TIP
To freeze Complete the recipe to the end of step 3. Open-freeze, then wrap and freeze.
To use Thaw for about 1 hour, then complete the recipe.

Apple Crumble Cupcakes

Preparation Time 20 minutes • **Cooking Time** 25 minutes, plus cooling • **Makes 12** • **Per Cupcake** 215 calories, 10g fat (of which 6g saturates), 31g carbohydrate, 0.2g salt • **Easy**

320g (11½oz) eating apples, cored (about 2)
juice of 1 lemon
200g (7oz) self-raising flour, sifted
1 tsp baking powder
1 tsp ground cinnamon
125g (4oz) light soft brown sugar
2 medium eggs
100g (3½oz) unsalted butter, melted

FOR THE CRUMBLE
50g (2oz) plain flour
25g (1oz) unsalted butter, chilled and cut into cubes
15g (½oz) light soft brown sugar

1 Preheat the oven to 180°C (160°C fan oven), mark 4. Line a 12-hole muffin tin with paper muffin cases.

2 Make the crumble. Put the flour into a bowl and, using your fingertips, rub in the butter until it resembles coarse breadcrumbs. Stir in the sugar and set aside.

3 Coarsely grate the apples into a large bowl and mix in the lemon juice. Add the flour, baking powder, cinnamon and sugar. Put the eggs and melted butter into a jug and lightly beat together, then pour into the flour mixture. Stir with a spatula until just combined. Divide the mixture equally between the paper cases, then sprinkle the crumble equally over the top of each cake.

4 Bake for 25 minutes or until lightly golden and risen. Leave to cool in the tin for 5 minutes, then transfer to a wire rack to cool completely.

★ TO STORE
Store in an airtight container. They will keep for 3–5 days.

★ FREEZING TIP
To freeze *Complete the recipe. Open-freeze, then wrap and freeze.* ***To use*** *Thaw for about 1 hour, then serve.*

Peanut Butter Cupcakes

Preparation Time 30 minutes • **Cooking Time** 25 minutes, plus cooling and setting • **Makes 12** • **Per Cupcake** 363 calories, 17g fat (of which 7g saturates), 49g carbohydrate, 0.5g salt • **Easy**

75g (3oz) unsalted peanuts or cashew nuts, toasted

100g (3½oz) unsalted butter, softened

50g (2oz) light soft brown sugar

50g (2oz) dark muscovado sugar

3 medium eggs

175g (6oz) self-raising flour, sifted

½ tsp baking powder

FOR THE TOPPING

100ml (3½fl oz) milk

50g (2oz) cocoa powder

300g (11oz) icing sugar

100g (3½oz) peanut butter

chocolate sprinkles or vermicelli

1 Preheat the oven to 190°C (170°C fan oven), mark 5. Line a 12-hole muffin tin with paper muffin cases.

2 Whiz the peanuts or cashews in a food processor until finely ground. Set aside.

3 Using a hand-held electric whisk, whisk the butter with the light brown and muscovado sugars, or beat with a wooden spoon, until pale and creamy. Gradually whisk in the eggs until just combined. Using a metal spoon, fold in the flour, baking powder and finely ground nuts until combined. Divide the mixture equally between the paper cases.

4 Bake for 20 minutes or until golden and risen. Leave to cool in the tin for 5 minutes, then transfer to a wire rack to cool completely.

5 For the decoration, warm the milk in a small saucepan. Sift the cocoa and icing sugar into a bowl, then gradually stir in the warm milk until it forms a smooth icing.

6 Put a small spoonful of peanut butter on the top of each cake and then spoon the chocolate icing on to cover the peanut butter and to coat the top of the cupcake.

Decorate with sprinkles or vermicelli. Stand the cakes upright on the wire rack and leave for about 1 hour to set.

★ TO STORE
Store in an airtight container. They will keep for 3–5 days.

★ FREEZING TIP
To freeze *Complete the recipe to the end of step 4. Open-freeze, then wrap and freeze.*
To use *Thaw for about 1 hour, then complete the recipe.*

Rocky Road Cupcakes

Preparation Time 30 minutes • **Cooking Time** 15–20 minutes, plus cooling and setting • **Makes 9** •
Per Cupcake 360 calories, 20g fat (of which 11g saturates), 45g carbohydrate, 0.5g salt • **Easy**

100g (3½oz) unsalted butter,
   softened
125g (4oz) caster sugar
2 medium eggs
150g (5oz) self-raising flour, sifted
25g (1oz) glacé cherries, diced
25g (1oz) milk chocolate chips
25g (1oz) pinenuts

FOR THE TOPPING
100g (3½oz) milk chocolate
50ml (2fl oz) double cream
25g (1oz) mini marshmallows
25g (1oz) glacé cherries, finely
   chopped
1 x 37g bag Maltesers

1 Preheat the oven to 190°C (170°C
fan oven), mark 5. Line a 12-hole
muffin tin with 9 paper muffin
cases.

2 Using a hand-held electric whisk,
whisk the butter and sugar in a
bowl, or beat with a wooden spoon,
until pale and creamy. Gradually
whisk in the eggs until just
combined. Using a metal spoon,
fold in the flour, cherries, chocolate
chips and pinenuts until combined.
Divide the mixture equally between
the paper cases.

3 Bake for 15–20 minutes until
golden and risen. Leave to cool in
the tin for 5 minutes, then transfer
to a wire rack to cool completely.

4 For the topping, break the
chocolate into pieces, then put into
a heatproof bowl with the cream.
Set over a pan of gently simmering
water, making sure the base of the
bowl doesn't touch the water. Heat
until melted, stirring occasionally
until smooth.

5 Remove from the heat and, using
a small palette knife, spread a little
over the top of each cake. Decorate
each with marshmallows, cherries
and Maltesers. Stand the cakes
upright on the wire rack and leave
for about 1 hour to set.

★ TO STORE
*Store in an airtight container in the
fridge. They will keep for 2–3 days.*

★ FREEZING TIP
*To **freeze** Complete the recipe to the
end of step 3. Open-freeze, then wrap
and freeze.*
*To **use** Thaw for about 1 hour, then
complete the recipe.*

Coffee Walnut Whip Cupcakes

Preparation Time 30 minutes • **Cooking Time** 20–25 minutes, plus cooling and chilling • **Makes 12** •
Per Cupcake 409 calories, 26g fat (of which 11g saturates), 43g carbohydrate, 0.5g salt • **Easy**

100g (3½oz) walnuts
175g (6oz) unsalted butter, softened
150g (5oz) self-raising flour, sifted
175g (6oz) light soft brown sugar
3 medium eggs
1 tsp baking powder
50ml (2fl oz) milk

**FOR THE TOPPING AND
   DECORATION**
1 tbsp instant coffee granules
50g (2oz) unsalted butter, softened
200g (7oz) icing sugar, sifted
50g (2oz) walnuts, finely chopped

1 Preheat the oven to 190°C (170°C
fan oven), mark 5. Line a 12-hole
muffin tin with paper muffin cases.

2 Whiz the walnuts in a food
processor until finely ground.
Transfer to a large bowl. Add the
butter, flour, brown sugar, eggs,
baking powder and milk to the
ground walnuts. Using a hand-held
electric whisk, whisk together until
pale and creamy. Divide the mixture
equally between the paper cases.

3 Bake for 20–25 minutes until
golden and risen. Leave to cool in
the tin for 5 minutes, then transfer
to a wire rack to cool completely.

4 For the buttercream topping, put
2 tbsp boiling water into a small
bowl, add the coffee and stir to
dissolve. Put the butter, 100g
(3½oz) icing sugar and the coffee

mixture into a bowl and whisk until
combined. Chill for 30 minutes.

5 Remove the buttercream from the
fridge and gradually whisk in the
remaining icing sugar until smooth
and fluffy. Using a small palette
knife, spread a little buttercream
over the top of each cake. Put the
chopped walnuts into a shallow
bowl and lightly dip the top of each
cake into the walnuts.

⭐ TO STORE
*Store in an airtight container. They will
keep for 2–3 days.*

⭐ FREEZING TIP
To freeze *Complete the recipe to the
end of step 3. Open-freeze, then wrap
and freeze.*
To use *Thaw for about 1 hour, then
complete the recipe.*

Raspberry Ripple Cupcakes

Preparation Time 30 minutes • **Cooking Time** 20 minutes, plus cooling • **Makes 9** • **Per Cupcake** 385 calories, 26g fat (of which 16g saturates), 36g carbohydrate, 0.5g salt • **Easy**

50g (2oz) seedless raspberry jam
50g (2oz) fresh raspberries
125g (4oz) unsalted butter, softened
100g (3½oz) caster sugar
2 medium eggs
1 tbsp milk
150g (5oz) self-raising flour, sifted

**FOR THE TOPPING AND
   DECORATION**
150g (5oz) fresh raspberries
300ml (½ pint) whipping cream
50g (2oz) icing sugar, sifted

1 Preheat the oven to 190°C (170°C fan oven), mark 5. Line a 12-hole muffin tin with paper muffin cases.

2 Mix the raspberry jam with the raspberries, lightly crushing the raspberries. Set aside.

3 Using a hand-held electric whisk, whisk the butter and caster sugar in a bowl, or beat with a wooden spoon, until pale and creamy. Gradually whisk in the eggs and milk until just combined. Using a metal spoon, fold in the flour until just combined, then carefully fold in the raspberry jam mixture until just marbled, being careful not to over-mix. Divide the mixture equally between the paper cases.

4 Bake for 20 minutes or until golden and risen. Leave to cool in the tin for 5 minutes, then transfer to a wire rack to cool completely.

5 For the decoration, reserve 9 raspberries. Mash the remaining raspberries in a bowl with a fork. Pass through a sieve into a bowl to remove the seeds. Using a hand-held electric whisk, whisk the cream and icing sugar together until stiff peaks form. Mix the raspberry purée into the cream until combined.

6 Insert a star nozzle into a piping bag, then fill the bag with the cream and pipe a swirl on to the top of each cake. Decorate each with a raspberry.

★ TO STORE
Store in an airtight container in the fridge. They will keep for up to 2 days.

★ FREEZING TIP
To freeze *Complete the recipe to the end of step 4. Open-freeze, then wrap and freeze.*
To use *Thaw for about 1 hour, then complete the recipe.*

The Ultimate Carrot Cupcakes

★

Preparation Time 30 minutes • **Cooking Time** 20 minutes, plus cooling • **Makes 12** • **Per Cupcake** 255 calories, 12g fat (of which 4g saturates), 34g carbohydrate, 0.3g salt • **Easy**

150g (5oz) carrots
50g (2oz) raisins
175g (6oz) self-raising flour, sifted
½ tsp bicarbonate of soda
150g (5oz) light soft brown sugar
zest of 1 orange
½ tsp ground mixed spice
3 medium eggs
100ml (3½fl oz) sunflower oil
75ml (2½fl oz) buttermilk

FOR THE TOPPING AND DECORATION
50g (2oz) icing sugar, sifted
250g (9oz) mascarpone cheese
100g (3½oz) quark cheese
juice of ½ orange
red, yellow and green ready-made
    fondant icing (optional)

1 Preheat the oven to 190°C (170°C fan oven), mark 5. Line a 12-hole muffin tin with paper muffin cases.

2 Coarsely grate the carrots and put into a large bowl. Add the raisins, flour, bicarbonate of soda, brown sugar, orange zest and mixed spice. Put the eggs, oil and buttermilk into a jug and lightly beat together until combined. Pour the egg mixture into the flour and stir with a spatula until just combined.

3 Divide the mixture equally between the paper cases and bake for 20 minutes or until lightly golden and risen. Leave to cool in the tin for 5 minutes, then transfer to a wire rack to cool completely.

4 For the topping, mix the icing sugar with the mascarpone, quark and orange juice to a smooth icing. Using a small palette knife, spread a little of the icing over each cake. Use the coloured fondant to make small carrots, if you like, and decorate the cakes with them.

★ TO STORE
Store in an airtight container in the fridge. They will keep for up to 2 days.

★ FREEZING TIP
To freeze Complete the recipe to the end of step 3. Open-freeze, then wrap and freeze.
To use Thaw for about 1 hour, then complete the recipe.

Sticky Gingerbread Cupcakes

Preparation Time 35 minutes • Cooking Time 20 minutes, plus cooling • Makes 9 • Per Cupcake 386 calories, 17g fat (of which 11g saturates), 58g carbohydrate, 0.5g salt • Easy

175g (6oz) self-raising flour
75g (3oz) unsalted butter, chilled
　　and cut into cubes
¼ tsp bicarbonate of soda
2 tsp ground ginger
25g (1oz) stem ginger in syrup,
　　finely chopped, plus 3 tbsp syrup
　　from the jar
50g (2oz) dark muscovado sugar
50g (2oz) golden syrup
50g (2oz) treacle
juice of 1 orange
2 medium eggs, beaten

**FOR THE TOPPING AND
DECORATION**
100g (3½oz) unsalted butter,
　　softened
200g (7oz) icing sugar, sifted
3 tbsp syrup from the stem
　　ginger jar
1 tsp ground ginger
ready-made sugar flowers (optional)

1 Preheat the oven to 190°C (170°C fan oven), mark 5. Line a 12-hole muffin tin with 9 paper muffin cases.

2 Put the flour into a large bowl and, using your fingertips, rub in the butter until it resembles breadcrumbs. Stir in the bicarbonate of soda, ground ginger and stem ginger and set aside. Put the muscovado sugar, syrup, treacle and orange juice into a small saucepan and heat gently until the sugar dissolves. Leave to cool for 5 minutes.

3 Mix the eggs and warm sugar mixture into the flour mixture and stir with a spatula until just combined. Divide equally between the paper cases.

4 Bake for 20 minutes or until golden and risen. Remove from the oven and drizzle each cake with 1 tsp ginger syrup. Leave to cool in the tin for 5 minutes, then transfer to a wire rack to cool completely.

5 For the buttercream topping, put the butter into a bowl and whisk until fluffy. Add the icing sugar, ginger syrup and ground ginger. Whisk until light and fluffy. Using a small palette knife, spread a little buttercream over the top of each cake. Decorate with sugar flowers, if you like.

★ TO STORE
Store in an airtight container. They will keep for 3–5 days.

★ FREEZING TIP
To freeze *Complete the recipe to the end of step 4. Open-freeze, then wrap and freeze.*
To use *Thaw for about 1 hour, then complete the recipe.*

Lavender and Honey Cupcakes

Preparation Time 35 minutes • **Cooking Time** 15–20 minutes, plus cooling and setting • **Makes 9** •
Per Cupcake 316 calories, 13g fat (of which 8g saturates), 50g carbohydrate, 0.3g salt • **Easy**

125g (4oz) unsalted butter, softened
125g (4oz) runny honey
2 medium eggs
125g (4oz) self-raising flour, sifted
1 tsp baking powder

**FOR THE ICING AND
  DECORATION**
3 honey and lavender tea bags
2 tsp unsalted butter
250g (9oz) icing sugar, sifted
red and blue food colouring
purple sugar stars
edible silver dust (optional)

1 Preheat the oven to 190°C (170°C fan oven), mark 5. Line a 12-hole muffin tin with 9 paper muffin cases.

2 Using a hand-held electric whisk, whisk the butter and honey in a bowl, or beat with a wooden spoon, until combined. Gradually whisk in the eggs until just combined. Using a metal spoon, fold in the flour and baking powder until combined. Divide the mixture equally between the paper cases.

3 Bake for 15–20 minutes until golden and risen. Leave to cool in the tin for 5 minutes, then transfer to a wire rack to cool completely.

4 For the icing, infuse the tea bags in 50ml (2fl oz) boiling water in a small bowl for 5 minutes. Remove the tea bags and squeeze out the excess water into the bowl. Stir in the butter until melted. Put the icing sugar into a large bowl, add the infused tea mixture and stir to make a smooth icing. Add a few drops of blue and red food colouring until it is lilac in colour.

5 Spoon a little icing on top of each cake, to flood the tops, then sprinkle with stars. Stand the cakes upright on the wire rack and leave for about 1 hour to set. Dust with edible dust, if you like, when set.

 TO STORE
Store in an airtight container. They will keep for 3–5 days.

 FREEZING TIP
*To **freeze** Complete the recipe to the end of step 3. Open-freeze, then wrap and freeze.*
*To **use** Thaw for about 1 hour, then complete the recipe.*

St Clements Cupcakes

Preparation Time 40 minutes • **Cooking Time** 15–18 minutes, plus cooling and setting • **Makes 9** •
Per Cupcake 309 calories, 1g fat (of which trace saturates), 76g carbohydrate, 0g salt • **Easy**

1 small orange (about 200g/7oz)
175g (6oz) self-raising flour, sifted
100g (3½oz) caster sugar
100ml (3½fl oz) milk
1 medium egg, beaten
50g (2oz) unsalted butter, melted
1 tsp baking powder
zest of 1 large lemon

**FOR THE TOPPING AND
    DECORATION**
400g (14oz) royal icing sugar, sifted
juice and zest of 1 small orange
sugar star sprinkles
edible glitter (optional)

1 Preheat the oven to 190°C (170°C fan oven), mark 5. Line a 12-hole muffin tin with 9 paper muffin cases.

2 Grate the zest from the orange into a large bowl and set aside. Cut the top and bottom off the orange and stand it upright on a board. Using a serrated knife, cut away the pith in a downward motion. Roughly chop the orange flesh, discarding any pips. Put the chopped orange into a food processor and whiz until puréed.

3 Transfer the orange purée into the bowl with the zest. Add the flour, caster sugar, milk, egg, melted butter, baking powder and lemon zest. Stir with a spatula until just combined. Divide the mixture equally between the paper cases.

4 Bake for 15–18 minutes until golden and risen. Leave to cool in the tin for 5 minutes, then transfer to a wire rack to cool completely.

5 For the topping, put the icing sugar, orange juice and zest into a bowl and whisk for 5 minutes or until soft peaks form. Spoon a little over the top of each cake to flood the top, then sprinkle with the stars. Stand the cakes upright on the wire rack and leave for about 1 hour to set. Dust with edible glitter, if you like, when set.

★ TO STORE
Store in an airtight tin. They will keep for 3–5 days.

★ FREEZING TIP
To freeze Complete the recipe to the end of step 4. Open-freeze, then wrap and freeze.
To use Thaw for about 1 hour, then complete the recipe.

Cherry Bakewell Cupcakes

Preparation Time 30 minutes • **Cooking Time** 25 minutes, plus cooling and setting • **Makes 12** •
Per Cupcake 405 calories, 21g fat (of which 11g saturates), 53g carbohydrate, 0.4g salt • **Easy**

175g (6oz) unsalted butter, softened
175g (6oz) caster sugar
3 medium eggs
150g (5oz) self-raising flour, sifted
1 tsp baking powder
75g (3oz) ground almonds
1 tsp almond extract
75g (3oz) glacé cherries, finely
    chopped

**FOR THE TOPPING AND
    DECORATION**
1 tbsp custard powder
100ml (3½fl oz) milk
50g (2oz) unsalted butter, softened
250g (9oz) icing sugar, sifted
red sugar sprinkles

1 Preheat the oven to 190°C (170°C fan oven), mark 5. Line a 12-hole muffin tin with paper muffin cases.

2 Using a hand-held electric whisk, whisk the butter and caster sugar in a bowl, or beat with a wooden spoon, until pale and creamy. Gradually whisk in the eggs until just combined. Using a metal spoon, fold in the flour, baking powder, ground almonds, almond extract and cherries until combined. Divide the mixture equally between the paper cases.

3 Bake for 20 minutes or until golden and risen. Leave to cool in the tin for 5 minutes, then transfer to a wire rack to cool completely.

4 For the topping, put the custard powder into a jug and add a little of the milk to make a smooth paste. Put the remaining milk into a saucepan and bring just to the boil. Pour the hot milk on to the custard paste and stir. Return to the milk pan and heat gently for 1–2 minutes until it thickens. Remove from the heat, cover with dampened greaseproof paper to prevent a skin forming and cool completely.

5 Put the custard into a bowl and, using an electric whisk, whisk in the butter. Chill for 30 minutes.

6 Gradually whisk the icing sugar into the chilled custard mixture until you have a smooth, thick icing. Using a small palette knife, spread a little custard cream over the top of each cake, then decorate with sugar sprinkles. Stand the cakes upright on the wire rack and leave for about 1 hour to set.

★TO STORE
Store in an airtight container in the fridge. They will keep for 2–3 days.

★ FREEZING TIP
***To freeze** Complete the recipe to the end of step 3. Open-freeze, then wrap and freeze.*
***To use** Thaw for about 1 hour, then complete the recipe.*

Be Mine Cupcakes

Preparation Time 30 minutes • **Cooking Time** 15 minutes, plus cooling • **Makes 12** • **Per Cupcake** 289 calories, 15g fat (of which 9g saturates), 40g carbohydrate, 0.3g salt • **Easy**

125g (4oz) unsalted butter, softened
100g (3½oz) caster sugar
2 medium eggs
125g (4oz) self-raising flour, sifted
½ tsp baking powder
1 x 51g bar Turkish Delight, finely chopped
1 tbsp rosewater

FOR THE TOPPING AND DECORATION
75g (3oz) unsalted butter, softened
250g (9oz) icing sugar, sifted
2 tbsp rosewater
pink and white heart-shaped sugar sprinkles
about 12 Loveheart sweets (optional)

1 Preheat the oven to 190°C (170°C fan oven), mark 5. Line a 12-hole muffin tin with paper fairy cake cases.

2 Using a hand-held electric whisk, whisk the butter and caster sugar in a bowl, or beat with a wooden spoon, until pale and creamy. Gradually whisk in the eggs until just combined. Using a metal spoon, fold in the flour, baking powder, Turkish Delight and rosewater until combined. Divide the mixture equally between the paper cases.

3 Bake for 15 minutes or until golden and risen. Leave to cool in the tin for 5 minutes, then transfer to a wire rack to cool completely.

4 For the topping, put the butter into a bowl and whisk until fluffy. Add the icing sugar and rosewater and whisk until light and fluffy. Using a small palette knife, spread a little buttercream over the top of each cake. Decorate with sugar hearts, then top each with a Loveheart, if you like.

★ TO STORE
Store in an airtight container. They will keep for 3–5 days.

★ FREEZING TIP
To freeze Complete the recipe to the end of step 3. Open-freeze, then wrap and freeze.
To use Thaw for about 1 hour, then complete the recipe.

Tropical Burst Cupcakes

★

Preparation Time 35 minutes • **Cooking Time** 20 minutes, plus cooling and setting • **Makes 12** • **Per Cupcake** 256 calories, 8g fat (of which 1g saturates), 45g carbohydrate, 0.2g salt • **Easy**

200g (7oz) self-raising flour, sifted
½ tsp bicarbonate of soda
100g (3½oz) caster sugar
50g (2oz) ready-to-eat dried
    tropical fruit, finely chopped
3 medium eggs
100ml (3½fl oz) sunflower oil
75ml (2½fl oz) buttermilk
1 x 227g tin pineapple pieces,
    drained and finely chopped

**FOR THE TOPPING AND
    DECORATION**
225g (8oz) royal icing sugar, sifted
zest and juice of 1 lime
sugar decorations (optional)

1 Preheat the oven to 190°C (170°C fan oven), mark 5. Line a 12-hole muffin tin with paper muffin cases.

2 Put the flour, bicarbonate of soda, caster sugar and dried fruit into a large bowl. Put the eggs, oil and buttermilk into a jug and lightly beat together until combined. Pour the oil mixture and the pineapple pieces into the flour and stir with a spatula until just combined. Divide the mixture equally between the paper cases.

3 Bake for 20 minutes or until lightly golden and risen. Leave to cool in the tin for 5 minutes, then transfer to a wire rack to cool completely.

4 For the topping, put the icing sugar, lime juice and zest and 1 tbsp cold water into a bowl and whisk for 5 minutes or until soft peaks form. Using a small palette knife, spread a little over the top of each cake. Stand the cakes upright on the wire rack, scatter with sugar decorations, if you like, and leave for about 1 hour to set.

★ TO STORE
Store in an airtight container. They will keep for 3–5 days.

★ FREEZING TIP
*To **freeze** Complete the recipe to the end of step 3. Open-freeze, then wrap and freeze.*
*To **use** Thaw for about 1 hour, then complete the recipe.*

Red Nose Buns

Preparation Time 20 minutes • Cooking Time 12–15 minutes, plus cooling and setting • Makes 36 • Per Bun 39 calories, 1g fat (of which 1g saturates), 7g carbohydrate, 0g salt • Easy

50g (2oz) unsalted butter, very soft
50g (2oz) caster sugar
1 medium egg, beaten
50g (2oz) self-raising flour
¼ tsp baking powder
1 ripe banana, peeled and mashed

**FOR THE ICING AND
  DECORATION**
125g (4oz) icing sugar, sifted
about 1 tbsp orange juice
red glacé cherries or round red
  jelly sweets

1 Preheat the oven to 190°C (170°C fan oven) mark 5. Arrange about 36 petits fours cases on baking sheets.

2 Put the butter, caster sugar, egg, flour and baking powder into a food processor and whiz until smooth and well mixed. Add the banana and whiz for 1 minute. Put a teaspoonful of the mixture into each paper case.

3 Bake for 12–15 minutes until golden. Transfer to a wire rack to cool completely.

4 For the icing, mix the icing sugar with the orange juice until smooth and just thick enough to coat the back of a spoon. Top each bun with a small blob of icing and stick half a cherry or a sweet on each one. Stand the cakes upright on the wire rack and leave for about 1 hour to set.

 TO STORE
Store in an airtight container. They will keep for 3–5 days.

 FREEZING TIP
To freeze Complete the recipe to the end of step 3. Open-freeze, then wrap and freeze.
To use Thaw for about 1 hour, then complete the recipe.

Polka Dot Cupcakes

★

Preparation Time 30 minutes • **Cooking Time** 20 minutes, plus cooling • **Makes 12** • **Per Cupcake** 283 calories, 12g fat (of which 4g saturates), 42g carbohydrate, 0.2g salt • **Easy**

250g (9oz) plain flour, sifted
1 tbsp baking powder
100g (3½oz) caster sugar
1 tbsp vanilla extract
2 medium eggs
125ml (4fl oz) sunflower oil
175g (6oz) natural yogurt

**FOR THE TOPPING AND
  DECORATION**
50g (2oz) unsalted butter, softened
175g (6oz) icing sugar, sifted
25g (1oz) cocoa powder, sifted
mini Smarties or chocolate beans

1 Preheat the oven to 190°C (170°C fan oven), mark 5. Line a 12-hole muffin tin with paper muffin cases.

2 Put the flour, baking powder and caster sugar into a large bowl. Put the vanilla extract, eggs, oil and yogurt into a jug and lightly beat together until combined. Pour into the flour mixture and stir with a spatula until just combined. Divide the mixture equally between the paper cases.

3 Bake for 20 minutes or until lightly golden and risen. Leave to cool in the tin for 5 minutes, then transfer to a wire rack to cool completely.

4 For the topping, put the butter into a bowl and whisk until fluffy. Gradually add the icing sugar until combined. Add the cocoa powder and 2 tbsp boiling water and whisk until light and fluffy. Using a small palette knife, spread a little buttercream over the top of each cake. Decorate with mini Smarties or chocolate beans.

 TO STORE
Store in an airtight container. They will keep for 3–5 days.

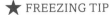 FREEZING TIP
__To freeze__ Complete the recipe to the end of step 3. Open-freeze, then wrap and freeze.
__To use__ Thaw for about 1 hour, then complete the recipe.

Mallow Madness Cupcakes

Preparation Time 40 minutes • **Cooking Time** 20–25 minutes, plus cooling and setting • **Makes 12** •
Per Cupcake 317 calories, 13g fat (of which 2g saturates), 49g carbohydrate, 0.1g salt • **Easy**

3 medium eggs
175g (6oz) self-raising flour, sifted
150g (5oz) caster sugar
175ml (6fl oz) sunflower oil
½ tsp baking powder
50g (2oz) white chocolate chips

**FOR THE TOPPING AND
  DECORATION**
125g (4oz) pink and white
  marshmallows
1 medium egg white
150g (5oz) caster sugar
a pinch of cream of tartar
pink sugar sprinkles

1 Preheat the oven to 190°C (170°C fan oven), mark 5. Line a 12-hole muffin tin with paper muffin cases.

2 Put the eggs, flour, sugar, oil and baking powder into a large bowl and, using a hand-held electric whisk, whisk until just combined. Add the chocolate chips and fold through. Divide the mixture equally between the paper cases.

3 Bake for 20–25 minutes until lightly golden and risen. Leave to cool in the tin for 5 minutes, then transfer to a wire rack to cool completely.

4 For the decoration, reserve 6 white marshmallows. Put the remaining marshmallows, the egg white, sugar and a pinch of cream of tartar into a heatproof bowl and whisk lightly using a hand-held electric whisk. Put the bowl over a pan of simmering water and whisk continuously, for about 7 minutes or until the marshmallows have melted and the mixture thickens sufficiently to stand in peaks.

5 Cut the reserved marshmallows in half. Spread a little of the icing over the top of each cake. Scatter with sugar sprinkles and top each with a marshmallow half. Stand the cakes upright on the wire rack and leave for about 1 hour to set.

⭐ TO STORE
Store in an airtight container. They will keep for 3–5 days.

⭐ FREEZING TIP
To freeze *Complete the recipe to the end of step 3. Open-freeze, then wrap and freeze.*
To use *Thaw for about 1 hour, then complete the recipe.*

Mini Green Tea Cupcakes

★

Preparation Time 40 minutes • **Cooking Time** 25 minutes, plus cooling and infusing • **Makes 12** •
Per Cupcake 282 calories, 13g fat (of which 8g saturates), 41g carbohydrate, 0.3g salt • **Easy**

100ml (3½fl oz) milk
2 tsp loose green tea leaves
100g (3½oz) unsalted butter,
  softened
125g (4oz) caster sugar
2 medium eggs
150g (5oz) self-raising flour, sifted
¼ tsp baking powder

**FOR THE TOPPING AND
  DECORATION**
3 tsp loose green tea leaves
about 75ml (2½fl oz) boiling water
75g (3oz) unsalted butter, softened
250g (9oz) icing sugar, sifted
ready-made sugar flowers

1 Preheat the oven to 190°C (170°C fan oven), mark 5. Line a 12-hole muffin tin with paper fairy cake or bun cases.

2 Put the milk into a small saucepan and bring to the boil. Add the green tea leaves and leave to infuse for 30 minutes.

3 Using a hand-held electric whisk, whisk the butter and caster sugar in a bowl, or beat with a wooden spoon, until pale and creamy. Gradually whisk in the eggs until just combined. Pass the green tea milk through a sieve into the bowl, then discard the tea. Using a metal spoon, fold in the flour and baking powder until combined. Divide the mixture equally between the paper cases.

4 Bake for 18–20 minutes until golden and risen. Leave to cool in the tin for 5 minutes, then transfer to a wire rack to cool completely.

5 For the topping, put the green tea leaves into a jug, add about 75ml (2½fl oz) boiling water and leave to infuse for 5 minutes. Put the butter into a bowl and whisk until fluffy. Gradually add the icing sugar and whisk until combined. Pass the green tea through a sieve into the bowl, then discard the tea. Continue to whisk until light and fluffy.

6 Insert a star nozzle into a piping bag, then fill the bag with the buttercream and pipe a swirl on to the top of each cake. Decorate each with a sugar flower.

★ TO STORE
Store in an airtight container. They will keep for 3–5 days.

★ FREEZING TIP
To freeze *Complete the recipe to the end of step 4. Open-freeze, then wrap and freeze.*
To use *Thaw for about 1 hour, then complete the recipe.*

Easter Cupcakes

Preparation Time 30 minutes • **Cooking Time** 30 minutes, plus cooling and setting • **Makes 6** •
Per Cupcake 378 calories, 27g fat (of which 8g saturates), 32g carbohydrate, 0.2g salt • **Easy**

2 medium eggs
75g (3oz) caster sugar
150ml (¼ pint) sunflower oil
150g (5oz) plain flour, sifted
½ tsp baking powder
1 tsp vanilla extract
15g (½oz) Rice Krispies

**FOR THE TOPPING AND
    DECORATION**
100g (3½oz) white chocolate,
    broken into pieces
15g (½oz) unsalted butter
25g (1oz) Rice Krispies
12 chocolate mini eggs

1 Preheat the oven to 180°C (160°C fan oven), mark 4. Line a 6-hole muffin tin with paper muffin cases.

2 Separate the eggs, putting the whites in a clean, grease-free bowl and the yolks in another. Add the sugar to the yolks and whisk with a hand-held electric whisk until pale and creamy. Then whisk in the oil until combined.

3 Whisk the egg whites until soft peaks form. Using a metal spoon, quickly fold the flour, baking powder, vanilla extract and Rice Krispies into the egg yolk mixture until just combined. Add half the egg whites to the egg yolk mixture to loosen, then carefully fold in the remaining egg whites. Divide the mixture equally between the paper cases.

4 Bake for 20–25 minutes until golden and risen. Leave to cool in the tin for 5 minutes, then transfer to a wire rack to cool completely.

5 For the topping, put the chocolate and butter into a heatproof bowl and place over a pan of barely simmering water, making sure the base of the bowl doesn't touch the water. Gently heat until the chocolate has melted, stirring occasionally until smooth. Remove the bowl from the heat, add the Rice Krispies and fold through until coated. Spoon the mixture on top of each cake, pressing down lightly, then top each with 2 chocolate eggs. Stand the cakes upright on the wire rack and leave for about 1 hour to set.

★ TO STORE
Store in an airtight container. They will keep for 3–5 days.

★ FREEZING TIP
To freeze *Complete the recipe to the end of step 4. Open-freeze, then wrap and freeze.*
To use *Thaw for about 1 hour, then complete the recipe.*

Sweet Shop Cupcakes

Preparation Time 30 minutes • **Cooking Time** 20 minutes, plus cooling and setting • **Makes 12** •
Per Cupcake 424 calories, 19g fat (of which 12g saturates), 64g carbohydrate, 0.6g salt • **Easy**

175g (6oz) unsalted butter, softened
175g (6oz) caster sugar
3 medium eggs
175g (6oz) self-raising flour, sifted
zest of 1 lemon
½ tsp baking powder
125g (4oz) lemon curd

**FOR THE TOPPING AND
  DECORATION**
75g (3oz) unsalted butter, softened
350g (12oz) icing sugar, sifted
50ml (2fl oz) milk
dolly mixtures, jelly beans or
  chocolate buttons

1 Preheat the oven to 190°C (170°C
fan oven), mark 5. Line a 12-hole
muffin tin with paper muffin cases.

2 Using a hand-held electric whisk,
whisk the butter and caster sugar in
a bowl, or beat with a wooden
spoon, until pale and creamy.
Gradually whisk in the eggs until
just combined. Using a metal spoon,
fold in the flour, lemon zest and
baking powder until combined.
Divide the mixture equally between
the paper cases.

3 Bake for 20 minutes or until
golden and risen. Leave to cool in
the tin for 5 minutes, then transfer
to a wire rack to cool completely.

4 Cut a small cone shape from the
top of each cake. Put a teaspoonful
of lemon curd into the hole in each
cake and then replace the cake
cone, pressing down lightly.

5 For the topping, put the butter
into a bowl and whisk until fluffy.
Gradually add half the icing sugar,
whisking until combined. Add the
milk and remaining icing sugar and
whisk until light and fluffy, then,
using a small palette knife, spread
a little over each cake. Stand the
cakes upright on the wire rack and

leave for about 30 minutes to set.
Decorate each cake with sweets
when set.

★ TO STORE
*Store in an airtight container. They will
keep for 2–3 days.*

★ FREEZING TIP
*To freeze Complete the recipe to the
end of step 3. Open-freeze, then wrap
and freeze*
*To use Thaw for about 1 hour, then
complete the recipe.*

Jewelled Cupcakes

Preparation Time 40 minutes • **Cooking Time** 30 minutes, plus cooling and setting • **Makes 12** • **Per Cupcake** 276 calories, 10g fat (of which 4g saturates), 46g carbohydrate, 0.4g salt • **Easy**

75g (3oz) unsalted butter, softened
150g (5oz) caster sugar
3 medium eggs
175g (6oz) self-raising flour, sifted
175g (6oz) mincemeat

FOR THE DECORATION
75g (3oz) apricot glaze (see page 280)
50g (2oz) toasted flaked almonds
50g (2oz) ready-to-eat apricots, chopped
12 glacé cherries
40g (1½oz) caster sugar
1 tbsp unsalted butter

1 Preheat the oven to 190°C (170°C fan oven), mark 5. Line a 12-hole muffin tin with paper muffin cases.

2 Using a hand-held electric whisk, whisk the butter and sugar in a bowl, or beat with a wooden spoon, until pale and creamy. Gradually whisk in the eggs until just combined. Using a metal spoon, fold in the flour and mincemeat until combined. Divide the mixture equally between the paper cases.

3 Bake for 20 minutes or until golden and risen. Leave to cool in the tin for 5 minutes, then transfer to a wire rack to cool completely.

4 For the decoration, brush each cake with a little apricot glaze, then scatter on a few almonds and apricots and a cherry. Stand the cakes upright on the wire rack.

5 Put the sugar and 1 tbsp cold water into a small pan and gently heat until the sugar dissolves. Increase the heat and bubble for 3–4 minutes until the sugar caramelises and turns golden in colour. Remove from the heat and quickly stir in the butter until combined. Being very careful, drizzle the hot caramel over the top of each cake. Leave for about 10 minutes to set.

★ TO STORE
Store in an airtight container. They will keep for 3–5 days.

★ FREEZING TIP
To freeze Complete the recipe to the end of step 3. Open-freeze, then wrap and freeze.
To use Thaw for about 1 hour, then complete the recipe.

Breakfast Cupcakes

★

Preparation Time 30 minutes • **Cooking Time** 20 minutes, plus cooling and setting • **Makes 12** • **Per Cupcake** 327 calories, 14g fat (of which 8g saturates), 48g carbohydrate, 0.3g salt • **Easy**

175g (6oz) unsalted butter, softened
100g (3½oz) caster sugar
3 medium eggs
75g (3oz) apricot jam
150g (5oz) self-raising flour, sifted
75g (3oz) oatbran
½ tsp baking powder

**FOR THE ICING AND
   DECORATION**
225g (8oz) icing sugar
1–2 tbsp orange juice
75g (3oz) mixed berry granola

1 Preheat the oven to 190°C (170°C fan oven), mark 5. Line a 12-hole muffin tin with paper muffin cases.

2 Using a hand-held electric whisk, whisk the butter and caster sugar in a bowl, or beat with a wooden spoon, until pale and creamy. Gradually whisk in the eggs until just combined. Using a metal spoon, fold in the apricot jam, flour, oatbran and baking powder until combined. Divide the mixture equally between the paper cases.

3 Bake for 20 minutes or until golden and risen. Leave to cool in the tin for 5 minutes, then transfer to a wire rack to cool completely.

4 For the icing, sift the icing sugar into a bowl, then add enough orange juice to achieve a smooth, thick icing. Spoon a little on top of each cake, then sprinkle with the granola. Stand the cakes upright on the wire rack and leave for about 1 hour to set.

 TO STORE
Store in an airtight container. They will keep for 3–5 days.

 FREEZING TIP
To freeze *Complete the recipe to the end of step 3. Open-freeze, then wrap and freeze.*
To use *Thaw for about 1 hour, then complete the recipe.*

Truffle Kisses Cupcakes

Preparation Time 40 minutes • **Cooking Time** 30 minutes, plus cooling and setting • **Makes 18** • **Per Cupcake** 317 calories, 20g fat (of which 10g saturates), 34g carbohydrate, 0.2g salt • **Easy**

150g (5oz) unsalted butter, softened
200g (7oz) caster sugar
3 medium eggs
75g (3oz) self-raising flour, sifted
200g (7oz) plain flour, sifted
½ tsp bicarbonate of soda
75g (3oz) roasted chopped
   hazelnuts
200ml (7fl oz) buttermilk
15g (½oz) dark chocolate, finely
   grated

**FOR THE TOPPING AND
DECORATION**
200ml (7fl oz) double cream
150g (5oz) dark chocolate

100g (3½oz) milk chocolate, finely
   chopped
18 small chocolate truffles
   (optional)

1 Preheat the oven to 180°C (160°C fan oven), mark 4. Line a 12-hole and a 6-hole muffin tin with paper muffin cases.

2 Using a hand-held electric whisk, whisk the butter and sugar in a bowl, or beat with a wooden spoon, until pale and creamy. Gradually whisk in the eggs until just combined. Using a metal spoon, fold in both flours, the bicarbonate of soda, hazelnuts, buttermilk and grated chocolate until combined. Divide the mixture equally between the paper cases.

3 Bake for 20–25 minutes until golden and risen. Leave to cool in the tin for 5 minutes, then transfer to a wire rack to cool completely.

4 For the topping, heat the cream in a small saucepan until nearly boiling. Finely chop 100g (3½oz) dark chocolate and put into a bowl along with all the milk chocolate. Pour the hot cream over the chocolate and leave to stand for 5 minutes, then stir gently until smooth. Chill the mixture for 15–20 minutes until thickened slightly.

5 Using a palette knife, spread a little chocolate cream over the top of each cake. Finely grate the remaining dark chocolate over the top of each cake. Finish each with a chocolate truffle, if you like. Stand the cakes upright on the wire rack and leave for about 1 hour to set.

 TO STORE
Store in an airtight container in the fridge. They will keep for 2–3 days.

★ FREEZING TIP
To freeze *Complete the recipe to the end of step 3. Open-freeze, then wrap and freeze.*
To use *Thaw for about 1 hour, then complete the recipe.*

Secret Garden Cupcakes

⭐

Preparation Time 45 minutes • **Cooking Time** 40 minutes, plus cooling • **Makes** 12 • **Per Cupcake** 398 calories, 20g fat (of which 13g saturates), 53g carbohydrate, 0.5g salt • **Easy**

200g (7oz) fresh strawberries, hulled and halved
200g (7oz) caster sugar
150g (5oz) unsalted butter, softened
3 medium eggs
200g (7oz) self-raising flour, sifted
½ tsp bicarbonate of soda
50ml (2fl oz) buttermilk

FOR THE TOPPING AND DECORATION
125g (4oz) unsalted butter, softened
250g (9oz) icing sugar, sifted
green food colouring
ladybird, bumble bee and butterfly sugar decorations (optional)

1 Preheat the oven to 190°C (170°C fan oven), mark 5. Line a 12-hole muffin tin with paper muffin cases.

2 Put the strawberries and 50g (2oz) caster sugar into a heatproof bowl and cover with clingfilm. Put over a pan of barely simmering water and cook gently for 30 minutes.

3 Meanwhile, using a hand-held electric whisk, whisk the butter and remaining caster sugar in a bowl, or beat with a wooden spoon, until pale and creamy. Gradually whisk in the eggs until just combined. Using a metal spoon, fold in the flour, bicarbonate of soda and buttermilk until combined. Divide the mixture equally between the paper cases.

4 Bake for 20 minutes or until golden and risen. Leave to cool in the tin for 5 minutes. Meanwhile, pass the strawberries and juice through a sieve into a shallow bowl. Discard the strawberries.

5 Using a cocktail stick, prick the top of the cakes all over. Dip the top of each cake into the strawberry syrup, then transfer to a wire rack to cool completely.

6 For the topping, put the butter into a bowl and whisk until fluffy. Gradually whisk in half the icing sugar, then add 1 tbsp boiling water, a little green food colouring and the remaining icing sugar and whisk until light and fluffy.

7 Insert a star nozzle into a piping bag, then fill the bag with the buttercream and pipe in a zigzag pattern on top of each cake. Decorate with the sugar ladybirds, butterflies and bumble bees, if you like.

⭐ TO STORE
Store in an airtight container. They will keep for 2–3 days.

Honeycomb Cream Cupcakes

Preparation Time 30 minutes • **Cooking Time** 20 minutes, plus cooling • **Makes 9** • **Per Cupcake** 480 calories, 25g fat (of which 15g saturates), 65g carbohydrate, 0.6g salt • **Easy**

125g (4oz) unsalted butter, softened
50g (2oz) caster sugar
2 medium eggs
75g (3oz) runny honey
125g (4oz) self-raising flour, sifted
50g (2oz) rolled oats
½ tsp baking powder
1 tbsp milk

**FOR THE TOPPING AND
  DECORATION**
125g (4oz) unsalted butter, softened
300g (11oz) golden icing sugar,
  sifted
2 tbsp milk
1 Crunchie bar, thinly sliced

1 Preheat the oven to 190°C (170°C fan oven), mark 5. Line a 12-hole muffin tin with 9 paper muffin cases.

2 Using a hand-held electric whisk, whisk the butter and caster sugar in a bowl, or beat with a wooden spoon, until pale and creamy. Gradually whisk in the eggs and honey until just combined. Using a metal spoon, fold in the flour, oats, baking powder and milk until combined. Divide the mixture equally between the paper cases.

3 Bake for 20 minutes or until golden and risen. Leave to cool in the tin for 5 minutes, then transfer to a wire rack to cool completely.

4 For the topping, put the butter into a bowl and whisk until fluffy. Gradually whisk in half the icing sugar, then add the milk and the remaining icing sugar and whisk until light and fluffy.

5 Insert a star nozzle into a piping bag, then fill the bag with the buttercream and pipe a swirl on to the top of each cake. When ready to serve, decorate each with a few slices of Crunchie.

 TO STORE
Store in an airtight container. They will keep for 2–3 days.

 FREEZING TIP
To freeze *Complete the recipe to the end of step 3. Open-freeze, then wrap and freeze.*
To use *Thaw for about 1 hour, then complete the recipe.*

Nutty Cupcakes

Preparation Time 40 minutes • **Cooking Time** 25 minutes, plus cooling and setting • **Makes 12** • **Per Cupcake** 338 calories, 23g fat (of which 10g saturates), 31g carbohydrate, 0.4g salt • **Easy**

150g (5oz) unsalted butter, softened
175g (6oz) self-raising flour, sifted
50g (2oz) caster sugar
100ml (3½fl oz) golden syrup
3 medium eggs
1 tsp baking powder
1 tsp ground mixed spice
50g (2oz) mixed chopped nuts

FOR THE TOPPING
3 tbsp double cream
1 tbsp milk
50g (2oz) milk chocolate, finely chopped
25g (1oz) dark chocolate, finely chopped
75g (3oz) roasted chopped hazelnuts

1 Preheat the oven to 190°C (170°C fan oven), mark 5. Line a 12-hole muffin tin with paper muffin cases.

2 Put the butter, flour, sugar, syrup, eggs, baking powder, mixed spice and nuts into a large bowl. Using a hand-held electric whisk, whisk together until pale and creamy. Divide the mixture equally between the paper cases.

3 Bake for 20 minutes or until golden and risen. Leave to cool in the tin for 5 minutes, then transfer to a wire rack to cool completely.

4 For the topping, heat the cream and milk in a small saucepan until nearly boiling. Put both chocolates into a bowl and pour the hot cream over them. Leave to stand for 5 minutes, then gently stir until smooth.

5 Put the hazelnuts into a shallow bowl. Dip the top of each cake into the chocolate cream, allow the excess to drip off, then dip into the hazelnuts until coated all over. Stand the cakes upright on the wire rack and leave for about 1 hour to set.

★ TO STORE
Store in an airtight container in the fridge. They will keep for 2–3 days.

★ FREEZING TIP
To freeze *Complete the recipe to the end of step 3. Open-freeze, then wrap and freeze.*
To use *Thaw for about 1 hour, then complete the recipe.*

Banoffee Cupcakes

Preparation Time 30 minutes • **Cooking Time** 20 minutes, plus cooling • **Makes 12** • **Per Cupcake** 404 calories, 16g fat (of which 10g saturates), 63g carbohydrate, 0.4g salt • **Easy**

175g (6oz) self-raising flour, sifted
½ tsp bicarbonate of soda
150g (5oz) light soft brown sugar
1 banana (about 150g/5oz), peeled
3 medium eggs
100g (3½oz) unsalted butter, melted
75ml (2½fl oz) buttermilk

FOR THE TOPPING AND DECORATION
150g (5oz) dulce de leche toffee sauce
75g (3oz) unsalted butter, softened
250g (9oz) golden icing sugar, sifted
mini fudge chunks (optional)

1 Preheat the oven to 190°C (170°C fan oven), mark 5. Line a 12-hole muffin tin with paper muffin cases.

2 Put the flour, bicarbonate of soda and brown sugar into a large bowl. Mash the banana with a fork in a small bowl. Put the eggs, melted butter and buttermilk into a jug and lightly beat together until combined. Pour into the flour mixture along with the mashed banana and stir with a spatula until just combined. Divide the mixture equally between the paper cases.

3 Bake for 18–20 minutes until lightly golden and risen. Leave to cool in the tin for 5 minutes, then transfer to a wire rack to cool completely.

4 For the decoration, whisk together the dulce de leche and butter in a bowl until combined. Gradually whisk in the icing sugar until light and fluffy. Use a palette knife to spread the buttercream on to the top of each cake. Decorate with the mini fudge chunks, if using.

★ TO STORE
Store in an airtight container. They will keep for 2–3 days.

★ FREEZING TIP
To freeze Complete the recipe to the end of step 3. Open-freeze, then wrap and freeze.
To use Thaw for about 1 hour, then complete the recipe.

Gluten-free Pistachio and Polenta Cupcakes

Preparation Time 35 minutes • **Cooking Time** 25 minutes, plus cooling • **Makes 12** • **Per Cupcake** 542 calories, 33g fat (of which 13g saturates), 56g carbohydrate, 0.6g salt • **Gluten Free** • **Easy**

150g (5oz) shelled pistachio nuts
175g (6oz) unsalted butter, softened
175g (6oz) caster sugar
3 medium eggs
200g (7oz) fine polenta
½ tsp baking powder
150g (5oz) ground almonds
zest of 2 lemons
2 tbsp milk

FOR THE ICING
75g (3oz) unsalted butter, softened
300g (11oz) icing sugar, sifted
juice of 2 lemons

1 Preheat the oven to 180°C (160°C fan oven), mark 4. Line a 12-hole muffin tin with paper muffin cases.

2 Whiz the pistachios in a food processor until really finely chopped.

3 Using a hand-held electric whisk, whisk the butter and caster sugar in a bowl, or beat with a wooden spoon, until pale and creamy. Gradually whisk in the eggs until just combined. Using a metal spoon, fold in the polenta, baking powder, ground almonds, lemon zest, milk and 100g (3½oz) ground pistachios until combined. Divide the mixture equally between the paper cases.

4 Bake for 25 minutes or until golden and risen. Leave to cool in the tin for 5 minutes, then transfer to a wire rack to cool completely.

5 For the icing, put the butter into a bowl and whisk until fluffy. Gradually whisk in half the icing sugar, then add the lemon juice and the remaining icing sugar, whisking until light and fluffy. Using a small palette knife, spread a little of the buttercream over the top of each cake, then sprinkle with a little of the remaining chopped pistachios.

★ TO STORE
Store in an airtight container. They will keep for 3–5 days.

★ FREEZING TIP
To freeze *Complete the recipe to the end of step 4. Open-freeze, then wrap and freeze.*
To use *Thaw for about 1 hour, then complete the recipe.*

Aniseed Cupcakes

Preparation Time 30 minutes • **Cooking Time** 20–25 minutes, plus cooling • **Makes 12** • **Per Cupcake** 291 calories, 15g fat (of which 9g saturates), 37g carbohydrate, 0.4g salt • **Easy**

125g (4oz) unsalted butter, softened
200g (7oz) caster sugar
2 medium eggs
200g (7oz) self-raising flour, sifted
25g (1oz) custard powder
2 tbsp caraway seeds
125ml (4fl oz) milk

**FOR THE TOPPING AND
    DECORATION**
75g (3oz) unsalted butter, softened
300g (11oz) icing sugar, sifted
2 tbsp Pernod
pale blue sugar sprinkles

1 Preheat the oven to 190°C (170°C fan oven), mark 5. Line a 12-hole muffin tin with paper muffin cases.

2 Using a hand-held electric whisk, whisk the butter and caster sugar in a bowl, or beat with a wooden spoon, until pale and creamy. Gradually whisk in the eggs until just combined. Using a metal spoon, fold in the flour, custard powder, caraway seeds and milk until combined. Divide the mixture equally between the paper cases.

3 Bake for 20–25 minutes until golden and risen. Leave to cool in the tin for 5 minutes, then transfer to a wire rack to cool completely.

4 For the topping, put the butter into a bowl and whisk until fluffy. Gradually whisk in half the icing sugar, then add the Pernod, 1 tbsp boiling water and the remaining icing sugar and whisk until light and fluffy. Using a small palette knife, spread a little of the buttercream over the top of each cake, then sprinkle with the blue sugar sprinkles.

 TO STORE

Store in an airtight container. They will keep for 3–5 days.

★ FREEZING TIP

__To freeze__ Complete the recipe to the end of step 3. Open-freeze, then wrap and freeze.
__To use__ Thaw for about 1 hour, then complete the recipe.

Mango and Passion Fruit Cupcakes

Preparation Time 30 minutes • **Cooking Time** 25 minutes, plus cooling • **Makes 12** • **Per Cupcake** 374 calories, 18g fat (of which 11g saturates), 52g carbohydrate, 0.4g salt • **Easy**

4 ripe passion fruit
about 75ml (2½fl oz) orange juice
150g (5oz) unsalted butter, softened
250g (9oz) plain flour, sifted
175g (6oz) caster sugar
3 medium eggs
1 tbsp baking powder
75g (3oz) ready-to-eat dried mango, finely chopped

FOR THE TOPPING AND DECORATION
100g (3½oz) cream cheese
25g (1oz) unsalted butter, softened
200g (7oz) icing sugar, sifted
1 large, ripe passion fruit
white sugar sprinkles

1 Preheat the oven to 180°C (160°C fan oven), mark 4. Line a 12–hole muffin tin with paper muffin cases.

2 Cut the passion fruit in half and pass the seeds and juice through a sieve into a jug. Discard the seeds. You need 150ml (¼ pint) liquid, so use the orange juice to top up the passion fruit juice.

3 Put the butter, flour, caster sugar, eggs, baking powder and passion fruit and orange juice into a large bowl. Using a hand-held electric whisk, whisk together, or beat with a wooden spoon, until pale and creamy. Add the chopped mango and fold through until combined. Divide the mixture equally between the paper cases.

4 Bake for 25 minutes or until golden and risen. Leave to cool in the tin for 5 minutes, then transfer to a wire rack to cool completely.

5 For the topping, whisk together the cream cheese and butter until fluffy. Gradually add the icing sugar until combined. Cut the passion fruit in half and pass the seeds and juice through a sieve into the icing. Discard the seeds. Stir to combine, then, using a small palette knife, spread a little over the top of each cake. Scatter on the sugar sprinkles.

★ TO STORE
Store in an airtight container in the fridge. They will keep for 2–3 days.

★ FREEZING TIP
To freeze Complete the recipe to the end of step 4. Open-freeze, then wrap and freeze.
To use Thaw for about 1 hour, then complete the recipe.

Marbled Chocolate Cupcakes

Preparation Time 40 minutes • **Cooking Time** 20 minutes, plus cooling • **Makes 12** • **Per Cupcake** 360 calories, 16g fat (of which 10g saturates), 54g carbohydrate, 0.5g salt • **Easy**

75g (3oz) unsalted butter, softened
150g (5oz) caster sugar
2 medium eggs
25g (1oz) self-raising flour, sifted
125g (4oz) plain flour, sifted
½ tsp bicarbonate of soda
2 tsp vanilla extract
150ml (¼ pint) buttermilk
25g (1oz) cocoa powder, sifted

FOR THE TOPPING
125g (4oz) unsalted butter, softened
350g (12oz) icing sugar, sifted
2 tsp vanilla extract
2 tbsp cocoa powder, sifted

1 Preheat the oven to 190°C (170°C fan oven), mark 5. Line a 12-hole muffin tin with paper muffin cases.

2 Using a hand-held electric whisk, whisk the butter and caster sugar in a bowl, or beat with a wooden spoon, until pale and creamy. Gradually whisk in the eggs until just combined. Using a metal spoon, fold in both flours, the bicarbonate of soda, vanilla extract and buttermilk until combined. Put half this mixture into another bowl and whisk in the cocoa powder. Then very lightly fold this mixture into the vanilla mixture, to create a marbled effect. Divide the mixture equally between the paper cases.

3 Bake for 20 minutes or until golden and risen. Leave to cool in the tin for 5 minutes, then transfer to a wire rack to cool completely.

4 For the topping, put the butter into a bowl and whisk until fluffy. Gradually whisk in half the icing sugar, then add the vanilla extract, 2 tbsp boiling water and the remaining icing sugar and whisk until light and fluffy. Put half the mixture into another bowl and whisk in the cocoa powder.

5 Insert a star nozzle into a piping bag, then fill the bag alternately with the vanilla and chocolate buttercreams. Pipe a swirl on to the top of each cake.

 TO STORE
Store in an airtight container. They will keep for 3–5 days.

 FREEZING TIP
To freeze Complete the recipe to the end of step 3. Open-freeze, then wrap and freeze.
To use Thaw for about 1 hour, then complete the recipe.

Sea Breeze Cupcakes

Preparation Time 40 minutes • **Cooking Time** 20 minutes, plus cooling and setting • **Makes 12** •
Per Cupcake 287 calories, 6g fat (of which 4g saturates), 61g carbohydrate, 0.1g salt • **Easy**

1 pink grapefruit (about 350g/12oz)
50g (2oz) ready-to-eat dried
  cranberries
250g (9oz) self-raising flour, sifted
125g (4oz) caster sugar
50ml (2fl oz) milk
1 medium egg, beaten
75g (3oz) unsalted butter, melted
1 tsp baking powder

**FOR THE ICING AND
  DECORATION**
300g (11oz) fondant icing sugar,
  sifted
red and yellow food colouring
50g (2oz) apricot glaze (see page
  280)
edible silver balls
cocktail umbrellas (optional)

1 Preheat the oven to 190°C (170°C
fan oven), mark 5. Line a 12-hole
muffin tin with paper muffin cases.

2 Grate the zest from half the
grapefruit into a bowl. Set aside. Cut
the top and bottom off the grapefruit
and stand it upright on a board. Using
a serrated knife, cut away the pith in
a downward motion. Cut in between
the membranes to remove the
segments. Whiz the segments in a
food processor until puréed.

3 Transfer the purée into the bowl
with the zest. Add the cranberries,
flour, caster sugar, milk, egg, melted
butter and baking powder and stir
with a spatula until just combined.

Divide the mixture equally between
the paper cases.

4 Bake for 20 minutes or until
golden and risen. Leave to cool in
the tin for 5 minutes, then transfer
to a wire rack to cool completely.

5 For the icing, put the icing sugar
into a bowl and add enough water
(2–4 tbsp) to make a smooth icing.
Add a few drops of food colouring to
make it pinky-orange in colour. Brush
the tops of the cakes with the apricot
glaze, then spoon a little icing on to
each cake to flood the top. Decorate

with the silver balls. Stand the cakes
upright on the wire rack and leave for
about 1 hour to set. Decorate with a
cocktail umbrella once set, if you like.

★ TO STORE
*Store in an airtight container. They will
keep for 3–5 days..*

★ FREEZING TIP
*To freeze Complete the recipe to the
end of step 4. Open-freeze, then wrap
and freeze.*
*To use Thaw for about 1 hour, then
complete the recipe.*

Toast and Marmalade Cupcakes

Preparation Time 30 minutes • **Cooking Time** 20–25 minutes, plus cooling and setting • **Makes 12**
Per Cupcake 336 calories, 10g fat (of which 2g saturates), 57g carbohydrate, 1.5g salt • **Easy**

150g (5oz) low-fat olive oil spread
200g (7oz) wholemeal self-raising
   flour, sifted
150g (5oz) light soft brown sugar
3 medium eggs
50g (2oz) marmalade
100ml (3½fl oz) milk
zest of 1 orange
50g (2oz) fresh wholemeal
   breadcrumbs

FOR THE ICING AND
   DECORATION
125g (4oz) marmalade
300g (11oz) icing sugar, sifted

1 Preheat the oven to 180°C (160°C fan oven), mark 4. Line a 12-hole muffin tin with paper muffin cases.

2 Put the low-fat spread, flour, brown sugar, eggs, marmalade, milk, orange zest and breadcrumbs into a large bowl. Using a hand-held electric whisk, whisk together until pale and creamy. Divide the mixture equally between the paper cases.

3 Bake for 20–25 minutes until golden and risen. Leave to cool in the tin for 5 minutes, then transfer to a wire rack to cool completely.

4 For the icing, pass the marmalade through a sieve into a bowl to remove the rind. Reserve the rind. Mix the icing sugar with the sieved marmalade in a bowl until it forms a smooth icing. Spoon a little icing on to each cake to flood the top, then scatter on the reserved rind. Stand the cakes upright on the wire rack and leave for about 1 hour to set.

★ TO STORE
Store in an airtight container. They will keep for 3–5 days.

★ FREEZING TIP
To freeze *Complete the recipe to the end of step 3. Open-freeze, then wrap and freeze.*
To use *Thaw for about 1 hour, then complete the recipe.*

Pretty Pink Cupcakes

Preparation Time 35 minutes • **Cooking Time** 20 minutes, plus cooling • **Makes 12** • **Per Cupcake** 361 calories, 14g fat (of which 6g saturates), 58g carbohydrate, 0.2g salt • **Easy**

150g (5oz) raw beetroot, peeled and
    finely grated
200g (7oz) self-raising flour, sifted
½ tsp bicarbonate of soda
150g (5oz) caster sugar
zest 1 orange
2 medium eggs
100ml (3½fl oz) sunflower oil
125ml (4fl oz) buttermilk

**FOR THE TOPPING AND
    DECORATION**
100g (3½oz) unsalted butter,
    softened
350g (12oz) icing sugar, sifted
50ml (2fl oz) milk
pink food colouring
ready-made pink or red sugar
    flowers (optional)

1 Preheat the oven to 190°C (170°C fan oven), mark 5. Line a 12-hole muffin tin with paper muffin cases.

2 Put the beetroot, flour, bicarbonate of soda, caster sugar and orange zest into a bowl. Put the eggs, oil and buttermilk into a jug and lightly beat together until combined. Pour the egg mixture into the flour and stir with a spatula until just combined. Divide the mixture equally between the paper cases.

3 Bake for 20 minutes or until lightly golden and risen. Leave to cool in the tin for 5 minutes, then transfer to a wire rack to cool completely.

4 For the topping, put the butter into a bowl and whisk until fluffy. Gradually whisk in half the icing sugar, then add the milk, a little pink food colouring and the remaining icing sugar and whisk until light and fluffy.

5 Insert a star nozzle into a piping bag, then fill the bag with the buttercream and pipe small swirls all the way around the top of each cake. Decorate with the sugar flowers, if using.

★ TO STORE
Store in an airtight container. They will keep for 3–5 days.

★ FREEZING TIP
To freeze Complete the recipe to the end of step 3. Open-freeze, then wrap and freeze.
To use Thaw for about 1 hour, then complete the recipe.

Small Cakes and Muffins

★

Chocolate Butterfly Cakes

Preparation Time 25 minutes • **Cooking Time** 15–20 minutes, plus cooling • **Makes 18** • **Per Cake** 170 calories, 7g fat (of which 4g saturates), 26g carbohydrate, 0.2g salt • **Easy**

125g (4oz) unsalted butter, very soft
125g (4oz) caster sugar
2 medium eggs, lightly beaten
   individually
125g (4oz) plain flour
25g (1oz) cocoa
½ tsp baking powder
1 tbsp milk
1 x quantity of buttercream icing
   (see page 282)

1 Preheat the oven to 190°C (170°C fan oven) mark 5. Put 18 paper cake cases into two bun trays.

2 Using a hand-held electric whisk, beat the butter and sugar together until soft and fluffy and lighter in colour. Beat in the eggs thoroughly, one at a time.

3 Sift the flour, cocoa and baking powder into the bowl and fold in gently until well mixed. Fold in the milk to give a soft, dropping consistency. Divide the mixture equally between the paper cases.

4 Bake for 15–20 minutes until risen and firm. Transfer to a wire rack to cool completely.

5 Slice off the top of each cake and cut the slice in half. Using a palette knife, spread buttercream on each cake. Put the 'butterfly wings' on top, with their curved sides facing towards each other.

★ TO STORE
Store in an airtight container. They will keep for up to two days.

★COOK'S TIP
Colour the buttercream with pink or green food colouring if you like, to match the theme of the party.

Apple Madeleines

★

Preparation Time 15 minutes • **Cooking Time** 8–10 minutes, plus cooling • **Makes 24** • **Per Madeleine** 106 calories, 6g fat (of which 4g saturates), 13g carbohydrate, 0.1g salt • **Easy**

150g (5oz) unsalted butter, melted and cooled, plus extra to grease
3 large eggs
150g (5oz) caster sugar
1 tsp vanilla extract
150g (5oz) plain flour, sifted
½ tsp baking powder
2 apples such as Cox's, peeled, cored and finely chopped
icing sugar to dust

1 Preheat the oven to 200°C (180°C fan oven) mark 6. Grease the madeleine tins.

2 Put the eggs and caster sugar into a bowl and, using a hand-held electric whisk, beat together until thick (this should take about 8 minutes), then add the vanilla extract. Quickly but gently, fold in the flour, baking powder and apples followed by the melted butter, making sure the butter doesn't settle at the bottom of the bowl. Spoon the mixture equally into the madeleine tins.

3 Bake for 8–10 minutes until golden, then remove from the tins and transfer to wire racks to cool completely. Dust with icing sugar before serving.

★ TO STORE
Store in an airtight container. They will keep for up to four days.

Spiced Carrot Muffins

Preparation Time 30 minutes • **Cooking Time** 20–25 minutes, plus cooling • **Makes 12** • **Per Muffin** 333 calories, 22g fat (of which 11g saturates), 31g carbohydrate, 0.5g salt • **Easy**

125g (4oz) unsalted butter, softened
125g (4oz) light muscovado sugar
3 pieces of preserved stem ginger, drained and chopped
150g (5oz) self-raising flour, sifted
1½ tsp baking powder
1 tbsp ground mixed spice
25g (1oz) ground almonds
3 medium eggs
finely grated zest of ½ orange
150g (5oz) carrots, grated
50g (2oz) pecan nuts, chopped
50g (2oz) sultanas
3 tbsp white rum or orange liqueur (optional)

FOR THE TOPPING AND DECORATION
200g (7oz) cream cheese
75g (3oz) icing sugar
1 tsp lemon juice
12 unsprayed rose petals (optional)

1 Preheat the oven to 180°C (160°C fan oven) mark 4. Line a 12-hole bun tin or muffin tin with paper muffin cases.

2 Beat the butter, muscovado sugar and stem ginger together until pale and creamy. Add the flour, baking powder, spice, ground almonds, eggs and orange zest and beat well until combined. Stir in the carrots, pecan nuts and sultanas. Divide the mixture equally among the paper cases.

3 Bake for 20–25 minutes until risen and just firm. A skewer inserted into the centre should come out clean. Transfer to a wire rack and cool completely.

4 For the topping, beat the cream cheese in a bowl until softened. Beat in the icing sugar and lemon juice to give a smooth icing that just holds its shape.

5 Drizzle each cake with a little liqueur, if using. Using a small palette knife, spread a little icing over each cake. Decorate with a rose petal, if you like.

★ TO STORE
Store in an airtight container. They will keep for up to one week.

★ FREEZING TIP
__To freeze__ Complete the recipe to the end of step 3. Once the muffins are cold, pack, seal and freeze.
__To use__ Thaw at cool room temperature and complete the recipe.

Blueberry Muffins

Preparation Time 10 minutes • **Cooking Time** 20–25 minutes, plus cooling • **Makes 12** • **Per Muffin** 218 calories, 2g fat (of which trace saturates), 49g carbohydrate, 0.5g salt • **Easy**

2 medium eggs
250ml (9fl oz) semi-skimmed milk
250g (9oz) golden granulated sugar
2 tsp vanilla extract
350g (12oz) plain flour
4 tsp baking powder
250g (9oz) blueberries, frozen
finely grated zest of 2 lemons

1 Preheat the oven to 200°C (180°C fan oven) mark 6. Line a 12-hole bun tin or muffin tin with paper muffin cases.

2 Put the eggs, milk, sugar and vanilla extract into a bowl and mix well.

3 In another bowl, sift the flour and baking powder together, then add the blueberries and lemon zest. Toss together and make a well in the centre.

4 Pour the egg mixture into the flour and blueberries and mix in gently – over-beating will make the muffins tough. Divide the mixture equally between the paper cases.

5 Bake for 20–25 minutes until risen and just firm. Transfer to a wire rack to cool completely. These are best eaten on the day they are made.

★FREEZING TIP
To freeze *Complete the recipe. Once the muffins are cold, pack, seal and freeze.* **To use** *Thaw at cool room temperature.*

★TRY SOMETHING DIFFERENT
Double Chocolate Chip Muffins
Omit the blueberries and lemon zest. Replace 40g (1½oz) of the flour with cocoa powder, then add 150g (5oz) chopped dark chocolate to the dry ingredients in step 3.

Bran and Apple Muffins

★

Preparation Time 20 minutes • **Cooking Time** 30 minutes • **Makes 10** • **Per Muffin** 137 calories, 1g fat (of which trace saturates), 31g carbohydrate, 0.3g salt • **Easy**

250ml (9fl oz) semi-skimmed milk
2 tbsp orange juice
50g (2oz) All Bran
9 ready-to-eat dried prunes
100g (3½oz) light muscovado sugar
2 medium egg whites
1 tbsp golden syrup
150g (5oz) plain flour, sifted
1 tsp baking powder
1 tsp ground cinnamon
1 eating apple, peeled and grated
demerara sugar to sprinkle

1 Preheat the oven to 190°C (170°C fan oven) mark 5. Line a bun tin or muffin tin with 10 paper muffin cases.

2 In a bowl, mix the milk and orange juice with the All Bran. Put to one side for 10 minutes.

3 Put the prunes into a food processor or blender with 100ml (3½fl oz) water and whiz for 2–3 minutes to make a purée, then add the muscovado sugar and whiz briefly to mix.

4 Put the egg whites into a clean, grease-free bowl and whisk until soft peaks form. Add the whites to the milk mixture with the syrup, flour, baking powder, cinnamon, grated apple and prune mixture. Fold all the ingredients together gently – don't over-mix.

5 Spoon the mixture into the muffin cases and bake for 30 minutes or until well risen and golden brown. Transfer to a wire rack to cool. Sprinkle with demerara sugar just before serving. These are best eaten on the day they are made.

★ FREEZING TIP
To freeze *Complete the recipe, but don't sprinkle with the sugar topping. Once the muffins are cold, pack, seal and freeze.*
To use *Thaw at cool room temperature. Sprinkle with the sugar to serve.*

Brown Sugar Muffins

★

Preparation Time 10 minutes • **Cooking Time** 30–35 minutes, plus cooling • **Makes 6** • **Per Muffin** 233 calories, 8g fat (of which 5g saturates), 38g carbohydrate, 0.4g salt • **Easy**

12 brown sugar cubes
150g (5oz) plain flour
1½ tsp baking powder
¼ tsp salt
1 medium egg, beaten
40g (1½oz) golden caster sugar
50g (2oz) unsalted butter, melted
½ tsp vanilla extract
100ml (3½fl oz) milk

1 Preheat the oven to 200°C (180°C fan oven) mark 6. Line a 6-hole bun tin or muffin tin with paper muffin cases.

2 Roughly crush the sugar cubes and put to one side. Sift the flour, baking powder and salt together.

3 Put the beaten egg, caster sugar, melted butter, vanilla extract and milk into a large bowl and stir to combine. Gently fold in the sifted flour. Spoon the mixture equally into the paper cases and sprinkle with the brown sugar.

4 Bake for 30–35 minutes until golden. Transfer to a wire rack to cool completely. These are best eaten on the day they are made.

★ TRY SOMETHING DIFFERENT
Apple and Cinnamon Muffins
Fold 5 tbsp ready-made chunky apple sauce and 1 tsp ground cinnamon into the mixture with the flour.
Maple Syrup and Pecan Muffins
Lightly toast 50g (2oz) pecan nuts and roughly chop. Fold half the nuts and 3 tbsp maple syrup into the mixture. Mix the remaining nuts with the crushed sugar and sprinkle over the muffins before baking. Drizzle with maple syrup to serve.

★ FREEZING TIP
To freeze *Complete the recipe. Once the muffins are cold, pack, seal and freeze.*
To use *Thaw at cool room temperature.*

Cherry and Almond Muffins

★

Preparation Time 10 minutes • **Cooking Time** 25 minutes, plus cooling • **Makes 12** • **Per Muffin** 230 calories, 6g fat (of which 1g saturates), 42g carbohydrate, 0.1g salt • **Easy**

225g (8oz) plain flour
1 tsp baking powder
a pinch of salt
75g (3oz) caster sugar
50g (2oz) ground almonds
350g (12oz) glacé cherries, roughly
    chopped
300ml (½ pint) milk
3 tbsp lemon juice
50ml (2fl oz) sunflower oil or
    melted butter
1 large egg
1 tsp almond extract
roughly crushed sugar cubes to
    decorate

1 Preheat the oven to 190°C (170°C fan oven) mark 5. Line a 12-hole bun tin or muffin tin with paper muffin cases.

2 Sift the flour, baking powder and salt together. Add the caster sugar and ground almonds, then stir in the chopped cherries.

3 Whisk the milk, lemon juice, oil or butter, the egg and almond extract together. Pour into the dry ingredients and stir until all the ingredients are just combined – the mixture should be lumpy. Do not over-mix or the muffins will be tough. Spoon the mixture equally into the paper cases and sprinkle with the crushed sugar cubes.

4 Bake for about 25 minutes or until golden and well risen.

5 Leave to cool in the tin for 5 minutes, then transfer to a wire rack to cool completely. These are best eaten on the day they are made.

★ FREEZING TIP
To freeze Complete the recipe. Once the muffins are cold, pack, seal and freeze.
To use Thaw at cool room temperature.

Chocolate Banana Muffins

Preparation Time 15 minutes • **Cooking Time** 20 minutes, plus cooling • **Makes 12** • **Per Muffin** 228 calories, 7g fat (of which 4g saturates), 40g carbohydrate, 0.5g salt • **Easy**

275g (10oz) self-raising flour
1 tsp bicarbonate of soda
½ tsp salt
3 large bananas, about 450g (1lb)
125g (4oz) golden caster sugar
1 large egg, beaten
50ml (2fl oz) semi-skimmed milk
75g (3oz) unsalted butter, melted
    and cooled
50g (2oz) plain chocolate, chopped

1 Preheat the oven to 180°C (160°C fan oven) mark 4. Line a 12-hole bun tin or muffin tin with paper muffin cases.

2 Sift the flour, bicarbonate of soda and salt together into a large mixing bowl and put to one side.

3 Peel the bananas and mash with a fork in a bowl. Add the caster sugar, egg, milk and melted butter and mix until well combined. Add this to the flour mixture, with the chopped chocolate. Stir gently, using only a few strokes, until the flour is only just incorporated – do not over-mix. The mixture should be lumpy. Spoon the mixture equally into the paper cases, half-filling them.

4 Bake for 20 minutes or until the muffins are well risen and golden. Transfer to a wire rack to cool completely. Serve warm or cold. These are best eaten on the day they are made.

★ FREEZING TIP
To freeze *Complete the recipe. Once the muffins are cold, pack, seal and freeze.*
To use *Thaw at cool room temperature.*

Wholemeal Banana Muffins

★

Preparation Time 15 minutes, plus soaking • **Cooking Time** 20–25 minutes • **Makes 6** • **Per Muffin** 341 calories, 13g fat (of which 2g saturates), 51g carbohydrate, 0.6g salt • **Easy**

butter to grease (optional)
50g (2oz) raisins
finely grated zest and juice of
    1 orange
125g (4oz) wholemeal flour
25g (1oz) wheatgerm
3 tbsp caster sugar
2 tsp baking powder
a pinch of salt
1 large egg, beaten
50ml (2fl oz) milk
50ml (2fl oz) sunflower oil
2 medium-sized ripe bananas,
    about 225g (8oz) when peeled,
    roughly mashed

FOR THE TOPPING
5 tbsp orange marmalade
50g (2oz) banana chips, roughly
    chopped
50g (2oz) walnuts, roughly chopped

1 Preheat the oven to 200°C (180°C fan oven) mark 6. Line a 6-hole bun tin or muffin tin with paper muffin cases. Put the raisins into a bowl, pour the orange juice over them and leave to soak for 1 hour.

2 Put the orange zest into a bowl with the flour, wheatgerm, sugar, baking powder and salt and mix together. Make a well in the centre.

3 In a separate bowl, mix the egg, milk and oil, then pour into the flour mixture and stir until just blended. Drain the raisins, reserving 1 tbsp

juice, and stir into the mixture with the bananas. Don't over-mix. Fill each muffin case two-thirds full.

4 Bake for 20–25 minutes until a skewer inserted into the centre comes out clean. Transfer to a wire rack to cool slightly.

5 For the topping, gently heat the marmalade with the reserved orange juice until melted. Simmer for 1 minute, then add the banana chips and walnuts. Spoon on top of the muffins. Serve while still warm.

★FREEZING TIP
To freeze Complete the recipe to the end of step 4. Once the muffins are cold, pack, seal and freeze.
To use Thaw at cool room temperature. Complete the recipe.

Honey and Yogurt Muffins

Preparation Time 15 minutes • **Cooking Time** 17–20 minutes • **Makes 12** • **Per Muffin** 180 calories, 6g fat (of which 4g saturates), 27g carbohydrate, 0.1g salt • **Easy**

225g (8oz) plain white flour
1½ tsp baking powder
1 tsp bicarbonate of soda
½ tsp each ground mixed spice and
    ground nutmeg
a pinch of salt
50g (2oz) ground oatmeal
50g (2oz) light muscovado sugar
225g (8oz) Greek yogurt
125ml (4fl oz) milk
1 egg
50g (2oz) butter, melted and cooled
4 tbsp runny honey

1 Preheat the oven to 200°C (180°C fan) mark 6. Line a 12-hole bun tin or muffin tin with paper muffin cases.

2 Sift the flour, baking powder, bicarbonate of soda, mixed spice, nutmeg and salt into a bowl. Stir in the oatmeal and sugar.

3 Mix the yogurt with the milk in a bowl, then beat in the egg, butter and honey. Pour on to the dry ingredients and stir in quickly until just blended – don't over-mix. Divide the mixture equally between the paper cases.

4 Bake for 17–20 minutes until the muffins are well risen and just firm. Leave to cool in the tin for 5 minutes, then transfer to a wire rack. Serve warm or cold. These are best eaten on the day they are made.

★ FREEZING TIP
To freeze *Complete the recipe. Once the muffins are cold, pack, seal and freeze.*
To use *Thaw at cool room temperature.*

Raspberry Millefeuilles

Preparation Time 40 minutes, plus chilling and standing • **Cooking Time** 40 minutes, plus cooling • **Serves 8** •
Per Serving 828 calories, 57g fat (of which 23g saturates), 65g carbohydrate, 1.4g salt • **Easy**

550g (1¼lb) puff pastry, thawed
   if frozen
flour to dust
25g (1oz) caster sugar, plus 3 tbsp
50g (2oz) hazelnuts, toasted and
   chopped
225g (8oz) raspberries
1 tbsp lemon juice
1 x quantity Confectioner's Custard
   (see Cook's Tip)
300ml (½ pint) double cream
50g (2oz) icing sugar, sifted

1 Cut the pastry into three and roll out each piece on a lightly floured surface into an 18 x 35.5cm (7 x 14in) rectangle. Put each on a baking sheet, prick and chill for 30 minutes.

2 Preheat the oven to 220°C (200°C fan oven) mark 7. Bake the pastry for 10 minutes, then turn the pieces over and cook for another 3 minutes. Sprinkle each sheet with 1 tbsp caster sugar and one-third of the nuts. Return to the oven for 8 minutes or until the sugar dissolves. Cool slightly, then transfer to wire racks to cool.

3 Sprinkle the raspberries with 25g (1oz) caster sugar and the lemon juice. Beat the custard until smooth and whip the cream until thick, then fold the cream into the custard with the raspberries and juices. Cover and chill.

4 Put the icing sugar into a bowl, then stir in 2 tbsp water. Trim each pastry sheet to 15 x 30.5cm (6 x 12in), then drizzle with the icing. Leave for 15 minutes.

5 Spoon half the custard over a sheet of pastry. Put another sheet on top and spoon on the remaining custard. Top with the final sheet and press down lightly. Leave for 30 minutes before slicing.

★ COOK'S TIP
Confectioner's Custard
Scrape the vanilla seeds from 1 vanilla pod into a pan. Add the pod and 450ml (¾ pint) milk, bring to the boil, then set aside for 30 minutes. Remove the vanilla pod. Whisk 4 large egg yolks and 75g (3oz) caster sugar until pale. Mix in 50g (2oz) plain flour. Strain in a quarter of the infused milk, mix, then stir in the remainder. Return to the pan and bring to the boil over a low heat, stirring. Pour into a bowl, cover with clingfilm, cool and chill for 3 4 hours.

Apple Shorties

Preparation Time 20 minutes • **Cooking Time** 30 minutes, plus cooling • **Makes 16** • **Per Square** 100 calories, 4g fat (of which 3g saturates), 17g carbohydrate, 0.1g salt • **Easy**

75g (3oz) unsalted butter, softened, plus extra to grease
40g (1½oz) caster sugar
75g (3oz) plain flour, sifted
40g (1½oz) fine semolina
1 cooking apple, about 175g (6oz), peeled and grated
125g (4oz) sultanas
½ tsp mixed spice
2 tbsp light muscovado sugar
1 tsp lemon juice

1 Preheat the oven to 190°C (170°C fan oven) mark 5. Grease an 18cm (7in) square shallow cake tin.

2 Beat the butter, caster sugar, flour and semolina together until the mixture is blended. Press the mixture into the prepared tin and level the surface. Bake for 15 minutes.

3 Meanwhile, mix the apple with the remaining ingredients. Spoon evenly over the shortbread and put back in the oven for a further 15 minutes.

4 Leave to cool in the tin for a few minutes, then cut into 16 squares. Leave to cool completely, then remove from the tin.

★ TO STORE
Store in an airtight container. They will keep for up to three days.

Citrus Eccles Cakes

★

Preparation Time 35 minutes, plus chilling • **Cooking Time** 12–15 minutes • **Makes 20** • **Per Cake** 161 calories, 10g fat (of which 6g saturates), 19g carbohydrate, 0.2g salt • **Easy**

**225g (8oz) puff pastry, thawed if
    frozen**
flour to dust
beaten egg to glaze
**50g (2oz) unsalted butter, melted,
    plus extra to grease**
caster sugar to sprinkle

FOR THE FILLING
175g (6oz) currants
**50g (2oz) chopped mixed candied
    peel**
50g (2oz) muscovado sugar
finely grated zest of 2 lemons

1 Preheat the oven to 220°C (200°C fan oven) mark 7. To make the filling, mix all the ingredients together in a bowl.

2 Roll out half the pastry on a lightly floured surface to a 51 x 20.5cm (20 x 8in) rectangle, then cut in half lengthways. Cut each strip crossways into five equal pieces. With the tip of a sharp knife, make rows of 2cm (¾ in) slits on each piece of pastry, spacing them 5mm (¼ in) apart and staggering alternate rows so that the pastry forms a lattice when pulled apart slightly. Brush the edges with beaten egg.

3 Divide the filling among the latticed pastries, placing it in the centre of each. Bring the edges of the pastry up over the filling, pinching them together to seal. Invert on to a lightly greased baking sheet, so that the neat lattice sides are uppermost. Brush the pastry with beaten egg and sprinkle lightly with caster sugar.

4 Bake for 12–15 minutes until puffed and golden. Pour a little melted butter into each cake, through the lattice. Serve warm.

Brazil Nut and Clementine Cakes

★

Preparation Time 30 minutes, plus cooling and freezing • **Cooking Time** 1¼ hours, plus cooling • **Makes 8** •
Per Cake 413 calories, 26g fat (of which 5g saturates), 41g carbohydrate, 0.1g salt • **Easy**

butter to grease
1 lemon
10 clementines
150g (5oz) brazil nuts
100ml (3½fl oz) mild olive oil
3 medium eggs
275g (10oz) golden caster sugar
1 tsp baking powder
2 tbsp brandy

TO DECORATE
mint sprigs
icing sugar

1 Grease eight 150ml (¼ pint) ramekin dishes and baseline with greaseproof paper. Wash the lemon and 4 clementines and put into a pan. Cover with boiling water, reduce the heat to a gentle simmer and cook for 30 minutes or until the clementines are tender.

2 Remove the clementines with a slotted spoon and set aside. Cook the lemon for a further 10 minutes or until tender. Drain, reserving 200ml (7fl oz) liquid, and cool slightly. Halve the fruit, remove the pips and roughly chop.

3 Preheat the oven to 180°C (160°C fan oven) mark 4. Grind the nuts in a food processor until finely chopped, then tip out and set aside. There's no need to wash the jug – add the cooked fruit and blend to a purée.

4 Put the oil, eggs and 125g (4oz) caster sugar into a mixing bowl and whisk until slightly thick and foamy. Stir in the ground nuts, fruit purée and baking powder. Divide among the ramekins. put on a baking sheet. Bake for 25 minutes or until slightly risen and firm to the touch. Leave to cool in the tin.

5 Peel the remaining clementines, remove the pips and divide into segments, then skin each segment. Heat the remaining sugar in a small pan with 150ml (¼ pint) of the reserved cooking liquid until the sugar dissolves. Bring to the boil and cook until a pale caramel in colour. Dip the base of the pan into cold water to stop the caramel cooking. Stir in the remaining liquid and the brandy. Return to the heat, stirring until the caramel has dissolved. Stir in the clementine segments.

6 Loosen the edges of the cakes, turn out on to individual plates and remove the paper lining. Pile the fruit segments on top and spoon the caramel over them. Decorate each with a mint sprig and a dusting of icing sugar.

White Chocolate Scones with Summer Berries

Preparation Time 20 minutes • **Cooking Time** 15 minutes, plus cooling • **Makes 16** • **Per Scone** 195 calories, 13g fat (of which 8g saturates), 19g carbohydrate, 0.3g salt • **Easy**

150g (5oz) mixed summer berries, such as strawberries, raspberries, blackberries and currants
1 tbsp lemon juice
3 tbsp redcurrant or blackcurrant jelly
75g (3oz) unsalted butter, diced, plus extra to grease
225g (8oz) self-raising flour, plus extra to dust
½ tsp baking powder
1 tbsp golden caster sugar
125g (4oz) good-quality white chocolate, finely chopped
1 medium egg, beaten
6 tbsp milk
142ml tub clotted cream, or lightly whipped cream
icing sugar to dust

1 Put the berries into a small bowl, slicing the strawberries if you're using them. Heat the lemon juice and jelly in a small pan, stirring until syrupy and smooth. Pour over the berries and put to one side to cool.

2 Preheat the oven to 200°C (180°C fan oven) mark 6. Lightly grease a baking sheet.

3 Put the flour, baking powder and caster sugar into a large bowl. Rub in the butter, then stir in the chocolate. Make a well in the centre, then add the egg and milk. Stir lightly with a round-bladed knife until the mixture just comes together into a soft dough – add a splash more milk if it looks too dry.

4 Turn out on to a floured surface and press into a rough round about 2.5cm (1in) deep – the dough doesn't need to be too smooth. Stamp out small rounds using a 4cm (1½in) cutter and put on the prepared baking sheet.

5 Bake the scones for 10–15 minutes until risen and golden, then remove from the oven and transfer to a wire rack to cool.

6 To serve, split open the scones and spread with clotted or whipped cream. Add a small spoonful of fruit, replace the tops and dust with icing sugar. These are best eaten on the day they are made.

Cheesecakes and Tortes ★

Chocolate Brandy Torte

Preparation Time 10 minutes • **Cooking Time** 45 minutes, plus cooling • **Cuts into 6 slices** • **Per Slice** 531 calories, 35g fat (of which 19g saturates), 47g carbohydrate, 0.5g salt • **Easy**

125g (4oz) unsalted butter, diced, plus extra to grease
225g (8oz) plain chocolate (at least 70% cocoa solids), broken into pieces
3 large eggs, separated
125g (4oz) light muscovado sugar
50ml (2fl oz) brandy
75g (3oz) self-raising flour, sifted
50g (2oz) ground almonds
icing sugar to dust
crème fraîche to serve

1 Preheat the oven to 180°C (160°C fan oven) mark 4. Grease a 20.5cm (8in) springform cake tin and baseline with baking parchment.

2 Melt the diced butter and chocolate in a heatproof bowl set over a pan of gently simmering water, making sure the base of the bowl doesn't touch the water, stirring occasionally. Take the bowl off the pan and leave to cool a little.

3 Put the egg yolks and muscovado sugar into a bowl and whisk together until pale and creamy, then whisk in the brandy and melted chocolate at a slow speed. Using a large metal spoon, fold in the flour and ground almonds. Put the mixture to one side.

4 Put the egg whites into a clean, grease-free bowl and whisk until soft peaks form. Beat a large spoonful of the egg white into the chocolate mixture to lighten it, then carefully fold in the remainder with a large metal spoon.

5 Pour the mixture into the prepared tin and bake for 45 minutes or until a skewer inserted into the centre comes out clean. Leave to cool in the tin for 10 minutes, then turn out on to a wire rack to cool completely. Remove the lining paper from the base of the cake when it's cold.

6 To serve, dust the top of the cake with sifted icing sugar and serve with crème fraîche.

★ TO STORE
Store in an airtight container. It will keep for up to three days.

★ FREEZING TIP
*To **freeze** Complete the recipe to the end of step 4, wrap, seal, label and freeze; it will keep for up to one month.*
*To **use** Thaw the torte at a cool room temperature for 2 hours. Dust with sifted icing sugar to serve.*

Almond and Orange Torte

Preparation Time 30 minutes • **Cooking Time** 1 hour 50 minutes, plus cooling • **Cuts into 12 wedges** •
Per Wedge 223 calories, 13g fat (of which 1g saturates), 22g carbohydrate, 0.1g salt • **Easy**

oil to grease
flour to dust
1 medium orange
3 medium eggs
225g (8oz) golden caster sugar
250g (9oz) ground almonds
½ tsp baking powder
icing sugar to dust
crème fraîche to serve

1 Grease and line, then oil and flour a 20.5cm (8in) springform cake tin. Put the whole orange into a small pan and cover with water. Bring to the boil, then cover and simmer for at least 1 hour or until tender (see Cook's Tip). Remove from the water and leave to cool.

2 Cut the orange in half and remove the pips. Whiz in a food processor or blender to make a smooth purée.

3 Preheat the oven to 180°C (160°C fan oven) mark 4. Put the eggs and caster sugar into a bowl and whisk together until thick and pale. Fold in the almonds, baking powder and orange purée. Pour the mixture into the prepared tin.

4 Bake for 40–50 minutes until a skewer inserted into the centre comes out clean. Leave to cool in the tin.

5 Release the clasp on the tin and remove the cake. Carefully peel off the lining paper and put the cake on a serving plate. Dust with icing sugar, then cut into 12 wedges. Serve with crème fraîche.

 TO STORE
Store in an airtight container. It will keep for up to three days.

★ COOK'S TIP
To save time, you can microwave the orange. Put it into a small heatproof bowl, cover with 100ml (3½fl oz) water and cook in a 900W microwave oven on full power for 10–12 minutes until soft.

Baked Ricotta Torte

Preparation Time 20 minutes, plus chilling • **Cooking Time** 40 minutes, plus cooling • **Serves 8** • **Per Serving** 354 calories, 26g fat (of which 15g saturates), 26g carbohydrate, 0.7g salt • **Easy**

125g (4oz) digestive biscuits, finely
    crushed (see Cook's Tip)
50g (2oz) unsalted butter, melted
75g (3oz) dark muscovado sugar
250g (9oz) ricotta cheese
grated zest of 1 lemon, plus 3 tbsp
    juice
300g (11oz) natural yogurt
25g (1oz) rice flour, or ground rice
3 large eggs
cocoa powder to dust
chocolate curls to decorate (see
    page 283)

1 Line the base of a 23cm (9in) springform cake tin with baking parchment. Put the crushed biscuits into a bowl, add the melted butter and stir until the mixture is well combined. Tip the crumb mixture into the cake tin and press evenly on to the base, using the back of a spoon. Chill for 1 hour or until firm.

2 Preheat the oven to 180°C (160°C fan oven) mark 4. Put the sugar into the processor and whiz for 1–2 minutes. Add the ricotta and whiz for 2–3 minutes, then add the lemon zest and juice, yogurt and rice flour or ground rice. Pulse to mix well, then add the eggs and combine. (Alternatively, put the sugar into a bowl and use a hand-held electric mixer to blend in the ricotta, then the lemon zest, juice, yogurt and flour. Briefly mix in the eggs.)

3 Pour the ricotta mixture over the biscuit base and bake for 40 minutes or until lightly set. Leave to cool in the tin, then chill in the tin until ready to serve.

4 Unmould the torte and liberally dust with cocoa powder. Top with chocolate curls to finish.

★COOK'S TIP
Crush the biscuits to a fine powder in a food processor. (Alternatively, put them into a plastic bag and crush with a rolling pin.)

Tiramisù Torte

★

Preparation Time 40 minutes, plus chilling • **Cooking Time** 45 minutes, plus cooling and chilling • **Cuts into 10 slices** • **Per Slice** 682 calories, 50g fat (of which 30g saturates), 51g carbohydrate, 0.9g salt • **Easy**

275g (10oz) amaretti biscuits, ratafias or macaroons
75g (3oz) unsalted butter, melted
700g (1½lb) mascarpone or cream cheese (at room temperature)
150g (5oz) caster sugar
3 medium eggs, separated
25g (1oz) plain flour, sifted
3 tbsp dark rum
½ tsp vanilla extract
175g (6oz) plain chocolate (at least 50% cocoa solids)
1 tbsp finely ground coffee
3 tbsp Tia Maria or other coffee liqueur

1 Put the biscuits into a food processor and whiz until finely ground. Add the melted butter and stir until well mixed. Tip the crumb mixture into a 23cm (9in) springform cake tin and, using the back of a spoon, press evenly over the base and 4cm (1½in) up the sides to form a shell. Chill for about 1 hour or until firm.

2 Preheat the oven to 200°C (180°C fan oven) mark 6. Using a wooden spoon or a hand-held electric whisk, beat the cheese until smooth. Add the sugar and beat again until smooth, then beat in the egg yolks. Transfer half of the mixture to another bowl and stir in the flour, rum and vanilla extract.

3 Melt the chocolate in a heatproof bowl set over a pan of gently simmering water, making sure the base of the bowl doesn't touch the water. Remove the bowl from the pan and cool slightly, then stir in the coffee and coffee liqueur. Stir into the remaining half of the cheese mixture.

4 Put the egg whites into a clean, grease-free bowl and whisk until soft peaks form, then fold half the egg whites into each flavoured cheese mixture. Spoon alternate mounds of the two mixtures into the biscuit case until full. Using a knife, swirl them together for a marbled effect.

5 Bake for 45 minutes (if necessary, lightly cover with foil if the top is browning too quickly). At this stage the torte will be soft in the middle.

6 Turn off the oven and leave the cheesecake inside, with the door slightly ajar, until cool; it will firm up during this time. Chill for several hours.

Sachertorte

★

Preparation Time 35 minutes • **Cooking Time** 45–55 minutes, plus cooling and setting • **Cuts into** 12 slices •
Per Slice 496 calories, 33g fat (of which 20g saturates), 45g carbohydrate, 0.7g salt • **A Little Effort**

175g (6oz) unsalted butter, at room
   temperature, plus extra to grease
175g (6oz) golden caster sugar
5 medium eggs, lightly beaten
3 tbsp cocoa powder
125g (4oz) self-raising flour
225g (8oz) plain chocolate (at least
   70% cocoa solids), broken into
   pieces, melted and cooled for
   5 minutes
4 tbsp brandy
1 x quantity warm Chocolate
   Ganache (see Cook's Tip)
12 lilac sugar-coated almonds, or
   50g (2oz) milk chocolate, melted

1 Preheat the oven to 190°C (170°C
fan oven) mark 5. Grease a 20.5cm
(8in) springform cake tin and line
with baking parchment.

2 Cream together the butter and
sugar until pale and fluffy. Gradually
beat in two-thirds of the beaten
eggs – don't worry if the mixture
curdles. Sift in the cocoa powder
and 3 tbsp flour, then gradually beat
in the remaining eggs. Fold in the
remaining flour. Fold in the melted
chocolate until evenly incorporated.
Stir in 2 tbsp brandy. Pour the
mixture into the prepared tin.

3 Bake for 45 minutes (if necessary,
cover loosely with foil if the top is
browning too quickly). To test if
done, insert a skewer into the centre
of the cake – it should come out
clean. Leave to cool in the tin for

30 minutes. Remove the cake from
the tin and put on a wire rack to
cool completely.

4 Drizzle with the remaining brandy,
then position the wire rack over a
tray. Ladle the ganache over the top
of the cake, letting it trickle down
the sides. Using a palette knife,
spread it evenly over the cake.
Decorate with almonds or melted
milk chocolate and leave for about
1 hour to set.

★ TO STORE
Store in an airtight container. It will keep
for up to one week.

★ COOK'S TIP
Chocolate Ganache
Melt 175g (6oz) plain chocolate (at least
70% cocoa solids), broken into pieces,
with 75g (3oz) butter and 4 tbsp warmed
double cream in a heatproof bowl over
a pan of gently simmering water,
making sure the base of the bowl doesn't
touch the water, stirring occasionally. Stir
the ganache until smooth

Luxury Chocolate Orange Torte

Preparation Time 30 minutes • **Cooking Time** 55 minutes–1 hour 5 minutes, plus cooling • **Cuts into 12 slices** •
Per Slice 231 calories, 12g fat (of which 3g saturates), 25g carbohydrate, 0.1g salt • **Gluten Free** • **A Little Effort**

75g (3oz) unsalted butter, diced,
    plus extra to grease
100g (3½oz) plain chocolate
    (at least 70% cocoa solids),
    broken into pieces
6 medium eggs
225g (8oz) golden caster sugar
150g (5oz) ground almonds, sifted
grated zest and juice of 1 orange
strawberries and raspberries to
    serve

1 Preheat the oven to 190°C (170°C fan oven) mark 5. Grease a 20.5cm (8in) springform cake tin and line with greaseproof paper.

2 Melt the butter and chocolate in a heatproof bowl set over a pan of gently simmering water, making sure the base of the bowl doesn't touch the water. Remove the bowl from the pan and set aside to cool a little.

3 Put the eggs and sugar into a large bowl and mix with a hand-held electric whisk until the volume has tripled and the mixture is thick and foamy – it will take 5–10 minutes. Add the ground almonds, orange zest and juice to the egg mixture, then gently fold together with a metal spoon.

4 Pour about two-thirds of the mixture into the prepared tin. Add the melted chocolate and butter to the remaining mixture and fold together. Add to the tin and swirl around just once or twice to create a marbled effect. Bake for 50 minutes–1 hour. Leave to cool in the tin.

5 Carefully remove the cake from the tin and slice. Serve with strawberries and raspberries.

★ TO STORE
Store in an airtight container. It will keep for up to three days.

Classic Baked Cheesecake

★

Preparation time 30 minutes, plus chilling • **Cooking time** 55 minutes, plus cooling and chilling • **Cuts into 12 slices** •
Per Slice 340 calories, 19g fat (of which 11g saturates), 36g carbohydrate, 1g salt • **Easy**

FOR THE BASE

125g (4oz) unsalted butter, melted,
plus extra to grease
250g pack digestive biscuits, finely
crushed (see page 155)

FOR THE FILLING

1 large lemon
2 x 250g cartons curd cheese
142ml carton soured cream
2 medium eggs
175g (6oz) golden caster sugar
1½ tsp vanilla extract
1 tbsp cornflour
50g (2oz) sultanas

1 Grease a 20.5cm (8in) springform cake tin. Put the biscuits into a bowl, add the melted butter and mix until well combined. Tip the crumb mixture into the prepared tin and press evenly on to the base, using the back of a spoon to level the surface. Chill for 1 hour or until firm.

2 Preheat the oven to 180°C (160°C fan oven) mark 4. To make the filling, grate the zest from the lemon and set aside. Halve the lemon, cut 3 very thin slices from one half and put to one side. Squeeze the juice from the rest of the lemon.

3 Put the lemon zest, lemon juice, curd cheese, soured cream, eggs, sugar, vanilla extract and cornflour into a large bowl. Using a hand-held electric whisk, beat together until thick and smooth, then fold in the sultanas. Pour the mixture into the tin and shake gently to level the surface.

4 Bake for 30 minutes Put the lemon slices, overlapping, on top. Bake for a further 20- 25 minutes until the cheesecake is just set and golden brown. Turn off the oven and leave the cheesecake inside, with the door ajar, until it is cool, then chill for at least 2 hours or overnight.

5 Remove the cheesecake from the fridge about 30 minutes before serving. Run a knife around the edge, release the side of the tin and remove. Cut the cheesecake into slices to serve.

Lemon and Orange Cheesecake

Preparation Time 30 minutes, plus cooling and chilling • **Cooking Time** 1¼ hours, plus cooling and chilling •
Cuts into 12 slices • **Per Slice** 530 calories, 40g fat (of which 24g saturates), 36g carbohydrate, 0.8g salt • **Easy**

150g (5oz) digestive biscuits
50g (2oz) Bourbon biscuits
50g (2oz) unsalted butter, melted
700g (1½lb) cream cheese
250g tub mascarpone cheese
225g (8oz) caster sugar
5 tsp plain flour
zest of 1 large orange and 1 lemon
1 vanilla pod, split along its length
3 large eggs, plus 2 large egg yolks,
   beaten

TO DECORATE
a few unsprayed rose petals
golden icing sugar

1 Preheat the oven to 180°C (160°C fan oven) mark 4. Line the base and sides of a deep 20.5cm (8in) springform tin with baking parchment.

2 Put the biscuits and butter into a food processor and whiz into crumbs. Tip the crumb mixture into the prepared tin and press evenly on to the base, using the back of a spoon to level the surface.

3 Bake for 15 minutes, then cool for 10 minutes. Reduce the oven temperature to 140°C (120°C fan oven) mark 1. Put the soft cheese into a large bowl with the mascarpone, sugar, flour and orange and lemon zest. Scrape in the vanilla seeds and beat until smooth. Slowly add the beaten eggs, keeping the mixture smooth. Pour the mixture into the tin and shake gently to level the surface. Bake for 1 hour.

4 Remove the cheesecake from the oven and leave to cool completely in the tin. Chill for 2 hours. Arrange unsprayed rose petals on top and dust with golden icing sugar to serve.

★GET AHEAD
*To **prepare ahead** Complete the recipe to the end of step 4, but don't decorate it. Chill for up to three days or freeze for up to one month.*
*To **use** Thaw overnight (if frozen) and decorate.*

Blueberry Cheesecake

⭐

Preparation Time 15 minutes, plus chilling • **Cooking Time** 45 minutes, plus cooling and chilling • **Cuts into 8 slices** •
Per Slice 376 calories, 24g fat (of which 14g saturates), 36g carbohydrate, 0.4g salt • **Easy**

1 large sponge flan case, 23–25.5cm
   (9–10in) diameter
butter to grease
300g (11oz) cream cheese
1 tsp vanilla extract
100g (3½oz) golden caster sugar
150ml (¼ pint) soured cream
2 medium eggs
2 tbsp cornflour

FOR THE TOPPING
150g (5oz) blueberries
2 tbsp redcurrant jelly

1 Preheat the oven to 180°C (160°C
fan oven) mark 4. Use the base of a
20.5cm (8in) springform cake tin to
cut out a circle from the flan case,
discarding the edges. Grease the
tin and baseline with greaseproof
paper, then put the flan base into it.
Press down with your fingers.

2 Put the cream cheese, vanilla,
sugar, soured cream, eggs and
cornflour into a food processor
and whiz until evenly combined.
Pour the mixture over the flan base
and shake gently to level the
surface. Bake for 45 minutes or until
just set and pale golden. Turn off
the oven and leave the cheesecake
inside, with the door ajar, for about
30 minutes. Leave to cool, then chill
for at least 2 hours.

3 To serve, put the blueberries into
a pan with the redcurrant jelly and
heat through until the jelly has

melted and the blueberries have
softened slightly – or place in a
heatproof bowl and cook on full
power in a 900W microwave for
1 minute. Spoon them over the
top of the cheesecake. Cool and
chill for 15 minutes before serving.

⭐TRY SOMETHING
DIFFERENT
*Use raspberries or other soft berries
instead of blueberries.*

Orange and Chocolate Cheesecake

★

Preparation Time 45 minutes • **Cooking Time** 2–2¼ hours, plus cooling • **Cuts into 12 slices** • **Per Slice** 767 calories, 60g fat (of which 37g saturates), 53g carbohydrate, 1.2g salt • **Easy**

225g (8oz) chilled unsalted butter, plus extra to grease
250g (9oz) plain flour, sifted
150g (5oz) light muscovado sugar
3 tbsp cocoa powder
chocolate curls to decorate (see page 283, optional)

FOR THE TOPPING
2 oranges
800g (1lb 12oz) cream cheese
250g (9oz) mascarpone cheese
4 large eggs
225g (8oz) golden caster sugar
2 tbsp cornflour
½ tsp vanilla extract
1 vanilla pod

1 Preheat the oven to 180°C (160°C fan oven) mark 4. Grease a 23cm (9in) springform cake tin and baseline with baking parchment.

2 Cut 175g (6oz) butter into cubes. Melt the remaining butter and set aside. Put the flour and cubed butter into a food processor with the sugar and cocoa powder. Whiz until the texture of fine breadcrumbs. (Alternatively, rub the butter into the flour in a large bowl by hand or using a pastry cutter. Stir in the sugar and cocoa.) Pour in the melted butter and pulse, or stir with a fork, until the mixture comes together.

3 Spoon the crumb mixture into the prepared tin and press evenly on to the base, using the back of a metal spoon to level the surface. Bake for 35–40 minutes until lightly puffed; avoid over-browning or the biscuit base will have a bitter flavour. Remove from the oven and allow to cool. Reduce the oven temperature to 150°C (130°C fan oven) mark 2.

4 Meanwhile, make the topping. Grate the zest from the oranges, then squeeze the juice – you will need 150ml (¼ pint). Put the cream cheese, mascarpone, eggs, sugar, cornflour, grated orange zest and vanilla extract into a large bowl.

Using a hand-held electric whisk, beat the ingredients together thoroughly until well combined.

5 Split the vanilla pod in half lengthways and, using the tip of a sharp knife, scrape out the seeds and add them to the cheese mixture. Beat in the orange juice and continue whisking until the mixture is smooth.

6 Pour the cheese mixture over the cooled biscuit base. Bake for about 1½ hours or until pale golden on top, slightly risen and just set around the edge. The cheesecake should still be slightly wobbly in the middle; it will set as it cools. Turn off the oven and leave the cheesecake inside, with the door ajar, to cool for 1 hour. Remove and allow to cool completely (about 3 hours), then chill.

7 Just before serving, unclip the tin and transfer the cheesecake to a plate. Scatter chocolate curls on top to decorate, if you like.

Marbled Chocolate Cheesecake

Preparation Time 25 minutes, plus chilling • **Cooking Time** 45 minutes, plus cooling and chilling • **Cuts into 18 squares** •
Per Square 325 calories, 27g fat (of which 14g saturates), 18g carbohydrate, 0.5g salt • **Easy**

150g (5oz) digestive biscuits, finely
   crushed (see page 155)
100g (3½oz) ground almonds
75g (3oz) unsalted butter, melted
75g (3oz) plain chocolate
5 large eggs, separated
150g (5oz) golden caster sugar
600g (1lb 5oz) cream cheese
1½ tsp vanilla bean paste
golden icing sugar to dust (optional)

1 Line the base and sides of a 33 x 23 x 5cm (13 x 9 x 2in) roasting tin with greaseproof paper, leaving the excess hanging over the sides. Put the biscuits into a bowl, add the almonds and butter and mix until well combined. Tip the crumb mixture into the prepared tin and press evenly on to the base, using the back of a spoon to level the surface. Chill for about 1 hour or until firm.

2 Preheat the oven to 170°C (150°C fan oven) mark 3. Melt the chocolate in a heatproof bowl set over a pan of gently simmering water, making sure the base of the bowl doesn't touch the water. Don't stir, or it will congeal. Remove the bowl from the pan and leave to cool slightly.

3 Put the egg whites into a clean, grease-free bowl and whisk until soft peaks form. Add 25g (1oz) sugar and whisk until stiff peaks form. In a separate bowl, using the same whisk, mix the cream cheese, remaining sugar, yolks and vanilla. Using a metal spoon, stir a spoonful of egg white into the cheese mixture. Carefully fold in the remaining whites. Put a quarter of the mixture into the egg white bowl. Fold the chocolate into it. Pour the vanilla mixture over the biscuit base, dollop spoonfuls of chocolate mixture on top and marble using a knife.

4 Bake for 45 minutes or until set. Cool in the tin, then chill for 2 hours.

5 Remove from the tin and dust with icing sugar, if you like.

 TO STORE
Store in an airtight container. It will keep for up to one week.

Raspberry Cheesecake

★

Preparation Time 25 minutes, plus chilling • **Cooking Time** 5 minutes, plus chilling • **Cuts into 10 slices** •
Per Slice 270 calories, 19g fat (of which 10g saturates), 20g carbohydrate, 0.5g salt • **Easy**

100g (3½oz) unsalted butter,
  melted, plus extra to grease
25g (1oz) blanched almonds, lightly
  toasted, then finely chopped
225g (8oz) almond butter biscuits,
  finely crushed (see page 155)
a few drops of almond extract
450g (1lb) raspberries
300g (11oz) Greek yogurt
150g (5oz) low-fat cream cheese
1 tbsp powdered gelatine
2 medium egg whites
50g (2oz) icing sugar

1 Grease a 20.5cm (8in) round springform cake tin. Mix the almonds with the crushed biscuits and melted butter and add the almond extract. Tip the crumb mixture into the prepared tin and press evenly on to the base, using the back of a spoon to level the surface. Chill for 1 hour or until firm.

2 To make the filling, purée 225g (8oz) raspberries in a blender, then press through a sieve. Put three-quarters of the purée to one side and return the rest to the blender. Add the yogurt and cheese, then whiz to blend. Transfer to a bowl. Sprinkle the gelatine over 2 tbsp water in a heatproof bowl and leave to soak for 2–3 minutes. Put the bowl over a pan of simmering water until the gelatine has dissolved.

3 Whisk the egg whites with the sugar until thick and shiny. Fold into the cheese mixture. Arrange half the remaining berries over the biscuit base, then pour the cheese mixture over the berries. Add the reserved purée and swirl with a knife to marble. Top with the remaining berries and chill for 3–4 hours.

Toffee Cheesecake

Preparation time 15 minutes, plus chilling • **Cooking time** 45 minutes–1 hour • **Cuts into 10 slices** • **Per Slice** 379 calories, 24g fat (of which 13g saturates), 34g carbohydrate, 1.1g salt • **Easy**

300g pack digestive biscuits, finely crushed (see page 155)
125g (4oz) unsalted butter, melted

FOR THE FILLING
450g (1lb) curd cheese
140ml (4½fl oz) double cream
juice of ½ lemon
3 medium eggs, beaten
50g (2oz) golden caster sugar
6 tbsp dulce de leche toffee sauce, plus extra to drizzle

1 Put the biscuits into a bowl, add the butter and mix to combine well. Tip the crumb mixture into a 20.5cm (8in) springform cake tin and press evenly into the base and up the sides, then chill for about 1 hour or until firm.

2 Preheat the oven to 200°C (180°C fan oven) mark 6. To make the filling, put the curd cheese and cream into a food processor or blender and whiz until smooth. Add the lemon juice, eggs, sugar and toffee sauce, then blend again until smooth. Pour into the chilled biscuit case and bake for 10 minutes. Reduce the oven temperature to 180°C (160°C fan oven) mark 4, then bake for 45 minutes or until set and golden brown.

3 Turn off the oven and leave the cheesecake inside, with the door ajar, until it is cool. When completely cool, chill for at least 2 hours to firm up the crust.

4 To remove the cheesecake from the tin, run a knife around the edge of the cake. Open the tin carefully, then use a palette knife to ease the cheesecake out. Cut into wedges, put on a serving plate and drizzle with toffee sauce.

★ COOK'S TIP
To slice the cheesecake easily, use a sharp knife dipped into a jug of boiling water and then wiped dry.

White Chocolate and Ginger Cheesecake with Cranberry Sauce

★

Preparation Time 25 minutes, plus chilling • **Cooking Time** 1 hour 40 minutes, plus cooling and chilling • **Cuts into 10 slices** • **Per Slice** 494 calories, 36g fat (of which 22g saturates), 36g carbohydrate, 0.7g salt • **Easy**

175g (6oz) gingernut biscuits
50g (2oz) unsalted butter, melted
150g (5oz) white chocolate
250g (9oz) mascarpone cheese
400g (14oz) cream cheese
4 medium eggs, beaten
100g (3½oz) golden caster sugar
75g (3oz) stem ginger, finely
    chopped
icing sugar to dust

FOR THE SAUCE
175g (6oz) fresh cranberries
60g (2½oz) golden caster sugar
1 tsp ground ginger

1 Line the base and sides of a 23cm (9in) loose-bottomed cake tin with greaseproof paper. Whiz the biscuits in a food processor to make fine crumbs. Pour into a bowl and stir in the butter. Tip the crumb mixture into the prepared tin and press evenly on to the base, using the back of a spoon to level the surface. Chill for about 1 hour or until firm.

2 Preheat the oven to 150°C (130°C fan oven) mark 2. Put 100g (3½oz) chocolate into a heatproof bowl set over a pan of gently simmering water, making sure the base of the bowl doesn't touch the water, and leave to melt. Cool slightly. Put the mascarpone and cream cheese into a large bowl and beat together until smooth. Stir in the eggs, caster sugar, stem ginger and melted white chocolate.

3 Pour into the prepared tin and bake in the centre of the oven for 1½ hours or until the cheesecake just wobbles slightly when the tin is tapped. Leave in the tin, place on a wire rack and allow to cool. When cold, chill for at least 4 hours.

4 To make the sauce, heat the cranberries, sugar and ground ginger in a pan with 100ml (3½fl oz) water. Simmer for 5 minutes or until the cranberries burst. Blend until smooth, then push through a sieve into a bowl and leave to chill.

5 Remove the cake from the tin and transfer to a plate. Dust with icing sugar, grate the remaining chocolate over the top and serve with the cranberry sauce.

★ FREEZING TIP
To freeze *Complete the recipe to the end of step 4. Wrap the whole tin in clingfilm; put the sauce in a freezerproof container. Freeze both. They will keep for up to one month.*
To use *Thaw in the fridge.*

Baked Orange Cheesecake

★

Preparation Time 35 minutes • **Cooking Time** about 1 hour, plus cooling • **Cuts into 8 slices** • **Per Slice** 543 calories, 47g fat (of which 29g saturates), 27g carbohydrate, 0.6g salt • **Easy**

3 medium eggs, separated
125g (4oz) caster sugar
3 × 200g tubs cream cheese
6 tbsp crème fraîche or thick Greek
   yogurt
125g (4oz) plain chocolate
zest of 2 large oranges

TO DECORATE
orange segments
chocolate curls (see page 283)
strips of deep-fried orange peel
   (optional, see Cook's Tip)
icing sugar to dust

1 Preheat the oven to 180°C (160°C fan oven) mark 4. Line the base of a 23cm (9in) springform cake tin with baking parchment.

2 Beat the egg yolks with 50g (2oz) sugar until pale in colour and thick. Add the cheese and crème fraîche or yogurt and beat until smooth.

3 Melt the chocolate in a large bowl set over a pan of simmering water, making sure the base of the bowl doesn't touch the water. Add one-third of the cheese mixture to the chocolate and mix until smooth.

4 Add the orange zest to the remaining cheese mixture.

5 Whisk the egg whites in a clean, grease-free bowl until stiff, then gradually whisk in the remaining sugar until the mixture is stiff and shiny. Fold one-third of the egg whites into the chocolate mixture, spoon into the prepared cake tin and smooth the top. Fold the remaining egg whites into the orange mixture, spoon on top of the chocolate mixture and smooth the surface.

6 Bake in the oven for 40–45 minutes until the centre is just firm to the touch. Turn off the oven and leave the cheesecake inside, with the door ajar, until it is cool, then chill for at least 2 hours or overnight.

8 Take the cheesecake out of the tin. Decorate with orange segments, chocolate curls and strips of deep-fried orange peel, if you like. Dust with icing sugar.

★COOK'S TIP
Deep-fried Orange Peel
Pare the peel thinly and deep-fry in a small amount of hot oil until crisp; drain on kitchen paper. Leave to cool, then use as required.

Warm Ginger Ricotta Cake

Preparation Time 25 minutes • **Cooking Time** 1¼ hours, plus cooling • **Cuts into 8 slices** • **Per Slice** 494 calories, 36g fat (of which 21g saturates), 38g carbohydrate, 0.8g salt • **Easy**

75g (3oz) unsalted butter, melted,
    plus extra to grease
225g (8oz) digestive biscuits, finely
    crushed (see page 155)
200g (7oz) cream cheese
225g (8oz) ricotta cheese
4 tbsp double cream
3 medium eggs, separated
1 tbsp cornflour
1 piece of preserved stem ginger
    in syrup, finely chopped, plus
    1 tbsp syrup
125g (4oz) icing sugar
Ginger and Whisky Sauce to serve
    (optional, see Cook's Tips)

1 Preheat the oven to 200°C (180°C fan oven) mark 6. Grease a 20.5cm (8in) springform cake tin. Put the biscuits into a bowl, add the melted butter and mix to combine. Tip just over half the crumb mixture into the prepared tin and press evenly into the base and up the sides.. Put to one side while you make the filling.

2 Beat together, or whiz in a processor, the cheeses, cream, egg yolks, cornflour, ginger and syrup. Transfer to a bowl.

3 Put the egg whites into a clean, grease-free bowl and whisk until soft peaks form. Gradually whisk in the icing sugar, keeping the mixture stiff and shiny. Fold into the ginger mixture. Spoon on to the biscuit base. Smooth the surface. Sprinkle the top with the remaining crumbs.

4 Bake for 30 minutes. Reduce the oven temperature to 180°C (160°C fan oven) mark 4, cover the cake loosely with foil and bake for a further 45 minutes. The cake should be just set in the centre. Cool for 15 minutes on a wire rack.

5 Serve warm, with Ginger and Whisky Sauce, if you like.

★ **COOK'S TIPS**
● *Ginger and Whisky Sauce*
Gently heat 300ml (½ pint) single cream with 2 tsp preserved stem ginger syrup and 1 tsp whisky. Serve just warm, with the cake.
● *The cake may also be served with sliced oranges soaked in ginger syrup and Cointreau.*

Children's Cakes and Cookies

Sleeping Beauty's Castle

★

Preparation Time 1 hour • **Serves** 35 • **Per Serving** 425 calories, 8g fat (of which 3g saturates), 86g carbohydrate, 0.2g salt • A Little Effort

1 x white ready-iced square 23cm (9in) sponge cake

5 raspberry or strawberry Swiss rolls, about 9cm (3½in) long

450g (1lb) white ready-to-roll icing (sugar paste)

icing sugar to dust

apricot glaze (see page 280)

1 x white ready-iced round 15cm (6in) sponge cake

2 x quantity of pink buttercream icing (see page 282)

5 ice cream sugar cones

FOR THE DECORATION

multicoloured sprinkles

red, pink, yellow, green and white writing icing

sugar flowers

paper flag

small round pink sweets or pink edible balls

1 Put the square cake on a 30.5cm (12in) square cake board. Measure the circumference of a Swiss roll with a piece of string. Divide the ready-to-roll icing into five pieces. Lightly dust a worksurface with icing sugar, then roll out each piece of icing thinly into a rectangle the length of the Swiss roll by the length of the piece of string. Neaten the edges with a sharp knife. Brush each piece of icing with apricot glaze and roll around a Swiss roll, gently working the edges together to seal.

2 Put the round cake in the centre of the square cake. Put a dollop of buttercream at each corner of the square cake and position four of the Swiss rolls, with the sealed edge facing inwards, to make towers. Smooth pink buttercream over four of the cones and spread a little on top of each tower. Dip the tips of the cones in sprinkles, then fix on top of the towers. Using red writing icing, draw a simple window, divided by four panes, at the top of each tower.

3 At the front of the castle, use red writing icing to draw a door with a doorknob. Use pink and yellow writing icing to draw small flowers around the castle and below the windows. Fix a few sugar flowers to the walls with writing icing. Connect the flowers with green writing icing to represent stems. Use the green icing to draw clumps of grass around the base of the wall. Stick a sugar flower to the paper flag with writing icing.

4 Position the remaining Swiss roll in the centre of the round cake. Cover the remaining cone with buttercream, dip in sprinkles and position on top of the round cake, fixing with a little buttercream. Draw on windows and decorate with sugar flowers as before. Make blobs of white writing icing, just touching each other, around the edges of the cones and decorate with pink sweets or edible balls. Stick the paper flag into the central tower.

★ GET AHEAD

To prepare ahead *Complete the recipe up to one day in advance.*

Ballet Shoe Cake

Preparation Time 45 minutes • **Cooking Time** 25–30 minutes, plus cooling • **Serves 12–15** • **Per Serving** 410 calories, 10g fat (of which 6g saturates), 82g carbohydrate, 0.5g salt • **A Little Effort**

butter to grease
1 x 4-egg quantity of lemon
    Victoria sponge mixture (see
    page 278)
good-quality lemon curd for filling
apricot glaze (see page 280)
700g (1½lb) white ready-to-roll
    icing (sugar paste)
red or pink food colouring
icing sugar to dust

FOR THE DECORATION
½ x quantity of royal icing (see
    page 282), coloured deep pink
sugar flowers and edible silver balls
pink or red ribbon

1 Grease two 20.5cm (8in) round sandwich tins and line with greaseproof paper. Make and bake the sponge mixture according to the instructions on page 278. Leave to cool in the tins for 5 minutes, then turn out on to a wire rack, remove the lining paper and leave to cool completely. Sandwich the cold cakes together with the lemon curd. Brush the cake with apricot glaze.

2 Set aside a small piece of the ready-to-roll icing to make the ballet shoes. Knead a few drops of the red or pink food colouring into the remaining icing to make it pale pink. Dust a worksurface lightly with icing sugar and roll out the icing to make a circle 5cm (2in) bigger than the top of the cake. Cover the cake with the icing, smoothing it out evenly across the top and down the sides, using your hand. Trim away any excess from the base.

3 Make a pair of ballet shoes using the reserved icing. Position the ballet shoes on top of the cake and stick in place with a dab of royal icing. Pipe scrolls (elongated S-shapes) around the cake and fix the sugar flowers in between with a dot of icing. Decorate the scrolls and flowers with silver balls. For a finishing touch, tie a ribbon around the cake.

 GET AHEAD
To prepare ahead *Complete the recipe up to one day in advance.*

 COOK'S TIP
Save time and buy plastic ballet shoes for decoration from a supermarket or specialist cake decorating shop.

★ TRY SOMETHING DIFFERENT
For a football theme, replace the ballet shoes with a miniature pair of plastic football boots and ice the cake in the relevant team colours.

Happy Birthday Cake

★

Preparation Time 1 hour • **Cooking Time** 25 minutes, plus cooling and drying • **Serves 10** • **Per Serving** 711 calories, 27g fat (of which 10g saturates), 112g carbohydrate, 0.5g salt • **A Little Effort**

butter to grease
1 x 4-egg quantity of Victoria
    sponge mixture (see page 278)
1 x quantity of buttercream icing
    (see page 282)
900g (2lb) white marzipan or ready-
    to-roll icing (sugar paste)
red, blue and green food colourings
gold stars to decorate (optional)

1 Grease two 18cm (7in) square cake tins and line with greaseproof paper. Make and bake the sponge mixture according to the instructions on page 278. Leave to cool in the tins for 5 minutes, then turn out on to a wire rack, remove the lining paper and leave to cool completely.

2 Sandwich the cold cakes together with all but 2 tbsp buttercream. Put the cake on a cake board and spread the reserved buttercream smoothly over the top and sides. Set aside.

3 Cut off one-third of the marzipan or icing and roll out thinly to fit the top of the cake. Cut to size. Knead the trimmings together with the remaining marzipan or icing.

4 Divide the remaining marzipan or icing into three pieces. Colour each piece red, blue or green respectively. Roll out each piece thinly and cut into an oblong measuring 18 x 10cm (7 x 4in). Knead the trimmings together, keeping the colours separate.

5 Cut each coloured oblong into strips measuring 18 x 2cm (7 x ¾in). Separate the strips and lay two strips of different colours alongside each other on the worksurface, to fit the depth of one side of the cake. Lightly roll the strips together to join them, keeping them straight. Run a palette knife underneath the strips to ensure that they move freely.

6 Stick the joined strips along one side of the cake and trim to fit. Repeat on each side of the cake. Position the white square of marzipan or icing on top of the

cake. Cut the remaining coloured strips into 1cm (½in) widths and position around the top of the cake.

7 Roll out the marzipan or icing trimmings thinly. Using small alphabet cutters, cut out letters to make 'Happy Birthday'. Arrange in the centre of the cake – brush the backs of the letters with a little water to stick down. Mould any remaining trimmings into balloon shapes with strings and arrange them on top of the cake. Leave to dry in a cool place. Add gold stars, if using (remove before serving).

Clown Cake

Preparation Time 45 minutes • **Serves 15** • **Per Serving** 300 calories, 8g fat (of which 2g saturates), 55g carbohydrate, 0.1g salt • **Easy**

25g (1oz) each of white, green, black and blue ready-to-roll icing (sugar paste)
50g (2oz) red ready-to-roll icing (sugar paste)
black and yellow writing icing
1 x white ready-iced 20.5cm (8in) sponge cake

1 First make the shapes for the clown's face. Roll out the white ready-to-roll icing and cut out two ovals for eyes. Roll out half the red icing and cut out a crescent shape for the mouth. Mark a smiley line along the centre of the mouth with black writing icing. Knead the trimmings and the other piece of red icing together and roll into a ball for his nose. Roll out a small piece of green icing and, using a star-shaped cutter, stamp out two stars for his cheeks.

2 Brush the backs of the shapes with water and position on the cake. Roll out the black icing and cut out two small circles to make pupils for the eyes, then stick on to the white ovals. Use the black and yellow writing icing to give him eyebrows and a swirl of hair.

3 Roll out the blue icing and cut out two sides of a bow tie. Roll the trimmings into a ball and flatten slightly to make the centre knot. Fix the two bow-tie pieces to the bottom edge of the cake with writing icing. Position the knot on top. Use the yellow writing icing to pipe polka dots on the tie.

★ GET AHEAD
To prepare ahead *Complete the recipe up to one day in advance.*

Hickory Dickory Dock Cake

Preparation Time 45 minutes • **Cooking Time** 20–25 minutes, plus cooling • **Serves 10** • **Per Serving** 455 calories, 12g fat (of which 7g saturates), 87g carbohydrate, 0.3g salt • **Easy**

butter to grease
1 x 3-egg quantity of Victoria
   sponge mixture (see page 278)
1 x quantity of buttercream icing
   (see page 282)
450g (1lb) white ready-to-roll icing
   (sugar paste)
blue food colouring
toy mouse or small sugar mouse
   to decorate
coloured ribbon

1 Grease two 18cm (7in) round cake tins and line with greaseproof paper. Make and bake the sponge mixture according to the instructions on page 278. Leave to cool in the tins for 5 minutes, then turn out on to a wire rack, remove the lining paper and leave to cool completely.

2 Sandwich the cold cakes together with all but 2 tbsp buttercream. Put the cake on a plate or cake board and spread the reserved buttercream smoothly over the top and sides (reserving a tiny amount of buttercream to stick the sugar mouse). Set aside.

3 Cut off 100g (3½oz) of the ready-to-roll icing and set aside. Roll out the rest thinly and cover the cake, smoothing out any creases with your hands as you go. Trim away the icing around the base of the cake and reserve the trimmings.

4 Knead the remaining icing with the trimmings and a few drops of food colouring. Roll out thinly. Cut out two strips, measuring half the diameter of the cake, to make the hands of the clock. Trim one end of each hand into an arrow shape and shorten one piece to form the little hand. Use the offcut to cut out a circular pivot for the ends of the hands. Cut out the numbers one to twelve with small number cutters.

5 Brush the backs of the numbers with water and arrange on the cake to resemble a clock face. Fix on the hands of the clock in the same way, setting them at one o'clock. Stick the sugar mouse, if using, on the face of the clock with a dot of the reserved buttercream, or put the toy mouse in position. Tie a ribbon around the cake.

★ GET AHEAD
To prepare ahead _Complete the recipe up to one day in advance._

Space Rocket Cake

Preparation Time 40 minutes • **Serves 6** • **Per Serving** 564 calories, 10g fat (of which 5g saturates), 122g carbohydrate, 0.6g salt • **Easy**

brown or black food colouring
900g (2lb) white ready-to-roll icing (sugar paste)
icing sugar to dust
1 ready-made Madeira cake slab
apricot glaze (see page 280)
ice cream sugar cone
6 chocolate mini rolls
6 candles with holders
red and black writing icing
edible silver balls to decorate

1 First, make the surface of the moon. Knead a few drops of food colouring into half the ready-to-roll icing to make a brown or grey, lunar-like colour. Roll out a square of the icing to fit a 30.5cm (12in) cake board, but first, stick pieces of the icing on the board to make rocks and press some in the centre so that they look like craters. Lay the square of icing over the rocks and craters and smooth to fit.

2 To make the spaceship, dust a worksurface lightly with icing sugar and roll out three-quarters of the remaining white icing thinly. Brush the Madeira cake with apricot glaze and stick the sugar cone to one of the short ends with more glaze. Lay the white icing over the top and mould around the shape, smoothing it with your hands and tucking the joins underneath. Fix on the lunar landscape with a dab of apricot glaze.

3 Slice one end off each mini roll so that you can see the icing inside. Stack up into a pyramid shape. Roll out the remaining white icing into a strip and neaten the edges with a sharp knife. Wrap around the pyramid, moulding gently as you go. Leave the ends of the rolls exposed and insert candles in holders as shown. Put the rocket section against the bottom of the spaceship, fixing with apricot glaze.

4 With black writing icing, write 'NASA 69' (or appropriate year) and mark panels on the body of the rocket. Decorate with silver balls. Use red writing icing to draw stripes over the rocket section.

5 As a finishing touch, put a candleholder and candle in each chocolate rocket and light when ready to serve.

★ GET AHEAD
To prepare ahead *Complete the recipe up to one day in advance.*

Knight's Castle

Preparation Time 1 hour • **Cooking Time** 45 minutes, plus cooling • **Serves 25** • **Per Serving** 258 calories, 11g fat (of which 6g saturates), 38g carbohydrate, 0.4g salt • **A Little Effort**

1 x 4-egg quantity of chocolate
  Victoria sponge mixture (see
  page 278)
1 x 3-egg quantity of chocolate
  Victoria sponge mixture (see
  page 278)
2 x quantities of chocolate
  buttercream icing (see page 282)
white writing icing
milk chocolate matchsticks
4 paper flags attached to cocktail
  sticks

1 Make and bake the 4-egg cake in a 20.5cm (8in) square tin, and the 3-egg cake in an 18cm (7in) square tin, according to the instructions on page 278. Leave to cool in the tins for 5 minutes, then turn out on to a wire rack, remove the lining paper and leave to cool completely.

2 Trim the top of the large cake to make it flat. Place the cake, cut side down, in the centre of a plate or 30.5cm (12in) cake board. Cover the large cake with two-thirds of the chocolate buttercream.

3 Neaten the edges of the smaller cake and cut into nine equal squares. To form a tower, put two squares on top of each other, sandwiched with buttercream, at one corner of the large cake, then secure with a cocktail stick. Cover with chocolate buttercream. Repeat with the remaining squares in the other three corners of the cake

(you'll have one square left over, which you can discard or eat).

4 With the white writing icing, draw arrow slits on each tower. In the centre of the main facing wall, stick a row of chocolate sticks to make a drawbridge. Stick a flag into each tower.

★ GET AHEAD
To prepare ahead *Complete the recipe up to one day in advance.*

Tiger Cake

Preparation Time 1½ hours • **Cooking Time** 20–25 minutes, plus cooling and drying • **Serves 8** • **Per Serving** 451 calories, 16g fat (of which 9g saturates), 76g carbohydrate, 0.4g salt • **A Little Effort**

butter to grease
1 x 3-egg quantity of chocolate
  Victoria sponge mixture (see
  page 278)
chocolate and hazelnut spread for
  the filling
1 x quantity of frosting (see
  page 283)
yellow (or orange), black and red
  (or pink) food colourings
200g (7oz) ready-to-roll icing (sugar
  paste)
2 green jelly diamonds and 2 sticks
  of spaghetti
cornflour to dust

1 Grease two 18cm (7in) round sandwich tins and line with greaseproof paper. Make and bake the sponge mixture according to the instructions on page 278. Leave to cool in the tins for 5 minutes, then turn out on to a wire rack, remove the lining paper and leave to cool completely.

2 Sandwich the two layers together with the chocolate and hazelnut spread. Put the cake on a 25.5cm (10in) round cake board or a round tray.

3 Colour the frosting yellow (or orange). Using a palette knife, spread the frosting to cover the top and sides of the cake, leaving it slightly fluffed up to give a furry effect.

4 Colour 75g (3oz) icing black, 25g (1oz) pink and 25g (1oz) yellow (or orange). Leave the remaining icing white. Roll out the pink and yellow icing and one-third of the white icing. Cut three 2cm (¾in) rounds of pink, two 5cm (2in) rounds of yellow and two 2.5cm (1in) ovals of white.

5 Make ears by gently pulling the yellow rounds to make them rounded at one end. Dampen them with a little water in the centre and attach a pink circle to each one to make inner ears. Pinch them together at the bottom to make

them curve like ears. Leave to dry over a rolling pin, pink-side down, for about 30 minutes. Position on the cake, pressing gently into the frosting.

6 Position the white ovals to make the eyes. Dampen with a little water and attach the jelly diamonds for pupils. Place the remaining pink circle as a tongue. Divide the unrolled white icing in half and roll into two flattened balls. Place them above the pink tongue to form the tiger's cheeks. Break the spaghetti into 10cm (4in) lengths and insert these 'whiskers' into the side of the cheeks.

7 Roll a nut of the black icing into a nose, mark two nostrils and place on top of the two white cheeks. Dust the worksurface with cornflour and roll out the remaining black icing thinly. Using a knife, cut out a variety of curved stripes, as shown, and arrange on the cake. Add a strip to each jelly diamond 'eye' to make the pupil.

 GET AHEAD
To prepare ahead *Complete the recipe up to one day in advance.*

Creepy-crawly Cake

Preparation Time 1½ hours plus drying • **Cooking Time** 25–30 minutes, plus cooling and drying • **Serves 12** •
Per Serving 534 calories, 26 fat (of which 17g saturates), 76g carbohydrate, 0.6g salt • **A Little Effort**

butter to grease
1 x 4-egg quantity of chocolate
  Victoria sponge mixture (see
  page 278)
½ x quantity of chocolate
  buttercream icing (see page 282)

FOR THE DECORATION
225g (8oz) white ready-to-roll icing
  (sugar paste)
assorted food colourings, including
  black and brown
red and black liquorice bootlaces
  and jelly creepy-crawly sweets,
  such as snakes and frogs
a little glacé icing (see page 282)

FOR THE ICING
450g (1lb) icing sugar, sifted
225g (8oz) butter, softened
few drops of vanilla extract
green food colouring

1 To make a trap door, use 125g
(4oz) ready-to-roll icing. Knead in a
few drops of brown food colouring
and roll out to a thickness of 5mm
(¼ in), then use a small tumbler to
cut out a circle. Place on a baking
tray lined with baking parchment
and leave in a cool place overnight
to dry.

2 Use the remaining white and
brown icing to make a selection of
spiders and beetles, colouring the
icing accordingly. Use the liquorice
to make spiders' legs. Pipe eyes on
the creatures with white glacé icing.
Allow to dry overnight.

3 The next day, grease two 20.5cm
(8in) round sandwich tins and line
with greaseproof paper. Make and
bake the sponge mixture according
to the instructions on page 278.
Leave to cool in the tins for 5 minutes,
then turn out on to a wire rack,
remove the lining paper and leave
to cool completely. Sandwich the
cold cakes together with chocolate
buttercream. Cut out a hole 1cm
(½in) deep and 6.5cm (2½in) wide in
the centre of the cake. Discard (or
eat) the trimmings.

4 To make the icing, beat the icing
sugar into the butter with the
vanilla. Beat in the food colouring.
Put the cake on a board or plate and
cover with the green icing. Secure
the trap door over the hole in the
middle of the cake. Prop open with
a cocktail stick painted with brown
food colouring, or a chocolate
matchstick. Arrange the creatures
over the cake. Make sure that some
creepy-crawlies are crawling out of
the trap door. Leave to dry.

★ GET AHEAD
To prepare ahead *Complete the recipe
up to one day in advance.*

Hedgehogs, Ladybirds and Tortoises

★

Preparation Time 1 hour • **Cooking Time** 15 minutes, plus cooling • **Makes 15** • **Per Cake** 178 calories, 4g fat (of which 2g saturates), 37g carbohydrate, 0.1g salt • **A Little Effort**

50g (2oz) butter, plus extra to grease
50g (2oz) caster sugar
1 medium egg, beaten
50g (2oz) self-raising flour
1 tbsp milk
1 x quantity of chocolate buttercream icing (see page 282)
75g (3oz) red ready-to-roll icing (sugar paste)
black and brown writing icing
125g (4oz) green ready-to-roll icing (sugar paste)
50g (2oz) brown ready-to-roll icing (sugar paste)
apricot jam

FOR THE DECORATION
chocolate sprinkles and milk and white chocolate drops
edible silver or gold balls
dolly mixture sweets

1 Preheat the oven to 180°C (160°C fan oven) mark 4. Liberally grease 15 holes in bun tins with rounded bases.

2 Cream the butter and sugar together until light and fluffy. Gradually beat in the egg. Fold in the flour and milk. Divide the mixture among the 15 holes of the bun tins and bake for about 15 minutes. Remove from the tin and cool on a wire rack.

3 Make the hedgehogs. Cover five of the cold buns with chocolate buttercream, shaping it to form a snout. Decorate with chocolate sprinkles, silver or gold balls for eyes and a dolly mixture sweet for the nose.

4 Make the ladybirds. Roll out the red icing thinly and use to cover a further five buns. Using black writing icing, pipe wings, spots and a smile on the ladybirds and use chocolate drops for eyes.

5 Make the tortoises. Cover the remaining buns with green icing. Use brown writing icing to draw 'shell' markings and add white chocolate drops. Make the heads, legs and tails from brown icing and attach to the bodies with a little jam. Add silver balls for eyes.

★ GET AHEAD
To prepare ahead *Complete the recipe up to one day in advance.*

Toadstool

Preparation Time 1½ hours • **Cooking Time** 40 minutes, plus cooling • **Serves 12** • **Per Serving** 433 calories, 10g fat (of which 6g saturates), 87g carbohydrate, 0.3g salt • **A Little Effort**

butter to grease

1 x 3-egg quantity of Victoria sponge mixture (see page 278)

700g (1½lb) white ready-to-roll icing (sugar paste)

brown, red, green and yellow food colourings

½ x quantity of buttercream icing (see page 282)

cornflour to dust

sugar flowers, dolly mixtures and butterfly decorations

1 Preheat the oven to 190°C (170°C fan oven) mark 5. Grease a 900g (2lb) food can and a 1.1 litre (2 pint) pudding basin and baseline with baking parchment. It doesn't matter how big the basin is, as long as it holds at least 1.1 litres (2 pints). A wide, shallow cake makes a better-looking toadstool.

2 Make the cake mixture according to the instructions on page 278. Half-fill the food can and put the remaining mixture into the pudding basin. Bake for about 30 minutes for the 'stalk' in the food can and 40 minutes for the 'mushroom cap' in the pudding basin. Transfer the can and basin to a wire rack to cool.

3 Take 350g (12oz) ready-to-roll icing. Colour a walnut-sized piece with brown food colouring and the rest red. Colour 125g (4oz) green and leave the remaining 225g (8oz) white. Roll out the green icing and cut into a kidney shape as a 'grass' base. Fix to a cake board with a little water. Unmould the cakes. Using the food can that the stalk was baked in as a template, cut a semi-circle from one side of the grass.

4 Reserve 50g (2oz) white icing and set aside; colour the rest yellow. Roll out the yellow icing into a long oblong to fit the stalk. Trim to neaten the edges. Spread buttercream thinly around the stalk cake then, holding the cake by the ends, set it at one end of the icing.

Roll up the icing around the stalk and press the seam together. With a dab of buttercream, fix the stalk upright in the cut-out semi-circle in the green icing. Spread the top with buttercream.

5 Roll out the red icing to fit the mushroom cap. Set the cake flat on the worksurface and cover the upper surface thinly with buttercream. Lay the red icing over the cake and smooth in place. Trim around the base of the cake. Dust the worksurface lightly with cornflour and carefully turn the cake upside down.

6 Colour the remaining buttercream dark brown. Insert a small, fluted nozzle into a piping bag, then fill the bag with the buttercream. Mark a circle in the centre of the base of the mushroom cap, where the stalk will fit. Pipe lines of buttercream radiating from this, to look like the 'gills' of a toadstool. Be sure to cover the sponge and red icing join. Carefully turn the cake the right way up and set on top of the stalk.

7 Roll out the reserved white icing and the brown icing. Cut the white icing into dots. Arrange on top of the toadstool, using a little buttercream to fix them. Cut the brown icing into a door and windows and fix to the stalk in the same way. Decorate the 'grass' with sugar flowers, sweets and butterflies.

 GET AHEAD

To prepare ahead Complete the recipe up to one day in advance.

Gingerbread Footballers

Preparation Time 5 minutes, plus chilling • Cooking Time 12–15 minutes, plus cooling and setting • Makes 20 •
Per Biscuit 157 calories, 6g fat (of which 4g saturates), 26g carbohydrate, 0.2g salt • Easy

125g (4oz) cold butter, diced, plus
   extra to grease
350g (12oz) plain flour, plus extra
   to dust
1 tsp bicarbonate of soda
2 tsp ground ginger
175g (6oz) light soft brown sugar
4 tbsp golden syrup
1 medium egg, beaten
assorted writing icings
star and football decorations
   (optional)

1 Lightly grease three baking sheets with butter. Sift the flour, bicarbonate of soda and ginger into a mixing bowl. Rub in the butter until the mixture resembles fine breadcrumbs, then stir in the sugar. (Alternatively, use a food processor.) Beat the syrup with the egg, then stir into the flour mixture and mix to make a dough. Knead until smooth, then divide in half and wrap in clingfilm. Chill for 30 minutes.

2 Preheat the oven to 190°C (170°C fan oven) mark 5. Turn out the dough on to a lightly floured worksurface and cut in half. Roll out each half until about 5mm (¼in) thick. Using a gingerbread man cutter, cut out shapes. Repeat with the second half of the dough. Re-roll the trimmings until all of the dough has been used. Put the gingerbread men on the prepared baking sheets.

3 Bake for 12–15 minutes until golden brown. Leave on the baking sheets to cool slightly, then transfer to wire racks to cool completely.

4 When the gingerbread has cooled completely, decorate the footballers. Using black writing icing, give each man a pair of eyes and a dot for a nose. Use red icing for a mouth and black or yellow icing for hair. Choosing the colour(s) of your child's favourite football strip, draw an outline around the edge of the gingerbread to represent a shirt and shorts, then fill in the shirt with stripes if you like. Use contrasting icing to write a number on the front of each shirt. Decorate the shorts with stars, if you like, and attach footballs with a dot of writing icing. Leave to set for about 30 minutes. Remember to remove non-edible decorations before eating.

★ TO STORE
Store in an airtight container. They will keep for up to one week.

Jewel Biscuits

Preparation Time 30 minutes, plus chilling • Cooking Time 10–15 minutes, plus cooling • Makes 18 •
Per Biscuit 164 calories, 6g fat (of which 4g saturates), 29g carbohydrate, 0.1g salt • A Little Effort

125g (4oz) butter, very soft
175g (6oz) plain white flour, sifted,
    plus extra to dust
50g (2oz) caster sugar
½ tsp vanilla extract
milk
18 coloured boiled sweets
1 x quantity glacé icing (see
    page 282)
edible coloured balls to decorate

1 Line three baking sheets with baking parchment. Put the butter, flour, sugar and vanilla extract into a bowl and bring together with a fork or wooden spoon to form a dough – add a drop of milk if the mixture looks too dry. Turn out on to a lightly floured worksurface and knead briefly to bring the dough together. Wrap in clingfilm and chill for 30 minutes.

2 Preheat the oven to 180°C (160°C fan oven) mark 4. Roll out the dough until it is about 3mm (⅛ in) thick (sprinkle the surface of the dough with flour if it starts to stick). Using novelty biscuit cutters, cut out different shapes and arrange on the prepared baking sheets. Using small cutters, cut a shape from the middle of each biscuit and put a sweet in each hole.

3 Bake for 10–15 minutes until the biscuits are pale golden brown and the sweets have melted. Leave to set for a minute, then transfer to a wire rack to cool completely. When the biscuits are cold, decorate with glacé icing and edible balls.

 TO STORE
*Store in an airtight container. They will
keep for up to one week.*

Dinosaur Biscuits

Preparation Time 45 minutes, plus chilling • **Cooking Time** 10–15 minutes, plus cooling • **Makes 16** •
Per Biscuit 187 calories, 4g fat (of which 3g saturates), 37g carbohydrate, 0.1g salt • **A Little Effort**

25g (1oz) plain white flour, sifted, plus extra to dust

175g (6oz) plain wholemeal flour, sifted

1 tsp baking powder

75g (3oz) cold butter, diced

25g (1oz) caster sugar

25g (1oz) porridge oats

about 5 tbsp milk

450g (1lb) white ready-to-roll icing (sugar paste)

assorted food colourings

icing sugar to dust

assorted writing icings

1 Line three baking sheets with baking parchment. Put both flours and the baking powder into a large bowl and rub in the butter with your fingertips until the mixture resembles breadcrumbs. (Alternatively, use a food processor.) Stir in the caster sugar and oats.

2 Gradually add the milk and, using a flat-bladed knife, bring the mixture together until it forms a soft, but not too sticky dough. Turn out on to a lightly floured worksurface and knead briefly until smooth. Wrap in clingfilm and chill for 30 minutes.

3 Preheat the oven to 200°C (180°C fan oven) mark 6. Roll out the dough on a floured worksurface to a thickness of 3mm (⅛in). Using biscuit cutters, cut out dinosaur shapes. Put the biscuits on the prepared baking sheets and bake for 10–15 minutes until a pale golden colour. Leave on the baking sheets to cool slightly, then transfer to wire racks to cool completely.

4 When the biscuits are cold, divide the icing into three or four pieces. Colour each piece with a few drops of food colouring and knead until the colour is evenly distributed. Dust the worksurface and a rolling pin with icing sugar and roll out the icing. Use the biscuit cutters to cut out dinosaur shapes. Brush the underside of the icing shapes with a little water and stick to the biscuits. Use the writing icing to draw on scales, eyes and smiles.

★ TO STORE
Store in an airtight container. They will keep for up to one week.

★ COOK'S TIP
To save time, look out for coloured ready-to-roll icings, which are available in major supermarkets or specialist cake decorating shops.

Meringue Bones

★

Preparation Time 25 minutes • **Cooking Time** 1¼ hours, plus cooling • **Makes 16** • **Per Bone** 32 calories, 0g fat, 8g carbohydrate, 0g salt • **Gluten Free** • **Dairy Free** • **Easy**

2 medium egg whites, at room temperature
125g (4oz) caster sugar
cocoa powder to dust

1 Preheat the oven to 140°C (120°C fan oven) mark 1. Line two or three baking sheets with baking parchment. Whisk the egg whites in a large, clean, grease-free bowl. Add the sugar, one teaspoonful at a time, whisking between each addition until very stiff. The meringue should be very thick and glossy.

2 Spoon the meringue into a piping bag fitted with a 1cm (½ in) plain nozzle. Pipe a line of meringue on a baking sheet, about 8cm (3¼in) long. At each end, pipe two small blobs to form the nubs of the bones. Continue until all the mixture has been used.

3 Bake for about 1½ hours or until hard and dry. Remove from the baking parchment and cool on a wire rack. Pile the meringues on a plate and dust lightly with cocoa powder.

★ TO STORE
Store in an airtight container. They will keep for several weeks.

Special Treat Cakes

Black Forest Roulade

★

Preparation Time 35 minutes • **Cooking Time** 20 minutes, plus cooling and chilling • **Cuts into 10 slices** •
Per Slice 248 calories, 12g fat (of which 7g saturates), 33g carbohydrate, 0.1g salt • **Easy**

4 large eggs, separated
125g (4oz) golden caster sugar, plus
    extra to dust
125g (4oz) plain chocolate (at least
    70% cocoa solids), broken into
    pieces, melted and cooled a little
cocoa powder and icing sugar to
    dust

FOR THE FILLING
140ml (4½fl oz) whipping cream
1 tsp icing sugar
75g (3oz) Greek yogurt
2 x 425g cans morello cherries,
    drained, pitted and halved

1 Preheat the oven to 180°C (160°C fan oven) mark 4. Line a 33 x 23cm (13 x 9in) Swiss roll tin with baking parchment.

2 Whisk the egg yolks with the sugar in a large bowl until thick and creamy. Whisk in the melted chocolate. Whisk the egg whites in a clean, grease-free bowl until stiff peaks form. Fold into the chocolate mixture. Pour into the tin, level the surface and bake for 20 minutes or until firm to the touch. Leave to cool in the tin for 10–15 minutes.

3 Put a sheet of baking parchment on the worksurface and dust with caster sugar. Carefully turn out the roulade on to the parchment and peel off the lining parchment. Cover with a damp cloth and leave to cool for 30 minutes.

4 To make the filling, lightly whip the cream with the icing sugar, then fold in the yogurt. Spread over the cold roulade and scatter the cherries on top. Roll up from one of the narrow ends, using the baking parchment to help. Chill for 30 minutes. Slice the roulade and serve, dusted with cocoa powder and icing sugar.

Chocolate and Chestnut Roulade

★

Preparation Time 20 minutes • **Cooking Time** 20–25 minutes, plus cooling • **Cuts into 10 slices** • **Per Slice** 409 calories, 28g fat (of which 17g saturates), 36g carbohydrate, 0.3g salt • **Gluten Free** • **Easy**

a little vegetable oil
6 medium eggs, separated
200g (7oz) caster sugar, plus extra
   to dust
2–3 drops vanilla extract
50g (2oz) cocoa powder, sifted

FOR THE FILLING
125g (4oz) plain chocolate (at least
   50% cocoa solids), broken into
   pieces
300ml (½ pint) double cream
225g (8oz) unsweetened chestnut
   purée
200ml (7fl oz) full-fat crème fraîche
50g (2oz) icing sugar

1 Preheat the oven to 180°C (160°C fan oven) mark 4. Lightly oil a 33 x 20.5cm (13 x 8in) Swiss roll tin, then line it with baking parchment.

2 Whisk the egg yolks with the caster sugar and vanilla extract until pale and thick. Using a large metal spoon, fold in the cocoa powder. Put the egg whites into a clean, grease-free bowl and whisk until stiff peaks form, then fold into the cocoa mixture. Spoon into the prepared tin, spread evenly and bake for 20–25 minutes until just cooked – the top should be springy to the touch. Leave to cool in the tin for 10–15 minutes.

3 Put a sheet of baking parchment on the worksurface and dust with caster sugar. Carefully turn out the roulade on to the parchment, then leave to cool. Peel away the lining paper.

4 Meanwhile, make the filling. Melt the chocolate in a heatproof bowl set over a pan of gently simmering water, making sure the base of the bowl doesn't touch the water.

5 In a separate bowl, lightly whip the cream. Beat the chestnut purée into the chocolate until smooth; the mixture will be quite thick. Whisk in the crème fraîche and icing sugar. Beat 1 tbsp of the whipped cream into the chocolate mixture, then use a metal spoon to fold in half the remaining cream.

6 Spread the filling over the roulade, then spread the remaining cream on top. Roll up from one of the narrow ends, using the baking parchment to help. Lift on to a serving plate and dust with caster sugar.

Decadent Chocolate Cake

Preparation Time 30 minutes • **Cooking Time** 1½ hours, plus cooling and setting • **Cuts into 12 slices** •
Per Slice 687 calories, 49g fat (of which 23g saturates), 54g carbohydrate, 0.7g salt • **Easy**

225g (8oz) unsalted butter,
   softened, plus extra to grease
300g (11oz) plain chocolate, broken
   into pieces
225g (8oz) golden caster sugar
225g (8oz) ground almonds
8 large eggs, separated
125g (4oz) fresh brown
   breadcrumbs
4 tbsp apricot jam (optional)

FOR THE GANACHE
175g (6oz) plain chocolate, broken
   into pieces
75g (3oz) butter, softened
4 tbsp double cream

1 Preheat the oven to 180°C (160°C fan oven) mark 4. Grease a 23cm (9in) springform cake tin and line with greaseproof paper.

2 Melt the chocolate in a heatproof bowl set over a pan of gently simmering water, making sure the base of the bowl doesn't touch the water. Remove the bowl from the pan.

3 Put the butter and sugar into a large bowl and beat until light and creamy. Add the almonds, egg yolks and breadcrumbs. Beat well until thoroughly mixed. Slowly add the chocolate and carefully stir it in. Do not over-mix as the chocolate may seize up and become unworkable.

4 Put the egg whites into a clean, grease-free bowl and whisk until stiff peaks form. Add half the whites to the chocolate mixture and, using a large metal spoon, fold in lightly. Carefully fold in the remainder. Pour into the prepared tin and level the surface.

5 Bake for 1 hour 20 minutes or until the cake is firm to the touch and a skewer inserted into the centre comes out clean. Cool in the tin for 5 minutes, then transfer to a wire rack for 2–3 hours to cool completely.

6 Put the jam, if using, into a pan and melt over a low heat. Brush jam over the top and sides of the cake.

7 Melt the chocolate, butter and cream in a heatproof bowl set over a pan of gently simmering water, making sure the base of the bowl doesn't touch the water. Stir just once until smooth. Either raise the cake off the worktop on the upturned tin or put it (still on the rack) on a tray to catch the drips. Pour the ganache into the centre and tip the cake to let it run down the sides evenly, or spread it with a palette knife.

Chocolate Marble Cake

★

Preparation Time 20 minutes • **Cooking Time** 45 minutes, plus cooling and setting • **Cuts into 8 slices** •
Per Slice 617 calories, 40g fat (of which 23g saturates), 59g carbohydrate, 1g salt • **Easy**

175g (6oz) unsalted butter, softened
175g (6oz) golden caster sugar
3 medium eggs
125g (4oz) self-raising flour, sifted
50g (2oz) ground almonds
1 tsp baking powder, sifted
finely grated zest of 1 orange
1 tbsp brandy
4 tbsp cocoa powder, sifted
1 x quantity Chocolate Ganache
  (see Cook's Tip)

FOR THE DECORATION
50g (2oz) golden granulated sugar
juice of 1 orange
8 small kumquats

1 Preheat the oven to 190°C (170°C
fan oven) mark 5. Line a 900g (2lb)
loaf tin with baking parchment.

2 Cream the butter with the caster
sugar until pale and light. Beat in
the eggs, one at a time. Fold the
flour, almonds and baking powder
into the bowl, then fold in the
orange zest and brandy. Put half the
mixture into a bowl and mix in the
cocoa powder. Spoon alternate
spoonfuls of both mixtures into the
tin. Shake the tin once, then drag a
skewer through the mixture. Bake
for 45 minutes or until a skewer
inserted into the centre comes out
clean. Turn the cake out on to a wire
rack to cool completely.

3 Peel off the lining paper, put the
cake back on the wire rack and
position over a tray. Pour the
chocolate ganache over the cake
to cover it completely. Leave to set
in a cool place for 30 minutes.

4 For the decoration, put the
granulated sugar into a pan.
Strain the orange juice into a jug,
add enough water to make 150ml
(¼ pint) and pour on to the sugar.
Heat gently to dissolve. Add the
kumquats and poach for 5–10
minutes, then leave to cool. Arrange

the kumquats on top of the cake.
Cut into slices to serve.

★COOK'S TIP
Chocolate Ganache
*Melt 200g (7oz) plain chocolate (at least
70% cocoa solids), broken into pieces,
with 75g (3oz) butter in a heatproof
bowl set over a pan of gently simmering
water, making sure the base of the bowl
doesn't touch the water, stirring
occasionally. Stir the ganache until
smooth.*

Black Forest Gâteau

★

Preparation Time 30 minutes • **Cooking Time** 50 minutes, plus cooling • **Cuts into 12 slices** • **Per Slice** 400 calories, 21g fat (of which 12g saturates), 53g carbohydrate, 0.4g salt • **A Little Effort**

125g (4oz) unsalted butter, melted
200g (7oz) plain flour
50g (2oz) cornflour
50g (2oz) cocoa powder, plus extra
   to dust
2 tsp espresso instant coffee
   powder
1 tsp baking powder
4 large eggs, separated
300g (11oz) golden caster sugar
2 x 300g jars morello cherries in
   syrup
2 tbsp kirsch
200ml (7fl oz) double cream
2 tbsp icing sugar, sifted
fresh cherries and chocolate curls
   (see page 283) to decorate

1 Preheat the oven to 180°C (160°C fan oven) mark 4. Brush a little of the melted butter over the base and sides of a 20.5cm (8in) cake tin, 9cm (3½in) deep. Line the base and sides of the tin with baking parchment.

2 Sift the flour, cornflour, cocoa powder, coffee powder and baking powder together three times – this helps to add air and makes sure all the ingredients are well mixed.

3 Put the egg yolks, sugar and 100ml (3½fl oz) cold water into a freestanding mixer and whisk for 8 minutes or until the mixture leaves a trail for 3 seconds.

4 Add the rest of the melted butter, pouring it around the edge of the bowl so the mixture doesn't lose any air, then quickly fold it in, followed by the sifted flour mixture in two batches.

5 Put the egg whites into a clean, grease-free bowl and whisk until stiff, then gently fold a spoonful into the cake mixture to loosen. Carefully fold in the rest of the egg whites, making sure there are no white blobs left. Pour into the prepared tin and bake in the oven for 45–50 minutes until a skewer inserted into the centre comes out clean. Leave to cool in the tin for 10 minutes, then turn out on to a wire rack to cool completely.

6 When the cake is cold, trim the top to make a flat surface. Turn the cake over so that the top becomes the base. Using a long serrated bread knife, carefully cut into three horizontally.

7 Drain the cherries, reserving 250ml (9fl oz) of the syrup. Put the syrup into a pan and simmer to reduce by half. Stir in the kirsch. Brush the hot syrup on to each layer of the cake – including the top – using all the liquid.

8 Lightly whip the cream with the icing sugar. Spread one-third over the bottom layer and cover with half the cherries. Top with the next cake layer and repeat with another third of the cream and the remaining cherries. Top with the final cake layer and spread with the remaining cream. Decorate with fresh cherries, chocolate scrolls and a dusting of cocoa powder.

Stollen Ring

★

Preparation Time 30 minutes, plus rising • **Cooking Time** about 25 minutes, plus cooling • **Cuts into 10 slices** •
Per Slice 268 calories, 7g fat (of which 3g saturates), 48g carbohydrate, 0.2g salt • **Easy**

450g (1lb) strong white bread flour,
    plus extra to dust
1 tbsp caster sugar
½ x 7g sachet fast-action dried yeast
¼ tsp salt
¼ tsp freshly grated nutmeg
2 large pinches of ground cloves
1 tsp mixed spice
225ml (8fl oz) milk
40g (1½oz) butter, melted, plus a
    little extra to grease
2 medium eggs
50g (2oz) sultanas
100–150g (3½–5oz) marzipan
icing sugar to dust
butter to serve

1 Put the flour, sugar, yeast, salt and the three spices into a large bowl and mix together. Make a well in the centre. Pour the milk into a pan and heat until lukewarm, then stir in the melted butter. Crack 1 egg into the well of dry ingredients and pour in half the milk mixture. Working quickly with your hands, mix thoroughly to form a soft but not sticky dough, adding extra milk as necessary.

2 Tip out the dough on to a floured worksurface, then knead for 5 minutes or until soft and elastic. Transfer to a lightly greased bowl, cover with a clean teatowel and leave to rise somewhere warm, but not hot, for 45 minutes.

3 Knead in the sultanas. Weigh the dough and divide into ten equal pieces. Line a large baking sheet with baking parchment and preheat the oven to 200°C (180°C fan oven) mark 6.

4 Knead the marzipan until soft, then cut into ten pieces. Using your fingers, flatten out one of the pieces of dough slightly, then put a marzipan chunk in the middle. Fold the dough around it, then squeeze together to make a neat ball. Repeat with the remaining pieces of dough.

5 Position the balls in a circle, just touching, on the baking sheet. Use the remaining egg to glaze the ring, then bake for 20–25 minutes until golden. Leave to cool on the baking tray – the stollen ring is quite fragile at this stage.

6 Carefully transfer to a serving platter or wooden board, dust with icing sugar and serve with butter.

★FREEZING TIP
To freeze Complete the recipe to the end of step 4. Leave the stollen on the baking sheet, wrap the whole sheet in clingfilm and freeze for up to one month.
To use Defrost at room temperature, then complete the recipe as step 5.

Best-ever Lemon Gâteau

Preparation Time 35 minutes • **Cooking Time** about 20 minutes, plus cooling and chilling • **Cuts into 8 slices** •
Per Slice 276 calories, 17g fat (of which 7g saturates), 28g carbohydrate, 0.2g salt • **Easy**

butter to grease
2½ tbsp semolina, plus extra to dust
6 large eggs, separated
150g (5oz) caster sugar
2 large lemons
40g (1½oz) ground almonds
3 tbsp plain flour
3 gelatine leaves
150ml (¼ pint) double cream
icing sugar to dust

1 Preheat the oven to 180°C (160°C fan oven) mark 4. Grease an 8cm (3¼in) deep, 20.5cm (8in) loose-bottomed round tin. Line the base with baking parchment and dust the sides with semolina.

2 Put 3 egg yolks, 50g (2oz) sugar and the zest of 1 lemon into a bowl and beat for 5 minutes. Fold in the semolina, almonds and flour.

3 Put 3 egg whites into a clean, grease-free bowl and whisk until stiff. Add 25g (1oz) sugar and beat for a few seconds. Fold 1 tbsp into the cake mix, then fold in the rest. Spoon into the prepared tin and level the surface. Bake for 15–20 minutes. Leave to cool in the tin.

4 Remove the sides of the tin and slide the cake on to a board, leaving the parchment in place. Slice the cake in half horizontally. Regrease and reline the sides of the tin with baking parchment, then put the cake half with the

paper attached into the tin, paper side down.

5 Put the gelatine into a bowl and cover with cold water. Leave for 5 minutes. Heat the juice of 1 lemon until simmering. Squeeze the excess water from the gelatine, then whisk into the lemon juice. Leave to cool. Whisk the remaining yolks and sugar with the zest of the other lemon until mousse-like. Fold the gelatine mixture into the sugar and lemon mixture.

6 Put the egg whites into a clean, grease-free bowl and whisk until stiff. Whisk the cream until it just holds its shape. Fold the cream into the yolk mix, then fold in the egg whites. Pour into the tin, cover and chill for 2 hours. Put the second cake layer over the mousse, cut side down. Cover and chill overnight.

7 Turn out the cake and peel off the paper. Dust with icing sugar. Heat a metal skewer in a gas flame and score lines on the top.

Lemon, Almond and Blueberry Gâteau

Preparation Time 25 minutes • **Cooking Time** 30–35 minutes, plus cooling • **Cuts into 10–12 slices** • **Per Slice** 189 calories, 5g fat (of which 1g saturates), 32g carbohydrate, 0.2g salt • **Easy**

4 large eggs
200g (7oz) golden caster sugar
1 tsp vanilla extract
75g (3oz) plain flour, sifted
50g (2oz) ground almonds
500g (1lb 2oz) fat-free Greek yogurt
3–4 tbsp maple syrup
zest of ½ lemon
225g (8oz) blueberries
15g (½oz) flaked almonds, toasted
icing sugar to dust (optional)

1 Preheat the oven to 180°C (160°C fan oven) mark 4. Line a 20.5cm (8in) cake tin with baking parchment.

2 Put the eggs, sugar and vanilla extract into a bowl and whisk with a hand-held electric whisk for 10 minutes or until the mixture is pale and mousse-like. Using a large metal spoon, fold in the flour and ground almonds, taking care not to over-mix and knock out the air. Pour into the prepared tin.

3 Bake for 30–35 minutes until golden and the cake is beginning to pull away from the sides of the paper. Turn the tin upside down on to a wire rack and leave to cool completely.

4 Beat the yogurt, syrup and lemon zest together. Cut the cake in half horizontally. Spread half the yogurt mixture over the base. Top with most of the blueberries. Replace the top, then spread the remaining mixture over it. Scatter the flaked almonds and remaining blueberries over the top. Dust with a little icing sugar, if you like.

★ GET AHEAD
To prepare ahead *Complete the recipe to the end of step 2. Wrap the tin in clingfilm and store in an airtight container. It will keep for up to two days.*
To use *Complete the recipe.*

Almond Toffee Meringues

★

Preparation Time 35 minutes • **Cooking Time** 22–25 minutes, plus cooling and drying • **Makes 4** •
Per Meringue 458 calories, 4g fat (of which trace saturates), 95g carbohydrate, 0.2g salt • **Easy**

oil to grease
25g (1oz) light muscovado sugar
100g (3½oz) egg whites (about
    3 medium eggs)
225g (8oz) caster sugar
25g (1oz) flaked almonds
lightly whipped cream to serve

**FOR THE MARINATED
    SUMMER FRUIT**
125ml (4fl oz) crème de cassis
juice of 1 orange
2 tbsp redcurrant jelly
200g (7oz) raspberries
4 nectarines, halved, stoned and
    sliced

1 To make the marinated fruit, put
the crème de cassis, orange juice
and redcurrant jelly into a small
pan. Heat gently to melt, then
bubble for 2–3 minutes until syrupy.
Pour into a large bowl to cool. Add
the raspberries and nectarines and
stir gently. Cover and chill.

2 Preheat the oven to 170°C
(150°C fan oven) mark 3 and
preheat the grill. Lightly oil a baking
sheet and sprinkle the muscovado
sugar over it. Grill for 2–3 minutes
until the sugar begins to bubble
and caramelise. Cool for about
15 minutes, then break the sugar
into a food processor and whiz to
a coarse powder.

3 Put the egg whites and caster
sugar into a large, clean bowl set
over a pan of gently simmering
water. Stir until the sugar has
dissolved and the egg white is warm
(about 10 minutes(. Remove from
the heat and place on a teatowel.
Beat with a hand-held electric whisk
for at least 15 minutes or until cold
and glossy and standing in stiff,
shiny peaks when the whisk is lifted.
Cover two baking sheets with
baking parchment. Fold half the
powdered sugar into the meringue
mixture. Spoon four oval mounds on
to the baking sheets, leaving plenty
of space between each. Sprinkle
with flaked almonds and the
remaining powdered sugar. Bake for
20 minutes, then turn off the heat
and leave in the oven to dry out
overnight. Serve with the marinated
fruit and lightly whipped cream.

★ COOK'S TIPS
● *Make sure the bowl does not touch the
hot water while you make the meringues.*
● *The flavour of the marinated fruit will
be even better if you chill it overnight. (If
the syrup thickens during chilling, stir in
1–2 tbsp orange juice.)*

Creamy Coffee and Praline Gâteau

★

Preparation Time 45 minutes • **Cooking Time** 25 minutes, plus cooling • **Cuts into 8 slices** • **Per Slice** 548 calories, 21g fat (of which 10g saturates), 83g carbohydrate, 0.2g salt • **For the Confident Cook**

50g (2oz) unsalted butter, melted,
    plus extra to grease
125g (4oz) plain flour, sifted, plus
    extra to dust
4 large eggs, separated
125g (4oz) caster sugar
1 tbsp coffee granules, dissolved in
    2 tsp boiling water

FOR THE PRALINE
50g (2oz) whole blanched hazelnuts
150g (5oz) caster sugar

FOR THE FILLING
500g (1lb 2oz) mascarpone cheese
250g (9oz) icing sugar, sifted
2 tbsp coffee granules, dissolved in
    1 tbsp boiling water

1 Preheat the oven to 190°C (170°C fan oven) mark 5. Grease two 18cm (7in) loose-based sandwich tins. Dust lightly with flour and tip out the excess.

2 Put the egg whites into a clean, grease-free bowl and whisk until soft peaks form. Whisk in one egg yolk; repeat with the other three yolks. Add the sugar, 1 tbsp at a time, and continue to whisk. The mixture should be thick enough to leave a trail when the whisk is lifted. Using a large metal spoon, fold half the flour into the mixture.

3 Mix the coffee into the melted butter, then pour around the edge of the egg mixture. Add the remaining flour and gradually fold in. Divide the mixture between the prepared tins and bake for 25 minutes or until risen and firm to the touch. Turn out on to a wire rack and leave to cool completely.

4 To make the praline, line a baking sheet with non-stick baking parchment and scatter the nuts on it. Dissolve the sugar in a heavy-based pan over a low heat, shaking the pan once or twice to help it dissolve evenly. Cook until it forms a dark golden-brown caramel. Pour over the nuts and leave to cool.

5 To make the filling, put the mascarpone and icing sugar into a large bowl, add the coffee and mix with a hand-held electric whisk. Slice each cake in half horizontally. Put one cake layer on a plate and spread with a quarter of the filling. Continue layering in this way, finishing with a layer of mascarpone filling.

6 Break the praline into two or three pieces and put into a plastic bag. Using a rolling pin, smash it into smaller pieces. Use to decorate the top of the cake.

Orange and White Chocolate Cake

★

Preparation Time 35 minutes, plus chilling • **Cooking Time** 40 minutes, plus cooling • **Cuts into 14 slices** •
Per Slice 544 calories, 35g fat (of which 18g saturates), 48g carbohydrate, 0.3g salt • **For the Confident Cook**

butter to grease
6 large eggs, separated
250g (9oz) golden caster sugar
150g (5oz) self-raising flour, sifted
150g (5oz) ground almonds
grated zest of 2 oranges and juice
    of 3 large oranges
100g (3½oz) golden granulated
    sugar
225ml (8fl oz) sweet white wine
350g (12oz) strawberries, thinly
    sliced

**FOR THE WHITE
    CHOCOLATE GANACHE**
225g (8oz) white chocolate,
    chopped
600ml (1 pint) double cream

1 Preheat the oven to 180°C (160°C fan oven) mark 4. Grease a 23cm (9in) round deep cake tin and line with baking parchment.

2 Put the egg whites into a clean, grease-free bowl and whisk until soft peaks form. Gradually beat in 50g (2oz) caster sugar and whisk until the mixture is stiff and glossy. Put the egg yolks and remaining sugar into another bowl and whisk until soft and mousse-like. Carefully stir in the flour, fold in one-third of the egg whites, then fold in the remaining egg whites, the ground almonds and orange zest. Pour the mixture into the prepared tin.

3 Bake for 35 minutes or until a skewer inserted into the centre comes out clean. Leave to cool in the tin for 10 minutes, then turn out on to a wire rack and leave to cool completely.

4 Put the orange juice, granulated sugar and wine into a small pan and stir over a low heat until the sugar has dissolved. Bring to the boil and bubble for 5 minutes or until syrupy. Cool and set aside.

5 To make the ganache, put the chocolate into a heatproof bowl with half the cream. Put the bowl over a pan of gently simmering water, making sure the base of the bowl doesn't touch the water, and leave until the chocolate melts, then stir to combine. Remove the bowl from the pan and cool, then beat with a wooden spoon until cold and thick. Whip the remaining cream lightly and beat a large spoonful into the chocolate cream to loosen it. Fold in the remainder. Chill for 2 hours.

6 Cut the cake in half horizontally, pierce all over with a skewer and put it, cut sides up, on a baking sheet. Drizzle the orange syrup over the cake and leave to soak in. Spread a quarter of the ganache over the base cake and scatter with 225g (8oz) strawberries. Cover with the top half of the cake and press down lightly. Using a palette knife, smooth the remaining ganache over the top and sides of the cake. Chill for up to 4 hours.

7 Decorate with the remaining strawberries and serve.

Toasted Hazelnut Meringue Cake

★

Preparation Time 10 minutes • **Cooking Time** about 30 minutes, plus cooling • **Cuts into 8 slices** • **Per Slice** 598 calories, 38g fat (of which 16g saturates), 57g carbohydrate, 0.1g salt • **Easy**

oil to grease
175g (6oz) skinned hazelnuts, toasted
3 large egg whites
175g (6oz) golden caster sugar
250g carton mascarpone cheese
285ml (9½fl oz) double cream
3 tbsp Bailey's Irish Cream liqueur, plus extra to serve
140g (4½oz) frozen raspberries
340g jar redcurrant jelly

1 Preheat the oven to 190°C (170°C fan oven) mark 5. Lightly oil two 18cm (7in) sandwich tins and baseline with baking parchment. Whiz the hazelnuts in a food processor until finely chopped.

2 Put the egg whites into a clean, grease-free bowl and whisk until stiff peaks form. Whisk in the sugar, a spoonful at a time. Using a metal spoon, fold in half the nuts. Divide the mixture between the tins and spread evenly. Bake in the middle of the oven for about 30 minutes, then leave to cool in the tins for 30 minutes.

3 To make the filling, put the mascarpone cheese into a bowl. Beat in the cream and liqueur until smooth. Put the raspberries and redcurrant jelly into a pan and heat gently until the jelly has melted. Sieve, then cool.

4 Use a palette knife to loosen the edges of the meringues, then turn out on to a wire rack. Peel off the baking parchment and discard. Put a large sheet of baking parchment on a board and sit one meringue on top, flat side down. Spread one-third of the mascarpone mixture over the meringue, then drizzle with raspberry purée. Top with the other meringue, then cover the whole cake with the rest of the mascarpone mixture. Sprinkle with the remaining hazelnuts. Carefully put the cake on to a serving plate and drizzle with more liqueur, if you like.

★ FREEZING TIP
To freeze *Freezing the meringue makes it slightly softer but no less tasty. Complete the recipe to the end of step 4, but don't put on serving plate or drizzle with more liqueur. Using the paper, lift the cake into the freezer, then freeze until solid. Once solid, store in a sturdy container in the freezer for up to one month.*
To use *Thaw overnight in the fridge, then complete the recipe.*

Pear and Almond Meringue Cake

Preparation Time 20 minutes • **Cooking Time** 50 minutes • **Cuts into 6 slices** • **Per Slice** 596 calories, 30g fat (of which 13g saturates), 77g carbohydrate, 0.8g salt • **Easy**

a few saffron strands
125g (4oz) unsalted butter, softened, plus extra to grease
300g (11oz) golden caster sugar
3 large eggs, plus 3 egg whites
150g (5oz) self-raising flour
1 tsp baking powder
75g (3oz) ground almonds
2 small pears, peeled, cored and chopped
25g (1oz) flaked almonds
icing sugar to dust

1 Preheat the oven to 180°C (160°C fan oven) mark 4. Put the saffron into a small heatproof bowl and add 2 tbsp boiling water. Leave to infuse. Lightly grease a 23cm (9in) round cake tin and line with baking parchment.

2 Using an electric whisk, cream the butter with 125g (4oz) caster sugar until smooth. Strain the saffron, then add the liquid and whole eggs, a little at a time, to the butter mixture, beating between each addition.

3 Sift in the flour and baking powder, then fold in, along with 50g (2oz) ground almonds. Stir in the pears, then spoon the mixture into the prepared tin, level the surface and bake for 20 minutes.

4 Put the egg whites into a clean, grease-free bowl and whisk until soft peaks form. Add the remaining sugar, a little at a time – the mixture should stay stiff. Fold in the remaining ground almonds.

5 Pull the oven shelf out slightly. Spoon the meringue over the cake and sprinkle with the flaked almonds. Bake for 30 minutes until a skewer inserted into the centre comes out clean. Dust with icing sugar.

Marshmallow Meringue Cake

★

Preparation Time 45 minutes, plus chilling, freezing and softening • **Cooking Time** 2½ hours, plus cooling • **Serves 10** •
Per Serving 479 calories, 24g fat (of which 14g saturates), 62g carbohydrate, 0.2g salt • **Gluten Free** • **For the Confident Cook**

225g (8oz) golden caster sugar
125g (4oz) light muscovado sugar
6 large eggs, separated
1 tsp cornflour
½ tsp vinegar
50g (2oz) flaked almonds, toasted
    (optional)
chocolate shavings and icing sugar
    to dust

FOR THE FILLING
Marshmallow Ice Cream (see
    Cook's Tip)
4 bananas, about 450g (1lb)

1 Preheat the oven to 130°C (110°C fan oven) mark ½. Line two baking sheets with baking parchment. Using a felt-tip pen, mark out a 23cm (9in) diameter circle on each, then turn the paper over.

2 Sift the caster and muscovado sugars together. Whisk the egg whites in a clean, grease-free bowl until they're stiff and dry. Whisk in the sugars, 1 tbsp at a time, until the mixture is glossy and very stiff – this will take about 5 minutes. Whisk in the cornflour and vinegar.

3 Spoon just over half the meringue on to one of the prepared baking sheets in a ring shape around the circumference of the circle and sprinkle with half the almonds, if using. Spread the remaining mixture evenly over the other circle to cover it completely. Sprinkle with the remaining almonds and bake for 2–2½ hours, then turn off the oven and leave the meringues inside, with the door ajar, to cool for 30 minutes.

4 About 30 minutes before serving, remove the ice cream from the freezer to soften. Put the meringue circle on a serving plate. Slice the bananas and scatter evenly over the base. Spoon the ice cream mixture over the bananas and put the meringue ring on top, pressing down gently. Decorate with chocolate shavings and a dusting of icing sugar, then serve immediately.

★ COOK'S TIP
Marshmallow Ice Cream
Bring 450ml (¾ pint) full-fat milk to scalding point in a small pan and add 1 tsp vanilla extract. Put 6 egg yolks into a bowl and pour the hot milk over them, whisking. Pour back into the cleaned pan and cook over a low heat, stirring until the mixture coats the back of a spoon. Put 200g (7oz) small white marshmallows in a bowl, strain the warm custard over them and stir until they have almost melted. Cool quickly, then cover and chill for 30 minutes. Fold 300ml (½ pint) lightly whipped double cream into the custard. Pour into a freezerproof container and freeze for 3–4 hours until just firm. (Alternatively, if you have an ice-cream maker, churn the custard until just firm.) Stir in 125g (4oz) chopped chocolate and freeze.

Tropical Fruit Cake

....

Preparation Time 40 minutes • **Cooking Time** 1 hour 20 minutes, plus cooling • **Cuts into 8 slices** • **Per Slice** 857 calories, 60g fat (of which 32g saturates), 74g carbohydrate, 0.3g salt • **For the Confident Cook**

125g (4oz) unsalted butter, softened
200g (7oz) caster sugar
grated zest of 1 orange and
    3 tbsp juice
2 large eggs, lightly beaten
a pinch of salt
125g (4oz) semolina
125g (4oz) desiccated coconut
200g (7oz) ground almonds
1 tsp baking powder
300ml (½ pint) double cream
icing sugar and vanilla extract
    to taste
1 mango, 1 papaya or pineapple,
    1 star fruit and 1 banana, peeled
    and sliced
6 lychees, peeled and stones
    removed
50g (2oz) coconut slices (see Cook's
    Tip)

FOR THE CITRUS SYRUP
pared zest of 1 orange and juice of
    2 oranges
pared zest of 1 lemon and juice of
    3 lemons
125g (4oz) caster sugar

1 Preheat the oven to 170°C (150°C fan oven) mark 3. Grease a 23cm (9in) springform cake tin and baseline with baking parchment.

2 To make the cake, whisk the butter and 125g (4oz) caster sugar together in a food processor (or use a hand-held electric whisk) until pale and fluffy. Beat the orange zest, eggs and salt together, then beat into the butter mixture, a spoonful at a time. Using a large metal spoon, fold in the semolina, desiccated coconut, ground almonds, baking powder and orange juice. Spoon the mixture into the prepared tin and level the surface.

3 Bake for 45–50 minutes until a skewer inserted into the centre comes out clean. Leave to cool in the tin for 15 minutes, then turn out on to a wire rack to cool completely.

4 Meanwhile, make the citrus syrup. Put the orange and lemon zests and juice, caster sugar and 450ml (¾ pint) water into a pan. Bring to the boil and bubble for 15–20 minutes until syrupy. Set aside to cool.

5 Cut about 1cm (½ in) from the centre of the cake, crumble and keep the crumbs to one side. Prick the cake with a fine skewer – without piercing right through, or the syrup will run through – and

spoon the syrup over it. Set aside 3 tbsp of the syrup.

6 Whisk the cream until it stands in soft peaks, then add the icing sugar and vanilla extract to taste. Carefully fold in the reserved cake crumbs, one-third of the prepared fruit and the reserved syrup. Stir gently to combine, taking care not to mash the fruit. Spoon on to the cake. Decorate with the remaining fruit and coconut slices.

7 For the topping, put the remaining 75g (3oz) caster sugar into a pan and add 50ml (2fl oz) water. Bring to the boil and bubble until the caramel turns a light brown. Carefully add 2 tbsp cold water. Drizzle over the cake while still warm and serve immediately.

★ COOK'S TIP
For fresh coconut slices, use a vegetable peeler to pare off thin slices, sprinkle with a little caster sugar and grill until lightly browned.

★ GET AHEAD
To prepare ahead *Complete the recipe to the end of step 3. Wrap the tin well in clingfilm and greaseproof paper and store in a cool place. It will keep for two to three days.*
To use *Complete the recipe.*

Chocolate Ginger Refrigerator Cake

Preparation Time 15 minutes • **Cooking Time** 10 minutes, plus chilling • **Makes 36 Squares** • **Per Square** 152 calories, 9g fat (of which 5g saturates), 17g carbohydrate, 0.2g salt • **Easy**

a little oil to grease
350g (12oz) plain chocolate, chopped
150g (5oz) unsalted butter, plus extra for greasing
75g (3oz) golden syrup
300g (11oz) crunchy ginger biscuits, roughly crushed
75g (3oz) flaked almonds
75g (3oz) dried cranberries
50g (2oz) white chocolate, roughly chopped

1 Lightly oil a deep 23cm (9in) square tin and line the base and sides with greaseproof paper.

2 Put the plain chocolate, butter and syrup into a heatproof bowl set over a pan of gently simmering water, making sure the base of the bowl doesn't touch the water. Leave for 5–10 minutes, without stirring, until melted, then stir everything to combine. Set aside to cool slightly.

3 Put the ginger biscuits into a large bowl with the almonds and cranberries. Pour the chocolate mixture into the bowl and stir well. Spoon into the prepared tin and level the surface.

4 Melt the white chocolate in a small heatproof bowl set over a pan of gently simmering water, making sure the base of the bowl doesn't touch the water, then drizzle over the top of the chocolate and biscuit mixture. Use a skewer to swirl the chocolate and create a marbled effect. Cover the tin with clingfilm, making sure it doesn't touch the chocolate. Chill for at least 4 hours or overnight.

5 Cut into squares to serve.

★ TO STORE
Cover and store in the fridge. It will keep for up to three weeks.

Iced Raspberry and Eggnog Trifle Cake

Preparation Time 35 minutes, plus cooling and freezing • **Cooking Time** 5 minutes • **Cuts into 12 slices** •
Per Slice 428 calories, 31g fat (of which 17g saturates), 34g carbohydrate, 0.3g salt • **Easy**

1½ tsp powdered gelatine
2 tbsp cornflour
150ml (¼ pint) milk
60g (2½oz) caster sugar
200ml (7fl oz) advocaat, plus
    4 tbsp extra
250g (9oz) Italian cantuccini
    biscuits, roughly crushed
600ml (1 pint) double cream
2 large egg whites
300g (11oz) frozen raspberries,
    thawed and lightly mashed, plus
    extra whole raspberries to
    decorate
1 tbsp icing sugar
fresh bay leaf sprig to decorate

1 Sprinkle the gelatine over 2 tbsp water in a small bowl and leave to stand for 5 minutes. Meanwhile, mix the cornflour with 5 tbsp milk in a pan. Stir in the remaining milk and the caster sugar. Bring to the boil and heat gently, stirring until the mixture has thickened. Stir in the soaked gelatine until it dissolves. Turn into a large bowl, stir in the 200ml (7fl oz) advocaat and leave to cool completely.

2 Line the base of a 20.5cm (8in) springform tin with baking parchment. Scatter the crushed biscuits evenly over the base, then drizzle with the 4 tbsp advocaat.

3 Whip half the cream until slightly thickened and fold into the Advocaat mixture. Put the egg whites into a clean, grease-free bowl and whisk until soft peaks form, then fold into the cream with a large metal spoon. Pour one-third of the mixture over the biscuit base and tap the tin on the surface so that the custard fills the gaps between the biscuits. Spoon half the mashed raspberries in a layer over the custard, making sure some of the fruit sits against the side of the tin (so that the raspberries show when the tin is removed). Add half the remaining custard, another layer of raspberries and the rest of the custard. Cover and freeze overnight.

4 Run a warm knife around the edges of the trifle cake to release it from the tin. Lift it out of the tin and peel away the paper. Return to the tin. Whip the remaining cream with the icing sugar and spread over the top. Freeze until firm.

5 Run a warm knife around the edges of the trifle to loosen. Carefully remove from the tin and put on to a flat serving plate. Transfer the trifle cake to the fridge for 3–4 hours before serving, then decorate with the whole raspberries and the bay leaf sprig to serve.

Italian Ice Cream Cake

Preparation Time 30 minutes, plus freezing and softening • **Cuts into 10 slices** • **Per Slice** 522 calories, 33g fat (of which 15g saturates), 46g carbohydrate, 0.2g salt • **Easy**

400g (14oz) fresh cherries, pitted and quartered
4 tbsp Amaretto liqueur
10 tbsp crème de cacao liqueur
200g (7oz) Savoiardi biscuits or sponge fingers
5 medium egg yolks
150g (5oz) golden caster sugar
450ml (¾ pint) double cream, lightly whipped
1 tbsp vanilla extract
75g (3oz) pistachio nuts or hazelnuts, roughly chopped
75g (3oz) plain chocolate (at least 70% cocoa solids), roughly chopped

2–3 tbsp cocoa powder
2–3 tbsp golden icing sugar

1 Put the cherries and Amaretto into a bowl, stir, cover with clingfilm and put to one side. Pour the crème de cacao into a shallow dish. Quickly dip a sponge finger into the liqueur on one side only, then cut in half lengthways to separate the sugary side from the base. Repeat with each biscuit.

2 Double-line a deep 24 x 4cm (9½ x 1½ in) round tin with clingfilm. Arrange the sugar-coated sponge finger halves, sugar side down, on the base of the tin. Drizzle with any remaining crème de cacao.

3 Put the egg yolks and caster sugar into a bowl and whisk until pale, light and fluffy. Fold in the cream, vanilla extract, nuts, chocolate and cherries with Amaretto. Spoon on top of the sponge fingers in the tin and cover with the remaining sponge finger halves, cut-side down. Cover with clingfilm and freeze for at least 5 hours.

4 Upturn the cake on to a serving plate and remove the clingfilm. Sift cocoa powder and icing sugar over the cake and cut into wedges. Before serving, leave at room temperature for 20 minutes if the weather is warm, 40 minutes at cool room temperature, or 1 hour in the fridge, to allow the cherries to thaw and the ice cream to become mousse-like.

★ COOK'S TIP
For a decorative top, use the tin to cut a template circle of greaseproof paper, then fold to make eight triangles. Cut these out. Put four on the cake and dust the uncovered cake with cocoa powder. Remove the triangles. Cover the cocoa with four triangles and dust the uncovered cake with icing sugar.

Banana and Chocolate Ice Cream Pie

★

Preparation Time 15 minutes, plus freezing • **Cuts into 8 slices** • **Per Slice** 406 calories, 26g fat (of which 15g saturates), 42g carbohydrate, 0.6g salt • **Easy**

500ml tub chocolate ice cream
**75g (3oz) butter, plus extra to
  grease**
**200g (7oz) plain chocolate digestive
  biscuits, crushed (see page 155)**
2 large bananas, sliced
juice of ½ lemon
**1 king-size Mars Bar, cut into thin
  slivers and chilled**

1 Take the ice cream out of the freezer to let it soften. Grease a 20.5cm (8in) loose-based fluted flan tin and baseline with greaseproof paper. Put the butter into a small pan and melt over a medium heat.

2 Put the biscuits into a bowl, add the melted butter and mix until well combined. Tip the crumb mixture into the prepared tin and press evenly on to the base, using the back of a spoon to level the surface.

3 Toss the bananas in the lemon juice and scatter over the base. Upturn the ice cream tub on to the bananas and use a palette knife to spread the ice cream evenly, covering the fruit. Scatter the Mars Bar slices over the ice cream and freeze for at least 1 hour. Slice to serve.

Refrigerator Cake

Preparation Time 10 minutes, plus chilling • **Cooking Time** 4 minutes • **Cuts into 12 slices** • **Per Slice** 411 calories, 24g fat (of which 14g saturates), 48g carbohydrate, 0.6g salt • **Easy**

175g (6oz) unsalted butter, cut into
   eight pieces, plus extra to grease
200g packet natural glacé cherries,
   halved
2 tbsp Kirsch
150g (5oz) dark chocolate with
   fruit, broken into pieces
200g (7oz) plain chocolate, broken
   into pieces
100g (3½oz) golden syrup
200g (7oz) digestive biscuits,
   roughly crushed (see page 155)

1 Grease a 20.5cm (8in) round tin and baseline with greaseproof paper. Put the cherries into a bowl, add the Kirsch and leave to soak.

2 Put all the chocolate, the butter and syrup into a large heatproof bowl. Microwave on medium for 2 minutes (based on a 900W oven), stir and cook for a further 2 minutes or until the chocolate has melted. Alternatively, put into a heatproof bowl set over a pan of simmering water, making sure the bottom of the bowl doesn't touch the water, and leave until melted.

3 Add half the soaked cherries and all the biscuits to the chocolate, then stir together. Spoon into the prepared tin and level the surface.

4 Arrange the remaining cherries around the edge of the cake and chill for at least 15 minutes.

5 Cut into wedges to serve.

★ TO STORE
Cover and store in the fridge. It will keep for up to two weeks.

Italian Ricotta Cake

Preparation Time 20 minutes, plus chilling • **Cuts into 10 slices** • **Per Slice** 502 calories, 37g fat (of which 17g saturates), 37g carbohydrate, 0.5g salt • **Easy**

350g (12oz) good-quality chocolate
   sponge cake
300ml (½ pint) double cream
50g (2oz) icing sugar, plus extra
   to dust
4 tbsp Kirsch or cherry brandy
250g (9oz) ricotta cheese
100g (3½oz) plain chocolate,
   chopped
100g (3½oz) natural glacé cherries,
   halved
100g (3½oz) pistachio nuts,
   chopped
a little cocoa powder, sifted, to dust

1 Use a little water to dampen a 1.8 litre (3¼ pint) freezerproof mixing bowl and line with clingfilm. Thinly slice the chocolate cake and use about two-thirds to line the base and sides of the bowl, leaving no gaps.

2 Whip the cream, icing sugar and liqueur until the mixture just holds its shape. Lightly beat in the ricotta cheese, then stir in the plain chocolate, cherries and nuts. Spoon the mixture into the bowl and smooth the surface.

3 Top with the remaining sponge, then fold over any excess cake around the sides of the bowl to cover the cream. Cover with clingfilm and chill for at least 4 hours or overnight.

4 Take off the clingfilm and turn the cake out on to a flat plate. Dust generously with cocoa, then with a thin layer of icing sugar. Cut into wedges and serve immediately.

★ GET AHEAD
To prepare ahead *Complete the recipe to the end of step 3, then freeze in the bowl for up to a month. The day before serving, transfer the bowl to the fridge.*
To use *Complete the recipe.*

Celebration Cakes ★

Birthday Parcel Cake

★

Preparation Time 1 hour • **Cooking Time** 25–30 minutes, plus cooling and drying • **Cuts into 10 slices** •
Per Slice 586 calories, 18g fat (of which 9g saturates), 105g carbohydrate, 0.5g salt • **A Little Effort**

butter to grease
1 x 4-egg quantity of Victoria
   sponge mixture (see page 278)
1 x quantity of buttercream icing
   (see page 282)

FOR THE ICING
450g (1lb) white ready-to-roll icing
   (sugar paste)
200g (7oz) ready-made marzipan or
   ready-to-roll icing (sugar paste)
red and green food colourings
icing sugar to dust
1 medium egg white, lightly beaten

1 Grease two 18cm (7in) square cake tins and line with greaseproof paper. Make and bake the sponge mixture according to the instructions on page 278. Leave to cool in the tins for 5 minutes, then turn out on to a wire rack, remove the lining paper and leave to cool completely.

2 Sandwich the cold cakes together with all but 2 tbsp buttercream. Put the cake on a plate or cake board and spread the reserved buttercream smoothly over the top and sides. Set aside.

3 Knead the 450g (1lb) icing until pliable. Put a small amount aside for the gift tag and thread, then roll out the remainder to a 30.5cm (12in) square. Place over the cake and trim small triangles out of the corners to avoid excess icing. Smooth over the joins.

4 For the decoration, knead the marzipan or icing until pliable. Divide into two pieces weighing 125g (4oz) and 75g (3oz). Knead a few drops of red food colouring into the larger piece until evenly coloured; knead the green colouring into the smaller piece.

5 Lightly dust the worksurface with icing sugar. Roll out the green marzipan or icing and cut into two strips, each measuring 30.5 x 2.5cm (12 x 1in). Then roll out the red marzipan or icing and cut into two

strips measuring 12.5 x 2cm (5 x ¾in); one strip measuring 7.5 x 2cm (3 x ¾in); and two strips measuring 5 x 2cm (2 x ¾in). Set aside.

6 Brush one side of the green strips with a little of the beaten egg white, then place them, moistened-side down, on top of the cake (in an off-centre cross) to look like ribbon on a parcel. Mark the edges of the ribbon with a fork.

7 Loop the two 12.5cm (5in) red strips to look like a bow and fix on top of the cake with egg white. Cut the 7.5cm (3in) and one of the 5cm (2in) strips in a V-shape to form the ends of the ribbon. Fix in place with egg white.

8 Use the remaining 5cm (2in) red strip to form the centre of the bow. If you like, use the reserved icing to make a tag and thread, then fix on the cake. Leave overnight to dry out and set.

★ COOK'S TIP
If you are particularly artistic, finish off the cake by drawing a design on the icing to make it look like wrapping paper. The simplest way to do this is to use edible food colouring pens. These are available from specialist cake decorating shops and look just like felt-tips. You can also use them to write a message on the tag.

Large Marbled Birthday Cake

Preparation Time 40 minutes • **Cooking Time** 40–45 minutes, plus cooling • **Cuts into 32 slices** • **Per Slice** 534 calories, 26g fat (of which 17g saturates), 76g carbohydrate, 0.6g salt • **Easy**

350g (12oz) unsalted butter, very
  soft, plus extra to grease
350g (12oz) caster sugar
450g (1lb) self-raising flour, sifted
3 tsp baking powder
6 medium eggs
6 tbsp milk
2 tsp vanilla extract
pink food colouring (or any other
  colour you like)
4 tbsp cocoa powder blended with a
  little hot water and cooled

FOR THE DECORATION
2 x 325g tubs ready-made vanilla
  buttercream icing

pink or red food colouring
writing icing
pink and white sugar flowers
butterfly decorations (optional)

1 Preheat the oven to 180°C (160°C fan oven) mark 4. Grease a 29 x 36cm (11½ x 14½ in) roasting tin, or the nearest equivalent, and line with greaseproof paper.

2 Put the butter, sugar, flour, baking powder, eggs, milk and vanilla extract into a bowl and beat with a hand-held electric whisk for

2 minutes or until smooth. Put about one-third of the cake mixture into a bowl, add a few drops of the food colouring and beat in. Put another third of the mixture into another bowl and add the cocoa powder and a little more milk if necessary. Mix well.

3 Put a dollop of plain cake mixture into the cake tin, then add a spoonful of chocolate mixture, followed by a spoonful of coloured mixture. Keep doing this until all the cake mixtures are in the tin.

4 Briefly swirl a skewer or knife through the mixture to give a marbled effect. Level the surface of the mixture and bake for 40–45 minutes or until the cake has shrunk away from the sides of the tin and springs back when pressed in the centre with your fingertips. Leave to cool in the tin.

5 Turn out the cake on to a worksurface and trim the edges to neaten. Place on a cake board with the smooth side uppermost. Tip the buttercream into a large bowl and mix in a few drops of food colouring until it is pale pink. Spread over the top and sides of the cake. Write your birthday message in the centre with the writing icing, then decorate with the sugar flowers. Fix in the butterflies, if using (remove these from the cut slice of cake before serving).

Celebration Chocolate Cake

Preparation Time 40 minutes • **Cooking Time** 1–1¼ hours, plus cooling • **Cuts into 16 slices** • **Per Slice** 161 calories, 9g fat (of which 3g saturates), 17g carbohydrate, 0.1g salt • **Gluten Free** • **Easy**

butter or sunflower oil to grease
200g (7oz) plain chocolate (at least 50% cocoa solids), broken into pieces
5 large eggs
125g (4oz) golden caster sugar
100g (3½oz) ground almonds
1 tbsp coffee liqueur, such as Tia Maria
fresh raspberries to decorate
icing sugar to dust

1 Grease a 12.5cm (5in) deep, round cake tin and line with greaseproof paper, making sure the paper comes 5–7.5cm (2–3in) above the tin.

2 Melt the chocolate in a heatproof bowl set over a pan of gently simmering water, making sure the base of the bowl doesn't touch the water. Remove the bowl from the pan and leave to cool slightly. Meanwhile, preheat the oven to 170°C (150°C fan oven) mark 3.

3 Separate all but one of the egg eggs, putting the whites to one side. Put the yolks, the whole egg and the sugar into the bowl of a freestanding mixer, or use a hand-held electric whisk. Whisk at high speed for 5 minutes or until the mixture is pale and leaves a ribbon trail when the whisk is lifted.

4 Set the mixer to a very low speed, add the chocolate and then the ground almonds and mix until evenly combined. Put to one side.

5 Put the egg whites into a clean, grease-free bowl and whisk until soft peaks form. Beat one quarter of the egg whites into the chocolate mixture to loosen, then fold in the rest.

6 Pour the mixture into the prepared tin. Bake for 1–1¼ hours until a skewer inserted into the centre of the cake for 30 seconds comes out hot. Make several holes in the cake with the skewer, then pour the liqueur over them. Leave to cool in the tin for 30 minutes, then turn out on to a wire rack to cool completely.

7 Transfer the cake to a plate, spoon raspberries on top and tie a ribbon around the cake. Dust with icing sugar.

Chocolate Mousse Roulade

★

Preparation Time 45 minutes, plus chilling • **Cooking Time** 40 minutes, plus cooling and chilling • **Cuts into 8 slices** •
Per Slice 510 calories, 30g fat (of which 16g saturates), 53g carbohydrate, 0.4g salt • **Gluten Free** • **For the Confident Cook**

6 large eggs, separated
150g (5oz) caster sugar, plus extra
  to sprinkle
50g (2oz) cocoa powder
frosted fruit and leaves to decorate

FOR THE FILLING
225g (8oz) milk chocolate, roughly
  chopped
2 large eggs, separated
125g (4oz) fresh or frozen
  cranberries, halved
50g (2oz) granulated sugar
grated zest and juice of ½ medium
  orange
200ml (7fl oz) double cream

1 Preheat the oven to 180°C (160°C fan oven) mark 4. Line a 30.5 x 20.5cm (12 x 8in) Swiss roll tin with baking parchment – it needs to stick up around the edges of the tin by 5cm (2in) to allow the cake to rise.

2 First, make the filling. Put the chocolate into a large heatproof bowl and add 50ml (2fl oz) water. Place over a pan of gently simmering water, making sure the base of the bowl doesn't touch the water. Leave to melt for 15–20 minutes. Remove the bowl from the pan and, without stirring, add the egg yolks, then stir until smooth. Put the egg whites into a clean, grease-free bowl and whisk until soft peaks form, then fold into the chocolate. Cover and chill for at least 2 hours.

3 Put the cranberries into a pan with the sugar, orange zest and juice and 100ml (3½ fl oz) water. Bring to a gentle simmer, then leave to barely simmer for 30 minutes, stirring occasionally until the cranberries are soft; there should be no liquid left in the pan. Remove from the heat and leave to cool.

4 To make the cake, put the egg yolks into a bowl and whisk with a hand-held electric whisk for 1–2 minutes until pale. Add the sugar and whisk until the mixture has the consistency of thick cream. Sift the cocoa powder over the mixture and fold in with a large metal spoon.

Put the egg whites into a clean, grease-free bowl and whisk until soft peaks form. Stir a spoonful of the egg whites into the chocolate mixture to loosen it, then fold in the remainder. Pour the mixture into the prepared tin.

5 Bake for about 25 minutes or until well risen and spongy. Leave to cool completely in the tin (it will sink dramatically).

6 Put a sheet of baking parchment on the worksurface and sprinkle with caster sugar. Turn the cold cake out on to the sugar and peel off the parchment. Spoon the chocolate filling on top and spread to within 2.5cm (1in) of the edge. Sprinkle on the glazed cranberries. Lightly whip the cream, spoon over the cranberries, then spread lightly to cover.

7 Holding a short edge of the baking parchment, gently lift and roll, pushing the edge down so it starts to curl. Keep lifting and rolling as the cake comes away from the paper. Don't worry if it cracks. Remove the paper. Chill for up to 8 hours. Decorate with frosted fruit and leaves to serve.

White Chocolate Mousse Cake

Preparation Time 30 minutes, plus freezing and thawing • **Cooking Time** 20–30 minutes • **Cuts into 10 slices** •
Per Slice 416 calories, 32g fat (of which 19g saturates), 27g carbohydrate, 0.2g salt • **Easy**

vegetable oil to grease
450g (1lb) white chocolate
285ml (9½fl oz) double cream
finely grated zest of 1 large orange
2 tsp orange liqueur, such as Grand
  Marnier
300g (11oz) Greek yogurt

1 Lightly oil a shallow 20.5cm (8in) round cake tin and line with baking parchment.

2 Break the chocolate into pieces, put into a large heatproof bowl with half the cream and melt over a pan of gently simmering water, making sure the base of the bowl doesn't touch the water. Leave for 20–30 minutes until the chocolate has melted. Don't stir – just leave it to melt.

3 Meanwhile, put the orange zest and liqueur into a small bowl. Set aside to soak. Whip the remaining cream until it just holds its shape.

4 Remove the bowl of melted chocolate from the pan and beat in the yogurt. Fold in the cream with the zest and liqueur mixture.

5 Spoon the mixture into the prepared tin, cover with clingfilm and freeze overnight. One hour before serving, transfer from the freezer to the fridge. Unwrap and put on a serving plate. Decorate, if you like (see Cook's Tip).

★ COOK'S TIP
If you like, you can decorate the mousse cake with a few halved strawberries, some blueberries and a handful of unsprayed rose petals, then dust with icing sugar.

★ FREEZING TIP
To freeze *Freeze as in step 5. It will keep, frozen, for up to one month.*
To use *Thaw as described in step 5.*

Kugelhopf

Preparation Time 45 minutes, plus soaking, chilling and rising • **Cooking Time** 50–55 minutes, plus cooling •
Cuts into 12 slices • **Per Slice** 382 calories, 22g fat (of which 11g saturates), 39g carbohydrate, 0.4g salt • **A Little Effort**

200g (7oz) raisins, black seedless
 if possible
3 tbsp light rum
2 tsp fast-action dried yeast
300g (11oz) plain white flour, plus
 extra to dust
4 large eggs
100ml (3½fl oz) milk
225g (8oz) unsalted butter,
 softened, plus extra to grease
75g (3oz) caster sugar
a pinch of salt
zest of 1 lemon
100g (3½oz) split blanched
 almonds, lightly toasted
icing sugar to dust
whole glacé fruits and nuts to
 decorate

1 Combine the raisins and rum, cover and soak overnight. Put the yeast and flour into a food mixer. Lightly whisk the eggs and milk and then, with the machine running on a slow speed, pour in the egg mixture and mix for 10 minutes or until the dough is very smooth, shiny and elastic. In another bowl, beat the butter, caster sugar, salt and lemon zest and then, with the mixer running, add to the dough, a spoonful at a time, until evenly incorporated. Turn the mixture into a large, lightly floured bowl. Cover with clingfilm and chill overnight.

2 Generously butter a 2 litre (3½ pint) kugelhopf ring mould. Press one-third of the almonds on to the sides of the mould. Chill. Roughly chop the remaining almonds. Mix by hand into the dough with the raisins and rum, then put into the mould, cover and leave for 3 hours in a warm place until it feels spongy and has risen to within 2cm (¾in) of the top of the mould.

3 Preheat the oven to 200°C (180°C fan oven) mark 6. Bake the kugelhopf on a shelf below the centre of the oven for 10 minutes. Cover with greaseproof paper, reduce the oven temperature to 190°C (170°C fan oven) mark 5 and bake for 40–45 minutes until the kugelhopf sounds hollow when you tap the mould. Cool in the tin for 15 minutes. Turn out on to a wire rack to cool completely. Decorate and serve dusted with icing sugar.

★ COOK'S TIPS
● *This cake is made with yeast, so it's best eaten within two days or it will go stale. If you have any left over, wrap and freeze in slices – it's tasty toasted or used for making bread and butter pudding.*
● *If you don't have a mixer with a beater attachment, use a food processor with a flat plastic blade.*

Cranberry Christmas Cake

★

Preparation Time 25 minutes, plus soaking and drying • **Cooking Time** 3–3½ hours, plus cooling • **Cuts into 24 slices** •
Per Slice 450 calories, 14g fat (of which 5g saturates), 77g carbohydrate, 0.2g salt • **A Little Effort**

250g (9oz) plump raisins
250g (9oz) plump sultanas
100g (3½oz) dried cranberries or
   blueberries
200g (7oz) natural glacé cherries,
   halved
200ml (7fl oz) vanilla vodka
150g (5oz) whole roasted almonds
200g (7oz) unsalted butter,
   softened, plus extra to grease
200g (7oz) unrefined dark
   muscovado sugar
4 medium eggs, beaten
100g (3½oz) plain flour, plus extra
   if needed

**FOR THE GLAZE, MARZIPAN
   AND ICING**
3 tbsp apricot jam
400g pack white marzipan
3 medium egg whites
2 tbsp lemon juice
2 tsp glycerine
675g (1lb 7oz) icing sugar, sifted,
   plus extra to dust

FOR THE DECORATION
fresh or frozen cranberries
sprigs of fresh bay leaves
icing sugar to dust

1 Put the dried fruit and cherries into a bowl. Add the vodka and stir, then cover and soak for 2–3 hours or overnight. Whiz the almonds in a food processor until coarsely chopped. Remove 75g (3oz) and set aside. Whiz the remainder until ground, then transfer to a bowl, cover and set aside.

2 Preheat the oven to 150°C (130°C fan oven) mark 2. Grease a 20.5cm (8in) round cake tin and line the base and sides with greaseproof paper.

3 Put the butter and sugar into a large mixing bowl, then beat with a hand-held electric whisk for 2–3 minutes until light and creamy. Gradually whisk in the beaten eggs, adding a little of the flour if the mixture starts to curdle. Stir in the ground and chopped almonds, along with any remaining flour. Add the soaked fruit and any unabsorbed vodka and mix well. Spoon the mixture into the prepared tin and level the surface.

4 Bake for 3–3½ hours until a skewer inserted into the centre comes out clean. Leave to cool in the tin, then remove, keeping it in the greaseproof paper. Wrap in a double thickness of foil until ready to decorate.

5 To glaze the cake, put the apricot jam into a small pan with 2 tsp cold water. Heat gently, then sieve into a bowl. Use a knife to level off the top of the cake, then turn it over and put on a cake board. Brush sieved jam over the top and sides.

6 To cover the cake with marzipan, roll out the marzipan on a surface lightly dusted with icing sugar, to 14cm (5½in) larger than the diameter of the cake. Lift it on to the

cake with the help of the rolling pin. Ease to fit and trim the edges to neaten. Leave to dry for 24 hours.

7 To ice the cake, put the egg whites into a large bowl and whisk with a balloon whisk until slightly frothy. There should be a layer of bubbles lying just across the surface of the egg whites. Add the lemon juice, glycerine and 2 tbsp icing sugar, then whisk until smooth. Whisk in the rest of the icing sugar, a little at a time, until the mixture is smooth, thick and forms soft peaks. Using a palette knife, smooth the icing over the top and sides of the cake. Use the tip of the knife to make peaks all over the cake. Leave to dry for at least 48 hours.

8 To decorate the cake, if using frozen cranberries to decorate, thaw and leave on a double sheet of kitchen paper for 20 minutes to soak up excess moisture. Snip off bay leaves in clusters of two or three, wash and dry thoroughly, then arrange on top of the cake with the cranberries. Dust lightly with icing sugar.

★ GET AHEAD
Unlike traditional Christmas cake recipes, this one doesn't need maturing, but it still keeps brilliantly.
To prepare ahead *Complete the recipe to the end of step 4 up to one month before Christmas.*
To use *Complete the recipe.*

Snowy Yule Log

Preparation Time 25 minutes • **Cooking Time** 15 minutes, plus cooling • **Cuts into 8 slices** • **Per Slice** 412 calories, 31g fat (of which 12g saturates), 33g carbohydrate, 0.1g salt • **Easy**

a little butter to grease
75g (3oz) plain flour
1 tsp baking powder
¼ tsp salt
4 medium eggs
150g (5oz) caster sugar
1 tsp vanilla extract
75g (3oz) ground almonds
284ml carton double cream
2 tbsp golden icing sugar, sifted, plus extra to dust
50g (2oz) flaked almonds, toasted

1 Preheat the oven to 180°C (160°C fan oven) mark 4. Grease a 33 x 23cm (13 x 9in) Swiss roll tin and line with greaseproof paper. Sift the flour, baking powder and salt together.

2 Using a hand-held electric whisk, beat the eggs, caster sugar and vanilla in a bowl for 5–10 minutes until pale and fluffy. The mixture is ready when it leaves a ribbon-like trail as you lift the beaters.

3 Using a large metal spoon, carefully fold in the ground almonds and the flour mixture, taking care not to beat too much air out of the mixture. Pour into the prepared tin and spread the mixture in a thin layer right to the edges.

4 Bake for 12–15 minutes until the edges begin to pull away from the sides of the tin and the cake springs back when you press it gently with a finger. Leave to cool in the tin.

5 Lightly whip the cream and icing sugar in a bowl until the mixture forms soft peaks. Put a sheet of greaseproof paper, larger than the cake, on the worksurface and dust heavily with icing sugar. Flip the cake on to the paper. Remove the tin and carefully peel away the attached paper.

6 Spread the cream over the cake and sprinkle with the flaked almonds. Using the greaseproof paper to help, roll up lengthways. Don't worry if cracks appear – they'll add to the log effect.

7 Carefully transfer to a serving plate. Dust with icing sugar and serve in slices.

★ TRY SOMETHING DIFFERENT
To decorate the Yule Log, melt 50g (2oz) dark chocolate in a heatproof bowl set over a pan of gently simmering water, making sure the base of the bowl doesn't touch the water. Wash 4 holly leaves and dry, then paint chocolate thickly on the shiny side of the leaves. Put on to a baking sheet lined with greaseproof paper and chill until the chocolate has set.
For the white holly leaves, repeat the process with 25g (1oz) good-quality white chocolate.
Fill a disposable piping bag with the remaining dark chocolate and cut off the tip. Write 'Noel' on a piece of greaseproof, then chill to set. Carefully peel away the holly leaves from the chocolate, and the greaseproof paper from the word 'Noel', and lay them on top of the log.

★ GET AHEAD
To prepare ahead *Complete the recipe to the end of step 6. Put the log on a freezeable serving dish and wrap in clingfilm. Freeze for up to one month.*
To use *Thaw overnight in the fridge and complete the recipe.*

Gluten-free Chocolate Cake

★

Preparation Time 30 minutes • **Cooking Time** 45 minutes–1 hour, plus cooling • **Cuts into 10 slices** • **Per Slice** 476 calories, 28g fat (of which 16g saturates), 60g carbohydrate, 0.3g salt • **Gluten Free** • **Easy**

125g (4oz) unsalted butter, softened, plus extra to grease
200g (7oz) light muscovado sugar
2 large eggs, lightly beaten
125g (4oz) gluten-free plain chocolate, broken into pieces, melted (see page 283) and left to cool slightly
100g (3½oz) natural yogurt
a few drops of vanilla extract
200g (7oz) brown rice flour
½ tsp wheat-free baking powder
1 tsp bicarbonate of soda

FOR THE ICING
150g (5oz) gluten-free plain chocolate, broken into pieces
150ml (¼ pint) double cream
large milk and plain or white chocolate buttons (gluten-free) to decorate

1 Preheat the oven to 180°C (160°C fan oven) mark 4. Grease a deep 18cm (7in) square cake tin and line with greaseproof paper.

2 Cream the butter and sugar together until light and fluffy. Gradually beat in the eggs, then the melted chocolate, yogurt and vanilla extract. Sift the rice flour, baking powder and bicarbonate of soda together, then beat into the mixture a little at a time. Pour into the prepared tin and bake for 45 minutes–1 hour or until a skewer inserted in the centre comes out clean. Leave to cool in the tin for 10 minutes, then transfer to a wire rack to cool completely.

3 To make the icing, put the chocolate into a heatproof bowl. Heat the cream to just below boiling point. Pour on to the chocolate and leave for 5 minutes, then beat until the chocolate has melted and the mixture is smooth. Cool until thickened, then spread all over the cake with a palette knife. Decorate the top and sides with alternate milk and plain or white chocolate buttons to create a polka-dot effect.

 TO STORE
Store in an airtight container. It will keep for up to three days.

Egg-free Chocolate Cake

Preparation Time 30 minutes, plus cooling • **Cooking Time** 1–1¼ hours, plus cooling • **Cuts into 12 slices** •
Per Slice 515 calories, 31g fat (of which 15g saturates), 59g carbohydrate, 0.4g salt • **Easy**

150ml (¼ pint) sunflower oil, plus
    extra to grease
75g (3oz) creamed coconut
25g (1oz) plain chocolate, broken
    into pieces
50g (2oz) cocoa powder
350g (12oz) self-raising flour
1 tsp baking powder
a pinch of salt
175g (6oz) light muscovado sugar

FOR THE ICING
350g (12oz) plain chocolate, broken
    into small pieces
150ml (¼ pint) double cream
white and milk chocolate Maltesers
    to decorate

1 Preheat the oven to 180°C (160°C fan oven) mark 4. Grease a 1.7 litre (3 pint), 30.5 x 10cm (12 x 4in) loaf tin and line with greaseproof paper.

2 Put the coconut into a heatproof bowl, pour on 425ml (14½fl oz) boiling water and stir to dissolve. Set aside to cool for 30 minutes.

3 Melt the chocolate in a heatproof bowl set over a pan of gently simmering water, making sure the base of the bowl doesn't touch the water. Stir until smooth, then remove the bowl from the pan and leave to cool slightly.

4 Sift the cocoa, flour, baking powder and salt into a bowl. Stir in the sugar and make a well in the middle. Add the coconut mixture, melted chocolate and oil. Beat to make a smooth batter. Pour the cake batter into the prepared tin.

5 Bake for 1–1¼ hours or until risen and just firm to the touch (if necessary, cover with foil after about 40 minutes if it gets too brown on top). Leave in the tin for 10 minutes, then transfer to a wire rack to cool. When cold, trim to neaten the edges.

6 To make the icing, put the chocolate into a heatproof bowl. Heat the cream to just below boiling point. Pour on to the chocolate and stir until melted. Leave to cool, beating occasionally, until thick – pop into the fridge for 30 minutes to help thicken if necessary.

7 Cut the cold cake in half horizontally and sandwich the layers together with one-third of the icing. Spread the rest evenly over the top and sides of the cake. Decorate the top of the cake with alternate rows of milk and white Maltesers. Lay an edging of alternate milk and white Maltesers around the base of the cake to decorate.

Tarts

Tarte Tatin

Preparation Time 30 minutes, plus chilling • Cooking Time about 1 hour, plus cooling • Cuts into 6 slices •
Per Slice 727 calories, 39g fat (of which 24g saturates), 94g carbohydrate, 0.7g salt • **Easy**

Sweet Shortcrust Pastry (see page
    284), made with 225g (8oz) plain
    flour, ¼ tsp salt, 150g (5oz)
    unsalted butter, 50g (2oz) golden
    icing sugar, 1 medium egg and
    2–3 drops vanilla extract
flour to dust

FOR THE FILLING
200g (7oz) golden caster sugar
125g (4oz) chilled unsalted butter
1.4–1.6kg (3–3½lb) crisp dessert
    apples, peeled and cored
juice of ½ lemon

1 To make the filling, sprinkle
the caster sugar over the base of
a 20.5cm (8in) tarte tatin tin or
ovenproof frying pan. Cut the butter
into slivers and arrange on the
sugar. Halve the apples and pack
them tightly, cut side up, on top of
the butter.

2 Put the tin or pan on the hob
and cook over a medium heat for
30 minutes (making sure it doesn't
bubble over or catch on the bottom)
or until the butter and sugar turn a
dark golden brown (see Cook's Tip).

Sprinkle with the lemon juice,
then allow to cool for 15 minutes.
Meanwhile, preheat the oven to
220°C (200°C fan oven) mark 7.

3 Put the pastry on a large sheet of
baking parchment. Roll out the
pastry to make a round 2.5cm (1in)
larger than the tin or pan. Prick
several times with a fork. Lay the
pastry over the apples, tucking the
edges down the side of the tin.
Bake for 25–30 minutes until
golden brown. Leave in the tin for
10 minutes, then carefully upturn
on to a serving plate. Serve warm.

★ COOK'S TIP
*When caramelising the apples in step 2,
be patient. Allow the sauce to turn a
dark golden brown – any paler and it
will be too sickly. Don't let it burn,
though, as this will make the caramel
taste bitter.*

Easy Pear and Toffee Tarte Tatin

Preparation Time 15 minutes • **Cooking Time** 25–30 minutes, plus cooling • **Cuts into 6 slices** • **Per Slice** 294 calories, 12g fat (of which 2g saturates), 46g carbohydrate, 0.5g salt • **Easy**

4 small, rosy pears, quartered and
    cored – no need to pee them
8 tbsp dulce de leche toffee sauce
225g (8oz) ready-rolled puff pastry
flour to dust
cream or vanilla ice cream to serve

1 Preheat the oven to 200°C (180°C fan oven) mark 6. Put the pears and toffee sauce into a large non-stick frying pan. Cook over a medium heat for 5 minutes or until the pears are well coated and the sauce has turned a slightly darker shade of golden brown.

2 Tip the pears and sauce into a 20.5cm (8in) non-stick sandwich or tart tin. Arrange the pears, skin side down, in a circle and leave to cool for 10 minutes.

3 If necessary, roll out the puff pastry on a lightly floured surface until it is wide enough to cover the tin. Lay it over the pears and press down on to the edge of the tin. Trim off any excess pastry. Prick the pastry all over, then bake for 20–25 minutes until well risen and golden.

4 Leave to cool for 5 minutes. To turn out, hold a large serving plate or baking sheet over the tart, turn over and give a quick shake to loosen. Lift off the tin. Serve the tart immediately, cut into wedges, with cream or ice cream.

★ TRY SOMETHING DIFFERENT
Replace the pears with 3–4 bananas, thickly sliced on the diagonal. Cook the dulce de leche for 5 minutes in step 1, stir in the bananas to coat, then arrange in the tin in an overlapping circle. Complete the recipe.

Almond and White Chocolate Tart with Pineapple

★

Preparation Time 1 hour, plus chilling • Cooking Time 55 minutes, plus cooling and setting • Cuts into 8 slices •
Per Slice 648 calories, 36g fat (of which 17g saturates), 77g carbohydrate, 0.5g salt • Easy

Sweet Shortcrust Pastry (see page
    284), made with 175g (6oz) plain
    flour, 50g (2oz) icing sugar,
    75g (3oz) butter, grated zest of
    1 large orange and 1 large
    egg yolk
flour to dust

FOR THE FILLING
100g (3½oz) white chocolate,
    broken into pieces
125g (4oz) unsalted butter
125g (4oz) icing sugar
2 large eggs, beaten
125g (4oz) ground almonds
1 tbsp plain flour
a few drops of vanilla extract

FOR THE TOPPING
1 medium pineapple, peeled and
    thinly sliced
icing sugar to sprinkle
125g (4oz) apricot jam

1 Roll out the pastry thinly on a lightly floured worksurface and line a 23cm (9in), 2.5cm (1in) deep, loose-based fluted tart tin. Chill for 20 minutes.

2 Preheat the oven to 200°C (180°C fan oven) mark 6. Prick the pastry base all over with a fork, then bake blind (see page 284). Remove from the oven. Reduce the oven temperature to 180°C (160°C fan oven) mark 4.

3 To make the filling, melt the chocolate in a heatproof bowl set over a pan of gently simmering water, making sure the base of the bowl doesn't touch the water. Remove the bowl from the pan and cool slightly.

4 Put the butter into a large bowl and, using a hand-held electric whisk, beat until creamy, then beat in the icing sugar until fluffy. Gradually beat the eggs into the butter mixture, a little at a time. Stir in the ground almonds, flour, melted chocolate and vanilla extract. Fill the pastry case with the mixture and smooth the top.

5 Bake for 25–30 minutes until just set in the middle. The mixture will puff in the oven and firm up on cooling. Cool for 15 minutes, then transfer to a wire rack to cool completely.

6 For the topping, sprinkle the pineapple heavily with icing sugar and put under a hot grill until the pineapple is glazed to a light caramel colour. Leave to cool. Put the jam into a small pan and warm over a low heat until melted. Simmer for 1–2 minutes, then sieve and put back in the pan (if the jam is a little thick, add a splash of water).

7 Arrange the pineapple over the tart and brush with a thin layer of warm jam. Allow the jam to set before serving.

Plum Tarte Tatin

★

Preparation Time 30 minutes, plus chilling • **Cooking Time** 30 minutes, plus cooling • **Cuts into 6 slices** •
Per Slice 488 calories, 28g fat (of which 17g saturates), 59g carbohydrate, 0.5g salt • **Easy**

75g (3oz) unsalted butter
125g (4oz) caster sugar
700g (1½lb) plums, halved and
   stoned
350g pack all-butter dessert pastry
flour to dust
crème fraîche or cream to serve

1 Melt the butter and sugar in a heavy-based frying pan. Cook, stirring, for 2–3 minutes until the sugar begins to turn light brown. Immediately add the plums and cook for 5 minutes or until the juices begin to run and the plums start to soften. Increase the heat and bubble until the juices are very syrupy. Lift the plums out of the pan into a 23cm (9in) shallow ovenproof dish or cake tin, with some of them cut side up, and pour the juice over them. Leave to cool.

2 Roll out the pastry on a lightly floured worksurface into a circle slightly larger than the dish and about 5mm (¼in) thick. Lay the pastry over the plums, tuck the edges down into the dish and make a few slits in the pastry with a knife to allow steam to escape. Chill for 20 minutes.

3 Preheat the oven to 220°C (200°C fan oven) mark 7. Bake for 20 minutes or until the pastry is golden. Cool for 5 minutes before carefully inverting on to a plate. Serve with crème fraîche or cream.

 FREEZING TIP
To freeze Complete the recipe to the end of step 2, then cover, wrap and freeze.
To use Bake from frozen at 220°C (200°C fan oven) mark 7 for 40 minutes or until the pastry is golden. Complete the recipe.

Plum and Almond Tart

★

Preparation Time 30 minutes, plus chilling • **Cooking Time** 40 minutes, plus cooling and setting • **Cuts into 8 slices** •
Per Slice 535 calories, 35g fat (of which 16g saturates), 50g carbohydrate, 0.5g salt • **Easy**

150g (5oz) unsalted butter, chilled
and diced
175g (6oz) plain flour, plus extra to
dust
7 tbsp soured cream

FOR THE FILLING
50g (2oz) unsalted butter
50g (2oz) caster sugar, plus extra
to dust
2 medium eggs, lightly beaten
100g (3½oz) ground almonds
1 tbsp Kirsch or 3–4 drops almond
essence
900g (2lb) plums, stoned and
quartered
50g (2oz) blanched almonds to
decorate
175g (6oz) redcurrant jelly

1 To make the pastry, put the butter
and flour into a food processor and
whiz for 1–2 seconds. Add the
soured cream and process for a
further 1–2 seconds until the dough
just begins to come together.
(Alternatively, rub the butter into the
flour in a large bowl by hand or
using a pastry cutter, then mix in the
soured cream.) Turn out on to a
lightly floured worksurface and
knead lightly for about 30 seconds
or until the pastry just comes
together. Wrap in clingfilm and chill
for 30 minutes.

2 To make the filling, put the butter
into a bowl and beat until soft, then
add the sugar and beat until light

and fluffy. Beat in the eggs,
alternating with the ground
almonds. Add the Kirsch or almond
essence, cover and set aside.

3 Roll out the pastry on a lightly
floured worksurface to a 30.5cm
(12in) circle, then transfer to a
baking sheet and prick all over with
a fork. Spread the almond mixture
over the pastry, leaving a 3cm (1¼in)
border all round. Scatter the plums
over the filling and fold the edges of
the pastry up over the fruit. Dust
with caster sugar, then chill for
20 minutes.

4 Preheat the oven to 220°C
(200°C fan oven) mark 7 and put a
baking tray in the oven to heat for
10 minutes. Put the tart, on its
baking sheet, on top of the hot
baking tray. Cook for 35–40
minutes until deep golden brown.

5 Leave the tart to cool for
10 minutes, then slide it on to a
wire rack. Arrange the almonds
among the fruit. Heat the redcurrant
jelly gently in a pan, stirring until
smooth, then brush generously
over the tart. Leave to set.

Marzipan and Kumquat Tart

Preparation Time 1¼ hours, plus chilling • **Cooking Time** 1 hour • **Cuts into 12 slices** • **Per Slice** 412 calories, 24g fat (of which 13g saturates), 46g carbohydrate, 0.5g salt • **Easy**

200g (7oz) plain flour, plus extra
   to dust
125g (4oz) unsalted butter, chilled
100g (3½oz) icing sugar
2 large egg yolks
250g (9oz) kumquats
150g (5oz) unsalted butter, softened
300g (11oz) marzipan, chilled and
   grated
2 large eggs
50g (2oz) self-raising flour
25g (1oz) caster sugar
300ml (½ pint) double cream
4 tbsp brandy
1 tbsp icing sugar, plus extra to
   dust

1 Whiz the plain flour and butter in a blender until the mixture resembles breadcrumbs. Add the icing sugar, egg yolks and 1 tsp cold water. Whiz until the dough just comes together. Tip on to a clean worksurface, knead lightly with your hands to bring it together, then wrap and chill for at least 1 hour.

2 Put the kumquats into a pan, cover with water and bring to the boil. Reduce the heat and simmer for 10 minutes. Drain, reserving the liquid, and leave to cool.

3 Roll out the pastry on a lightly floured surface – then use it to line a 27cm (10½in) round, 2.5cm (1in) deep loose-based flan tin. Chill for 30 minutes. Preheat the oven to 200°C (180°C fan oven) mark 6.

4 Line the pastry case with greaseproof paper and baking beans and bake blind for 20 minutes (see page 284). Remove the beans and paper and return to oven for 4–5 minutes until just dry to the touch. Remove from the oven. Reduce the heat to 180°C (160°C fan oven) mark 4.

5 Beat the butter in a bowl until creamy. Add the marzipan, eggs and self-raising flour. Beat until smooth. Reserve 12 kumquats and chop the remainder, discarding the pips. Add to the creamed mixture and spread inside the case. Slice each reserved kumquat into four. Arrange the slices in a star shape on top of the filling. Bake for 30 minutes or until pale golden and the surface is just firm.

6 Heat the caster sugar in a small pan with 5 tbsp reserved cooking liquid until the sugar dissolves, then cook until syrupy. Brush the glaze over the tart. Whip the cream with the brandy and the 1 tbsp icing sugar until thick. If you want to dust the tart with icing sugar, cover the kumquat 'star' with foil, then dust the area outside with icing sugar. Remove the foil and serve with the brandy cream.

Pear, Cranberry and Frangipane Tart

 ★

Preparation Time 30 minutes, plus chilling • **Cooking Time** 1 hour, plus cooling • **Cuts into 8 slices** • **Per Slice** 466 calories, 28g fat (of which 13g saturates), 48g carbohydrate, 0.6g salt • **Easy**

150g (5oz) caster sugar
2 small ripe pears
150g (5oz) unsalted butter, softened, plus extra to grease
175g (6oz) Hobnob biscuits, finely crushed (see page 155)
100g (3½oz) ground almonds
2 tbsp plain flour
1 tsp cornflour
1 tsp baking powder
2 medium eggs, beaten
1 tsp vanilla extract
25g (1oz) dried cranberries
25g (1oz) flaked almonds
icing sugar to dust
crème fraîche to serve

1 Put 50g (2oz) caster sugar in a pan with 500ml (18fl oz) water and dissolve over a gentle heat. Peel, halve and core the pears. Add to the sugar syrup. Cover the pan with a lid and simmer gently for 5–8 minutes, turning once. Transfer the pears and liquid to a bowl and leave to cool.

2 Lightly grease a 20.5cm (8in) loose-bottomed cake tin and line with greaseproof paper. Melt 25g (1oz) butter and mix in the crushed Hobnobs. Press into the base of the tin and chill for about 1 hour.

3 Preheat the oven to 180°C (160°C fan oven) mark 4. Cream the remaining butter and sugar together in a freestanding mixer (or use a hand-held electric whisk) until light and fluffy. Add the ground almonds, flour, cornflour and baking powder

and mix to combine. Add the eggs and vanilla extract. Mix until smooth. Stir in the cranberries and flaked almonds. Spoon the mixture on top of the biscuit base. Smooth the surface.

4 Remove the pears from the syrup and place on kitchen paper to soak up excess liquid. Slice one of the pear halves horizontally into 5mm (¼in) slices. Gently push down on the pear to fan out the slices slightly Place on top of the frangipane filling. Repeat with the remaining pear halves, spacing them evenly apart on top of the filling.

5 Bake for 45–50 minutes until the frangipane is golden, puffed and firm to the touch. Dust with icing sugar and serve with crème fraîche.

★ FREEZING TIP
To freeze *Complete the recipe to the end of step 4, then leave the tart, still in its tin, to cool completely. Once cool, wrap the entire tin in clingfilm, then freeze for up to one month.*
To use *Thaw overnight in the fridge and serve as in step 5.*

Fruit and Walnut Tart

Preparation Time 25 minutes, plus chilling • **Cooking Time** 1 hour 5 minutes, plus cooling • **Cuts into 8 slices** •
Per Slice 646 calories, 40g fat (of which 18g saturates), 68g carbohydrate, 0.6g salt • **Easy**

Sweet Shortcrust Pastry (see page
284), made with 225g (8oz) plain
flour, 125g (4oz) butter, 2 tbsp
golden icing sugar and 1 medium
egg

FOR THE FILLING
200g (7oz) clear honey
125g (4oz) unsalted butter, softened
125g (4oz) light muscovado sugar
3 medium eggs, beaten
grated zest and juice of 1 lemon
125g (4oz) walnuts, roughly
    chopped
125g (4oz) ready-to-eat dried
    apples and pears, roughly
    chopped, plus 3 dried pear slices
    to decorate

1 To make the filling, warm 175g
(6oz) honey in a small pan over a
low heat. Put the butter into a large
bowl with the sugar and beat with a
hand-held electric whisk until light
and fluffy. Add the eggs, lemon zest
and juice, walnuts, chopped apples
and pears and the warm honey. Stir
well and set aside.

2 Put the pastry between two
sheets of greaseproof paper and roll
out thinly. Peel off and discard the
top sheet of paper, then flip over
and use the pastry to line a 23cm
(9in) round or a 20.5cm (8in) square
loose-based tin. Prick all over with a
fork, cover with clingfilm and chill
for 30 minutes. Preheat the oven to
180°C (160°C fan oven) mark 4.

3 Bake the pastry case blind (see
page 284). Pour in the filling and
arrange the pear slices on top.
Brush with the remaining honey.
Put the tart on a baking sheet,
cover with foil and bake for
20 minutes. Remove the foil and
bake for a further 25 minutes or
until golden brown. Serve cool.

⭐ FREEZING TIP
To freeze *Complete the recipe.*
Cool the tart completely in the tin.
Wrap in foil and freeze for up to
one month.
To use *Remove from the freezer*
12 hours before serving and thaw
in the fridge.

Macadamia and Maple Tart

Preparation Time 15 minutes, plus freezing • **Cooking Time** about 40 minutes, plus cooling • **Cuts into 8 slices** •
Per Slice 608 calories, 38g fat (of which 11g saturates), 60g carbohydrate, 0.9g salt • **Easy**

225g (8oz) macadamia nuts, halved
350g (12oz) ready-made shortcrust
   pastry, thawed if frozen
flour to dust
75g (3oz) unsalted butter, softened
75g (3oz) dark muscovado sugar
3 medium eggs, beaten
1 tsp cornflour
50ml (2fl oz) maple syrup, plus
   extra to drizzle
225ml (8fl oz) golden syrup
grated zest of 1 lemon and 2 tbsp
   lemon juice
1 tsp vanilla extract

1 Put the macadamia nuts on a
baking sheet and toast under a
hot grill until golden brown.
Leave to cool.

2 Roll out the pastry on a lightly
floured worksurface and use to line
a 23cm (9in), 4cm (1½in) deep,
loose-based tart tin, leaving the
pastry hanging over the edges to
allow for shrinkage. Prick all over
with a fork, then freeze for
30 minutes.

3 Preheat the oven to 200°C (180°C
fan oven) mark 6. Bake the tart case
blind (see page 284). Using a sharp
knife, trim the overhanging pastry
to a neat edge.

4 Beat the butter with the sugar
until pale and creamy, then
gradually add the beaten eggs
and the cornflour. Stir in all the
remaining ingredients. The mixture
will look curdled, but don't panic.
Stir in the toasted nuts and pour
into the cooked pastry case.

5 Bake for 35–40 minutes until the
filling is just set. Leave to cool for
10 minutes before serving.

⭐ FREEZING TIP
To freeze *Complete the recipe, wrap
and freeze for up to one month.*
To use *Thaw overnight. Put on a
baking sheet, cover loosely with foil and
reheat at 200°C (180°C fan oven) mark
6 for 20 minutes.*

Pinenut and Honey Tart

Preparation Time 50 minutes, plus chilling • **Cooking Time** 1 hour, plus cooling • **Cuts into 6 slices** • **Per Slice** 863 calories, 54g fat (of which 26g saturates), 88g carbohydrate, 0.6g salt • **Easy**

250g (9oz) plain flour, plus extra
    to dust
200g (7oz) unsalted butter, softened
40g (1½oz) icing sugar
4 large eggs
100g (3½oz) pinenuts
200g (7oz) muscovado sugar
100ml (3½fl oz) clear honey
150ml (¼ pint) double cream
ice cream to serve

1 Put 225g (8oz) flour, 150g (5oz) butter and the icing sugar into a food processor and pulse until the mixture resembles fine crumbs. (Alternatively, rub the butter into the flour in a large bowl, by hand or using a pastry cutter, until it resembles fine crumbs. Stir in the icing sugar.) Add 1 egg. Pulse, or stir with a fork, until the mixture forms a ball. Wrap in clingfilm and chill for 30 minutes.

2 Preheat the oven to 200°C (180°C fan oven) mark 6. Roll out the pastry on a lightly floured worksurface and use to line a 23cm (9in) loose-based tart tin. Prick the base all over with a fork and bake blind (see page 284). Remove from the oven. Increase the oven temperature to 190°C (170°C fan oven) mark 5.

3 Sprinkle 75g (3oz) pinenuts over the pastry base. Melt 25g (1oz) butter and whisk with 175g (6oz) muscovado sugar, the honey, remaining eggs and the cream. Pour into the pastry case and bake for 25–30 minutes.

4 Pulse the remaining pinenuts, flour, butter and sugar until the mixture forms a crumbly texture. (Alternatively, rub the butter into the flour in a large bowl and stir in the pinenuts and sugar.) When the tart is cooked, remove it from the oven, sprinkle with the crumble mixture and return to the oven for 8–10 minutes.

5 Remove from the oven and leave to cool slightly. Serve warm, with ice cream.

Bramley Apple and Custard Tart

⭐

Preparation Time 30 minutes, plus chilling • **Cooking Time** about 2 hours, plus cooling and chilling • **Cuts into 12 slices** •
Per Slice 472 calories, 32g fat (of which 15g saturates), 46g carbohydrate, 0.5g salt • **Easy**

**750g (1lb 11oz) Bramley apples,
    peeled, cored and roughly
    chopped**
175g (6oz) golden caster sugar
**500g pack shortcrust pastry, chilled
flour to dust**
400ml (14fl oz) double cream
1 cinnamon stick
**3 large egg yolks, plus 1 large egg,
    beaten together**
2 dessert apples to decorate
**Apple Sauce (see Cook's Tip) to
    serve**

1 Cook the apples with 2 tbsp water
over a low heat until soft. Add 50g
(2oz) sugar and beat to make a
purée. Leave to cool.

2 Roll out the pastry on a lightly
floured worksurface and use to line a
20.5cm (8in), 4cm (1½in) deep,
loose-based fluted flan tin. Cover and
chill for 1 hour. Preheat the oven to
180°C (160°C fan oven) mark 4.
Bake the pastry case blind (see page
284). Remove from the oven.

3 Put the cream into a pan with 50g
(2oz) sugar and the cinnamon stick.
Bring slowly to the boil, then take
off the heat and remove the
cinnamon. Cool for 2–3 minutes
then beat in the egg yolks and egg.

4 Reduce the oven temperature to
170°C (150°C fan oven) mark 3.
Put the tart on a baking sheet, then
spoon the apple purée over the

pastry. Pour the cream mixture on
top and bake for 1–1½ hours or
until the custard is just set. Remove
the tart from the oven and leave to
cool in the tin, then chill.

5 To decorate, preheat the grill. Cut
the dessert apples into 5mm (¼in)
thick slices and lay them on a lipped
baking sheet. Sprinkle with 50g
(2oz) sugar and grill for 4–5 minutes
until caramelised, turn over and
repeat on the other side, then cool.
Remove the tart from the tin and
decorate with the apple slices. Serve
with Apple Sauce.

⭐ COOK'S TIP
Apple Sauce
*Pour 300ml (½ pint) apple juice into a
measuring jug. Mix 2 tbsp of the apple
juice with 1 tbsp arrowroot to make a
smooth paste. Pour the remaining apple
juice into a small pan and bring to a
gentle simmer. Add the arrowroot paste
and continue to heat, stirring constantly,
for 2–3 minutes until the sauce has
thickened slightly.*

Express Apple Tart

★

Preparation Time 10 minutes • **Cooking Time** 20 minutes • **Cuts into 8 slices** • **Per Slice** 197 calories, 12g fat (of which 0g saturates), 24g carbohydrate, 0.4g salt • **Easy**

375g pack ready-rolled puff pastry
500g (1lb 2oz) dessert apples, such as Cox's Orange Pippins, cored and thinly sliced, then tossed in the juice of 1 lemon
golden icing sugar to dust

1 Preheat the oven to 200°C (180°C fan oven) mark 6. Put the pastry on to a 28 x 38cm (11 x 15in) baking sheet and lightly roll a rolling pin over it to smooth down the pastry. Score lightly around the edge, leaving a 3cm (1¼in) border.

2 Put the apple slices on top of the pastry, within the border. Turn the edge of the pastry inwards to reach the edge of the apples, pressing it down and using your fingers to crimp the edge.

3 Dust heavily with icing sugar. Bake for 20 minutes or until the pastry is cooked and the sugar has caramelised. Serve warm, dusted with more icing sugar.

Rhubarb and Orange Crumble Tart

Preparation Time 25 minutes, plus chilling • Cooking Time about 40 minutes, plus cooling • Cuts into 8 slices •
Per Slice 518 calories, 37g fat (of which 22g saturates), 45g carbohydrate, 0.3g salt • **Easy**

200g (7oz) plain flour, plus extra
   to dust
125g (4oz) unsalted butter, cut
   into small pieces
25g (1oz) golden caster sugar
cream to serve

FOR THE FILLING
550g (1¼lb) rhubarb, cut into
   2.5cm (1in) pieces
50g (2oz) golden caster sugar
grated zest of 1 orange
juice of ½ orange

FOR THE CRUMBLE TOPPING
50g (2oz) plain flour
25g (1oz) ground almonds
50g (2oz) light muscovado sugar
25g (1oz) unsalted butter, cut into
   small pieces

1 To make the pastry, whiz the flour, butter and caster sugar in a food processor until it resembles fine crumbs. (Alternatively, rub the butter into the flour in a large bowl, by hand or using a pastry cutter, until it resembles fine crumbs. Stir in the sugar.) Add 2 tbsp cold water and whiz briefly again, or stir with a fork, to form a soft pastry. Wrap the pastry in clingfilm and chill for at least 30 minutes.

2 Roll out the pastry on a lightly floured worksurface and use to line a 10 x 35.5cm (4 x 14in) loose-based tin, or a 23cm (9in) round loose-based tart tin. Chill for 30 minutes.

Preheat the oven to 200°C (180°C fan oven) mark 6. Bake the tart case blind (see page 284).

3 Meanwhile, make the filling. Put the rhubarb, caster sugar, orange zest and juice into a pan and bring to the boil. Cook gently for 6–8 minutes until the rhubarb has just softened. Allow to cool.

4 To make the crumble topping, put the flour, almonds, muscovado sugar and butter into the food processor and whiz briefly until it resembles fine crumbs.

(Alternatively, rub the butter into the flour in a bowl, by hand or using a pastry cutter, until it resembles fine crumbs. Stir in the almonds and sugar.)

5 Spoon the rhubarb filling into the pastry case and level the surface. Top with the crumble mixture and bake for 20 minutes or until pale golden. Leave to cool slightly before serving with cream.

Caramelised Orange Tart

★

Preparation Time 15 minutes, plus chilling • **Cooking Time** 45 minutes, plus cooling • **Cuts into 8 slices** •
Per Slice 556 calories, 29g fat (of which 14g saturates), 70g carbohydrate, 0.5g salt • **Easy**

225g (8oz) plain flour, plus extra
    to dust
a pinch of salt
125g (4oz) unsalted butter, diced
2 tbsp golden icing sugar
1 medium egg yolk, beaten

FOR THE FILLING
juice of 1 lemon
juice of 1 orange
zest of 2 oranges
75g (3oz) unsalted butter
225g (8oz) golden granulated sugar
3 medium eggs, beaten
75g (3oz) ground almonds
2 tbsp orange liqueur

a few drops of orange food
    colouring (optional)

FOR THE DECORATION
100g (3½oz) golden caster sugar
pared zest of 1 orange, cut into
    slivers

1 Put the flour, salt, butter and icing sugar into a food processor and pulse until the mixture forms fine crumbs. (Alternatively, rub the fat into the flour, by hand or using a pastry cutter, then stir in the icing sugar.) Beat the egg yolk with 2 tbsp

cold water and add to the flour mixture. Process (or stir) until the crumbs make a dough. Knead lightly, wrap and chill.

2 To make the filling, put the juices, orange zest, butter, sugar and eggs into a heavy-based pan and heat gently, stirring, until thickened. Stir in the almonds, liqueur and food colouring, if using. Set aside.

3 Preheat the oven to 200°C (180°C fan oven) mark 6. Roll out the dough on a lightly floured worksurface and use to line a 23cm (9in) tin. Prick the base all over with a fork. Cover and chill for 10 minutes. Bake the pastry case blind (see page 284). Remove from the oven. Reduce the oven temperature to 180°C (160°C fan oven) mark 4. Pour the filling into the pastry case and bake for 20 minutes or until just firm. Cool in the tin.

4 To decorate, dissolve 50g (2oz) sugar in a pan with 300ml (½ pint) water. Add the orange zest and simmer for 10–15 minutes until the liquid has reduced and the zest is tender. Drain. Sprinkle the rest of the sugar over the tart. Caramelise under the grill, then leave to cool. Spoon the orange zest around the edge to serve.

Chocolate Orange Tart

Preparation Time 30 minutes, plus chilling • **Cooking Time** about 1 hour, plus cooling • **Cuts into 8 slices** •
Per Slice 441 calories, 28g fat (of which 17g saturates), 42g carbohydrate, 0.2g salt • **Easy**

Sweet Shortcrust Pastry (see page
  284), made with 150g (5oz) plain
  flour, a pinch of salt, 75g (3oz)
  unsalted butter, 25g (1oz) golden
  icing sugar, grated zest of
  1 orange and 2 large egg yolks
flour to dust
icing sugar to dust

FOR THE FILLING
175g (6oz) plain chocolate (at least
  50% cocoa solids), chopped
175ml (6fl oz) double cream
75g (3oz) light muscovado sugar
2 medium eggs
1 tbsp Grand Marnier or Cointreau

1 Roll out the pastry on a lightly
floured worksurface and use to line
a 20.5cm (8in) loose-based tart tin.
Prick the base all over with a fork,
put the tin on a baking sheet and
chill for 30 minutes. Preheat the
oven to 190°C (170°C fan oven)
mark 5.

2 Bake the pastry case blind (see
page 284). Remove from the oven
and put to one side. Reduce the
oven temperature to 170°C (150°C
fan oven) mark 3.

3 To make the filling, melt the
chocolate in a heatproof bowl set
over a pan of gently simmering
water, making sure the base of the
bowl doesn't touch the water.
Remove the bowl from the pan and
leave to cool for 10 minutes.

4 Put the cream, muscovado sugar,
eggs and liqueur into a bowl and
stir, using a wooden spoon to mix
thoroughly. Gradually stir in the
chocolate, then pour into the pastry
case and bake for 20 minutes or
until just set.

5 Serve warm or cold, dusted
liberally with icing sugar.

⭐ TRY SOMETHING
DIFFERENT
Omit the orange zest and replace the
Grand Marnier with crème de menthe.

Chocolate and Cherry Amaretti Tart

★

Preparation Time 30 minutes, plus marinating and chilling • **Cooking Time** 1½ hours, plus cooling • **Cuts into 8 slices** •
Per Slice 760 calories, 50g fat (of which 22g saturates), 67g carbohydrate, 0.8g salt • **Easy**

400g (14oz) pitted bottled or
   canned morello cherries, drained
3 tbsp brandy, sloe gin or almond-
   flavoured liqueur
150g (5oz) unsalted butter, softened
50g (2oz) icing sugar, plus extra
   to dust
1 small egg, beaten
225g (8oz) plain flour, plus extra
   to dust

FOR THE FILLING
100g (3½oz) plain chocolate,
   broken into pieces
125g (4oz) unsalted butter, softened
125g (4oz) caster sugar

3 large eggs, beaten
125g (4oz) ground almonds
25g (1oz) self-raising flour, sifted
50g (2oz) amaretti biscuits, finely
   crushed (see page 155)
75g (3oz) slivered or flaked
   almonds

1 Put the cherries into a bowl with the brandy, gin or liqueur and leave for 30 minutes or overnight. Put the butter, icing sugar and egg into a food processor and whiz until almost smooth. Add the flour and whiz until the mixture begins to

form a dough. (Alternatively, rub the fat into the flour, by hand or using a pastry cutter, to resemble fine crumbs, then stir in the icing sugar and egg.) Knead the pastry lightly, then wrap and chill for 30 minutes. Roll out the pastry on a lightly floured worksurface and use to line a 23cm (9in) loose-based fluted tart tin. Chill for 20 minutes.

2 Preheat the oven to 200°C (180°C fan oven) mark 6. Bake the pastry case blind (see page 284). Remove from the oven. Reduce the oven temperature to 150°C (130°C fan oven) mark 2.

3 To make the filling, melt the chocolate in a heatproof bowl set over a pan of gently simmering water, making sure the base of the bowl doesn't touch the water. Stir once or twice until smooth. Cool.

4 Beat the butter with the sugar until pale and fluffy. Gradually beat in the eggs, alternating with the ground almonds and flour. Fold in the melted chocolate and biscuits. Spoon one-third of the mixture into the pastry case. Spoon the cherries and juice over it. Spread the remaining filling over the cherries. Sprinkle on the slivered almonds and bake for about 1 hour. The tart will have a thin top crust but will be soft underneath. Leave in the tin for 10–15 minutes to firm up, then unmould, dust with icing sugar and serve warm.

Chocolate Espresso Tart

★

Preparation Time 30 minutes, plus chilling • **Cooking Time** 25 minutes, plus cooling and chilling • **Cuts into 10 slices** •
Per Slice 383 calories, 30g fat (of which 18g saturates), 30g carbohydrate, 0.2g salt • **Easy**

175g (6oz) plain flour, plus extra
   to dust
a pinch of salt
100g (3½oz) cold unsalted butter,
   diced
25g (1oz) caster sugar
1 medium egg, separated

FOR THE FILLING
200g bar good-quality dark
   chocolate (at least 64% cocoa
   solids), broken into squares
1 tbsp powered espresso coffee
284ml carton double cream
cocoa powder and chocolate curls
   (see page 283) to decorate

1 Sift the flour and salt into a bowl.
Rub in the butter until it resembles
fine breadcrumbs. Stir in the sugar.

2 Lightly beat the egg yolk with
2 tbsp ice-cold water. Using a flat-
bladed knife, stir enough of this
liquid into the flour mixture to make
it clump together without being
sticky or too dry. Bring together with
your hands and knead lightly until
smooth. Shape into a disc, wrap in
clingfilm and chill for 30 minutes.

3 Roll out the pastry on a lightly
floured surface to 3mm (⅛in) thick.
Use to line a round 20.5cm (8in) tin,
2.5cm (1in) deep. Prick the base all
over, then chill for 30 minutes.
Preheat the oven to 200°C (180°C
fan oven) mark 6. Put a baking sheet
in the oven to heat up.

4 Bake the pastry case blind
(see page 284) for 12–15 minutes
until the pastry is set. Remove the
beans and paper and bake for
5–10 minutes. Transfer to a wire
rack to cool.

5 Melt the chocolate and coffee in
a heatproof bowl set over a pan of
gently simmering water, making
sure the base of the bowl doesn't
touch the water. Stir once or twice.
Set aside to cool.

6 Put the egg whites into a clean,
grease-free bowl and whisk until

stiff. Using a metal spoon, fold into
the chocolate. Whisk the cream until
it just holds its shape, then fold into
the chocolate mixture. Pour into the
pastry case and chill until set.

7 Dust with cocoa and decorate
with chocolate curls to serve.

Classic Lemon Tart

Preparation Time 30 minutes, plus chilling • **Cooking Time** 50 minutes, plus cooling • **Cuts into 8 slices** •
Per Slice 385 calories, 23g fat (of which 13g saturates), 42g carbohydrate, 0.2g salt • **Easy**

butter to grease

plain flour to dust

Sweet Shortcrust Pastry (see page 284), made with 150g (5oz) plain flour, 75g (3oz) unsalted butter, 50g (2oz) icing sugar and 2 large egg yolks

peach slices and fresh or frozen raspberries, thawed, to decorate

icing sugar to dust

FOR THE FILLING

1 large egg, plus 4 large yolks

150g (5oz) caster sugar

grated zest of 4 lemons

150ml (¼ pint) freshly squeezed lemon juice (about 4 medium lemons)

150ml (¼ pint) double cream

1 Grease and flour a 23cm (9in), 2.5cm (1in) deep, loose-based flan tin. Roll out the pastry on a lightly floured worksurface into a circle – if the pastry sticks to the surface, gently ease a palette knife under it to loosen. Line the tin with the pastry and trim the excess. Prick the base all over with a fork. Chill for 30 minutes.

2 Preheat the oven to 190°C (170°C fan oven) mark 5. Put the tin on a baking sheet and bake the pastry case blind (see page 284). Remove from the oven, leaving the flan tin on the baking sheet. Reduce the oven temperature to 170°C (150°C fan oven) mark 3.

3 Meanwhile, to make the filling, put the whole egg, egg yolks and caster sugar into a bowl and beat together with a wooden spoon or balloon whisk until smooth. Carefully stir in the lemon zest, lemon juice and cream. Leave to stand for 5 minutes.

4 Ladle three-quarters of the filling into the pastry case, position the baking sheet on the oven shelf and ladle in the remainder. Bake for 25–30 minutes until the filling bounces back when touched lightly in the centre. Cool for 15 minutes to serve warm, or cool completely and chill. Decorate with peaches and raspberries and dust with icing sugar.

★ COOK'S TIP

Remember that ovens vary, so check the tart after 15 minutes of cooking. Turn round if cooking unevenly, otherwise the eggs might curdle.

Strawberry Tart

Preparation Time 40 minutes, plus chilling • **Cooking Time** 35–40 minutes, plus cooling • **Cuts into 6 slices** •
Per Slice 384 calories, 15g fat (of which 8g saturates), 57g carbohydrate, 0.2g salt • **Easy**

Sweet Shortcrust Pastry (see page 284), made with 125g (4oz) plain flour, a pinch of salt, 50g (2oz) golden caster sugar, 50g (2oz) unsalted butter and 2 medium egg yolks
flour to dust

FOR THE CRÈME PÂTISSIÈRE
300ml (½ pint) milk
1 vanilla pod, split, seeds separated
2 medium egg yolks
50g (2oz) golden caster sugar
2 tbsp plain flour
2 tbsp cornflour
50ml (2fl oz) crème fraîche

FOR THE TOPPING
450g (1lb) medium strawberries, hulled and halved
6 tbsp redcurrant jelly

1 To make the crème pâtissière, pour the milk into a pan with the vanilla pod and seeds. Heat gently to just below boiling, then remove from the heat. Put the yolks and sugar into a bowl, beat until pale, then stir in the flours. Discard the vanilla pod, then gradually mix the hot milk into the yolk mixture. Return to the pan and slowly bring to the boil, stirring, for 3–4 minutes until thick and smooth. Scrape into a bowl, cover with a circle of damp greaseproof paper and leave to cool.

2 Put the pastry between two sheets of greaseproof paper and roll out thinly. Use to line a 23cm (9in) loose-based flan tin. Prick with a fork, line with greaseproof paper and chill for 30 minutes.

3 Preheat the oven to 190°C (170°C fan oven) mark 5. Bake blind (see page 284) for 10–15 minutes. Remove the paper and beans, put back in the oven and bake for 10 minutes or until golden. Cool for 5 minutes, then remove from the tin and cool completely.

4 Add the crème fraîche to the crème pâtissière and beat until smooth. Spread evenly in the pastry case. Arrange the strawberry halves on top, working from the outside edge into the centre.

5 Heat the redcurrant jelly in a pan until syrupy, whisking lightly. Using a pastry brush, cover the strawberries with jelly. Serve within 2 hours.

★ COOK'S TIP
Serve within 2 hours of putting the tart together, otherwise the pastry will go soggy.

Coconut and Mango Tart

★

Preparation Time 35 minutes, plus chilling • Cooking Time 50 minutes, plus cooling and chilling • Cuts into 10 slices • Per Slice 253 calories, 18g fat (of which 11g saturates), 20g carbohydrate, 0.3g salt • **Easy**

125g (4oz) plain flour, plus extra
    to dust
75g (3oz) firm, unsalted butter
1 tbsp caster sugar
40g (1½oz) desiccated coconut
1 medium egg yolk
toasted coconut shreds to decorate
icing sugar to dust

FOR THE FILLING
2 small ripe mangoes, peeled,
    stoned and thinly sliced
75ml (2½fl oz) freshly squeezed
    orange juice
2 tbsp caster sugar, plus 75g (3oz)
3 medium eggs

15g (½oz) cornflour
400ml can coconut milk
150ml (¼ pint) double cream

1 To make the pastry, whiz the flour and butter in a food processor until the mixture resembles fine crumbs. Stir in the caster sugar and coconut. Add the egg yolk and about 2 tbsp cold water and pulse to make a firm dough. (Alternatively, rub the butter into the dry ingredients in a large bowl by hand or using a pastry cutter. Mix in the egg yolk and water.) Knead lightly, wrap and chill for 30 minutes.

Preheat the oven to 200°C (180°C fan oven) mark 6. Roll out the pastry on a lightly floured worksurface and use to line a 23cm (9in), 4cm (1½in) deep, loose-based flan tin. Bake the pastry case blind (see page 284). Remove from the oven. Reduce the oven temperature to 150°C (130°C fan oven) mark 2.

2 Meanwhile, to make the filling, put the mango slices into a heavy-based pan with the orange juice and 2 tbsp caster sugar. Bring to a simmer and cook gently for 3–5 minutes until the mango slices are softened but still retain their shape. Cool slightly.

3 Beat the eggs and the remaining sugar together in a bowl. Blend the cornflour with a little of the coconut milk in a pan. Add the remaining coconut milk. Bring to the boil, stirring until thickened. Remove from the heat and stir in the cream. Pour over the egg mixture, stirring until smooth.

4 Drain the mangoes, reserving the juice. Arrange in the pastry case. Stir the reserved juice into the coconut custard and ladle it over the mangoes. Bake for about 30 minutes or until the custard is just set; it will continue to firm up as it cools. Leave to cool, then chill for several hours or overnight.

5 Decorate with coconut shreds and dust with icing sugar to serve.

Glazed Cranberry and Orange Tart

★

Preparation Time 15 minutes • **Cooking Time** 6 minutes • **Cuts into 8 slices** • **Per Slice** 234 calories, 11g fat (of which 3g saturates), 29g carbohydrate, 0.2g salt • **Easy**

350g (12oz) fresh or frozen
    cranberries, defrosted
grated zest and juice of 1 orange
125g (4oz) golden caster sugar
½ tbsp arrowroot
250g tub mascarpone cheese
200ml (7fl oz) ready-made fresh
    custard with real vanilla
20.5cm (8in) cooked shortcrust
    pastry case

1 Tip the cranberries into a pan with the orange zest, juice and sugar and bring to the boil. Simmer for 5 minutes or until the cranberries are just softened and the syrup has reduced slightly. Using a slotted spoon, strain off the cranberries and set aside in a bowl, leaving the syrup in the pan.

2 Mix the arrowroot with 1 tbsp cold water, add to the pan and cook for 1 minute, stirring, until the syrup has thickened. Pour over the cranberries and leave to cool.

3 Tip the mascarpone and custard into a bowl and, using a hand-held electric whisk, mix until smooth. Spoon into the pastry case, top with the cranberry mixture and serve.

★ COOK'S TIP
A shop-bought pastry case helps to cut corners but, if you prefer, you can make a pie crust using the Sweet Shortcrust Pastry recipe on page 284.

Glazed Brandied Prune Tart

Preparation Time 25 minutes, plus soaking and chilling • **Cooking Time** 50 minutes • **Cuts into 8 slices** •
Per Slice 440 calories, 24g fat (of which 14g saturates), 47g carbohydrate, 0.2g salt • **Easy**

Sweet Shortcrust Pastry (see page
    284) made with 175g (6oz) plain
    flour, a pinch of salt, 75g (3oz)
    unsalted butter, 3 large egg yolks,
    75g (3oz) caster sugar, 1½ tsp
    water
flour to dust

FOR THE FILLING
250g (9oz) ready-to-eat dried
    prunes
5 tbsp brandy
1 vanilla pod, split
150ml (¼ pint) double cream
150ml (¼ pint) single cream
25g (1oz) caster sugar

2 large eggs
4 tbsp apricot jam and 2 tbsp
    brandy to glaze

1 To make the filling, put the prunes
into a small bowl, add the 5 tbsp
brandy, then cover and leave to soak
overnight or for several hours.

2 Roll out the pastry on a lightly
floured worksurface and use to line
a 23cm (9in), 2.5cm (1in) deep,
loose-based fluted flan tin. Chill for
30 minutes. Preheat the oven to
200°C (180°C fan oven) mark 6.

Prick the pastry base all over with a
fork, then bake blind (see page
284). Remove from the oven.
Reduce the oven temperature to
180°C (160°C fan oven) mark 4.

3 Put the vanilla pod into a pan with
the double cream. Bring just to the
boil. Remove from the heat and
leave to infuse for 20 minutes.
Remove the vanilla pod, rinse, dry
and store for reuse. Pour the cream
into a bowl. Add the single cream,
sugar and eggs and beat well.

4 Scatter the prunes in the pastry
case, then pour the cream mixture
around them. Bake for 30 minutes
or until the custard is turning golden
and is just set in the centre.

5 Meanwhile, sieve the jam into
a pan, add the 2 tbsp brandy and
heat gently until smooth. Brush the
glaze over the tart and serve warm
or cold.

Sweet Ricotta Tart

Preparation Time 25 minutes, plus chilling • **Cooking Time** 1 hour, plus cooling • **Cuts into 8 slices** • **Per Slice** 404 calories, 15g fat (of which 9g saturates), 60g carbohydrate, 0.3g salt • **Easy**

Sweet Shortcrust Pastry (see page
   284), made with 200g (7oz) plain
   flour, 75g (3oz) unsalted butter,
   50g (2oz) golden caster sugar and
   1 medium egg
flour to dust
icing sugar to dust

FOR THE FILLING
100g (3½oz) cracked wheat or
   bulgur wheat
200ml (7fl oz) milk
250g (9oz) ricotta cheese
150g (5oz) golden caster sugar
2 medium eggs
1 tbsp orange flower water
1 tsp vanilla extract
½ tsp ground cinnamon
1 piece – about 40g (1½oz) –
   candied peel, finely chopped

1 To make the filling, put the wheat into a pan, add the milk, then cover and bring to the boil. Reduce the heat and simmer for 5–8 minutes until all the liquid has been absorbed and the wheat still has a slight bite. Leave to cool.

2 Preheat the oven to 190°C (170°C fan oven) mark 5. Roll out the pastry on a lightly floured worksurface and use to line a 20.5cm (8in) loose-based sandwich tin. Prick the base all over with a fork. Cover and chill for 10 minutes. Knead together the trimmings, then wrap and chill.

Bake the pastry case blind (see page 284). Remove from the oven.

3 Put the ricotta into a bowl and add the sugar, eggs, orange flower water, vanilla extract and cinnamon. Beat well. Add the peel and cracked wheat and mix.

4 Roll out the pastry trimmings. Cut out six strips, each measuring 1 x 20.5cm (½ x 8in). Pour the filling into the pastry case. Lay the strips on top. Bake for 45 minutes. Leave in the tin for 10 minutes. Cool on a wire rack. Dust with icing sugar.

Mincemeat and Ricotta Tart

Preparation Time 45 minutes, plus chilling • **Cooking Time** about 1¼ hours, plus cooling • **Cuts into 8 slices** •
Per Slice 594 calories, 29g fat (of which 13g saturates), 78g carbohydrate, 0.3g salt • **Easy**

175g (6oz) plain flour, plus extra
   to dust
125g (4oz) unsalted butter, cut into
   cubes
25g (1oz) ground almonds
25g (1oz) caster sugar
1 large egg yolk

**FOR THE FILLING AND
TOPPING**
250g (9oz) ricotta cheese
25g (1oz) icing sugar, plus extra
   to dust
2 large egg yolks
3 tbsp double cream
700g (1½lb) mincemeat
grated zest of 1 lemon
1 tbsp brandy or lemon juice
25g (1oz) glacé cherries, sliced
2 tbsp flaked almonds

1 To make the pastry, whiz the flour and butter in a food processor until the mixture resembles fine crumbs. Add the ground almonds, sugar and egg yolk with 1 tbsp cold water. Pulse until the mixture just comes together. (Alternatively, rub the butter into the dry ingredients in a large bowl by hand or using a pastry cutter. Mix in the egg yolk and water.) Knead lightly, wrap and chill for at least 30 minutes.

2 Roll out the pastry on a lightly floured worksurface and use to line a 10 x 33cm (4 x 13in) loose-based tin. Prick the pastry base all over with a fork and chill for 30 minutes.

3 Preheat the oven to 190°C (170°C fan oven) mark 5. Bake the tart case blind (see page 284). Cool for 15 minutes. Reduce the oven temperature to 180°C (160°C fan oven) mark 4.

4 To make the filling, beat the ricotta with the icing sugar, egg yolks and cream. Spread over the pastry and bake for 20–25 minutes until lightly set.

5 Mix the mincemeat with the lemon zest and brandy or lemon juice and spoon over the tart. Scatter the glacé cherries and almonds on top and bake for 20 minutes. Cool slightly, then dust with icing sugar.

Vanilla Egg Custard Tart

Preparation Time 40 minutes, plus chilling • **Cooking Time** 1 hour, plus cooling • **Cuts into 6 slices** •
Per Slice 497 calories, 36g fat (of which 21g saturates), 36g carbohydrate, 0.4g salt • **Easy**

Sweet Shortcrust Pastry (see page
    284), made with 175g (6oz) plain
    flour, 125g (4oz) unsalted butter,
    25g (1oz) vanilla sugar, 1 tsp
    grated orange zest and 1 medium
    egg yolk
flour to dust
175g (6oz) raspberries (optional)
    to serve
vanilla sugar to dust

FOR THE VANILLA CUSTARD
2 large eggs
2 large egg yolks
40g (1½oz) golden caster sugar
450ml (¾ pint) single cream
½ vanilla pod, split lengthways

1 Roll out the pastry on a lightly
floured worksurface and use to line
a 20.5cm (8in), 4cm (1½in) deep,
loose-based fluted tart tin. Prick the
base all over with a fork. Chill for
30 minutes.

2 Preheat the oven to 200°C
(180°C fan oven) mark 6. Bake the
pastry case blind (see page 284).
Remove from the oven and cool
for 15 minutes. Reduce the oven
temperature to 150°C (130°C fan
oven) mark 2.

3 Meanwhile, make the vanilla
custard. Put the whole eggs, egg
yolks and sugar into a bowl and
beat well. Put the cream and vanilla
pod into a small pan over a very low
heat until the cream is almost

boiling. Pour on to the egg mixture,
whisking constantly, then strain into
the pastry case.

4 Put the tart back into the oven.
Bake for 45 minutes or until the
centre is softly set. Leave until cold,
then carefully remove from the tin.
Top with raspberries if you like, and
dust with vanilla sugar.

⭐ TRY SOMETHING
DIFFERENT
Chocolate Custard Tart
Replace 25g (1oz) of the flour with sifted
cocoa powder. For the custard, omit the
vanilla pod and heat 375ml (13fl oz)
single cream with 100g (3½oz) chopped
plain chocolate (70% cocoa solids), until
melted and just simmering.

Cinnamon Custard Tart

Preparation time 50 minutes, plus chilling and infusing • **Cooking time** 1½ hours, plus standing and cooling •
Cuts into 8 slices • **Per Slice** 664 calories, 34g fat (of which 20g saturates), 87g carbohydrate, 0.4g salt • **Easy**

250g (9oz) plain flour, plus extra
   to dust
100g (3½oz) unsalted butter
100g (3½oz) icing sugar
4 large eggs
450ml (¾ pint) milk
285ml (9½fl oz) double cream
1 vanilla pod, split
1 cinnamon stick, crumbled
275g (10oz) caster sugar
1 mango, 1 small pineapple,
   2 clementines and 125g (4oz)
   kumquats to serve

1 Put the flour, butter and icing sugar into a food processor and pulse until the mixture forms fine crumbs. (Alternatively, rub the fat into the flour by hand or using a pastry cutter, then stir in the icing sugar.) Beat 1 egg and add to the flour mixture with 1 tbsp water. Process (or stir) until the crumbs make a dough. Wrap in clingfilm and chill for 30 minutes.

2 Use the pastry to line a 23cm (9in) loose-based tart tin. Prick the base all over with a fork. Chill for 30 minutes.

3 Preheat the oven to 200°C (180°C fan oven) mark 6. Bake the pastry case blind (see page 284). Lightly whisk the remaining eggs. Use 1 tbsp egg to brush over the pastry. Return to the oven for 2 minutes. Remove from the oven. Reduce the oven temperature to 150°C (130°C fan oven) mark 2.

4 Put the milk, cream, vanilla pod and cinnamon into a pan and slowly bring to the boil. Leave to infuse for 20 minutes. Mix the whisked eggs with 150g (5oz) caster sugar. Stir the milk into the egg mixture, strain into a jug and pour into the tart. Cook for 40–50 minutes until the filling has just set. Turn the oven off and leave the tart in the oven for 15 minutes. Remove and cool in the tin for 20–30 minutes. Transfer to a wire rack to cool completely.

5 Make the caramelised fruit (see Finishing Touches). Cut the tart into portions and spoon the fruit over the top to serve.

⭐ FINISHING TOUCHES
To decorate, cut the fruits into thick slices and arrange on two non-stick baking sheets. Put the remaining caster sugar into a small, heavy-based pan and cook over a low heat until the sugar begins to dissolve, then turn up the heat and cook to a pale caramel. Cool a little and drizzle over the fruit. Allow to set. (The caramel will stay brittle for 1–2 hours.)

Classic Custard Tart

Preparation Time 25 minutes, plus chilling • **Cooking Time** 1¼ hours, plus cooling • **Cuts into 10 slices** •
Per Slice 399 calories, 28g fat (of which 16g saturates), 32g carbohydrate, 0.4g salt • **Easy**

**Sweet Shortcrust Pastry (see page
    284) made with 225g (8oz) plain
    flour, 175g (6oz) unsalted butter,
    50g (2oz) golden caster sugar,
    finely grated zest of 1 lemon,
    1 medium egg yolk**
plain flour to dust

FOR THE FILLING
8 large egg yolks
75g (3oz) golden caster sugar
450ml (¾ pint) single cream
nutmeg for grating

 COOK'S TIP
*Freeze the leftover egg whites in a clean
container. They will keep for up to three
months. Use to make meringues.*

1 Roll out the pastry on a lightly
floured worksurface to a 3mm (⅛in)
thickness. Use to line a 23cm (9in)
round, 4cm (1½in) deep flan tin.
Prick the base all over with a fork
and chill for 30 minutes.

2 Preheat the oven to 200°C (180°C
fan oven) mark 6. Put the flan tin on
a baking sheet and bake blind (see
page 284). Remove from the oven.
Reduce the oven temperature to
130°C (110°C fan oven) mark ½.

3 Using a wooden spoon, mix the
egg yolks with the sugar. Gradually
stir in the cream, then strain into a
jug to remove any eggy strands.
Pour the mixture into the pastry case
and bake for 40–50 minutes until
just set with a little wobble. Grate
plenty of nutmeg over the top and
cool in the tin on a wire rack. Serve
at room temperature.

Lavender and Goat's Cheese Tart

Preparation Time 30 minutes, plus chilling • **Cooking Time** about 1 hour 10 minutes, plus cooling and chilling •
Cuts into 12 slices • **Per Slice** 341 calories, 19g fat (of which 8g saturates), 37g carbohydrate, 0.6g salt • **Easy**

375g pack sweet shortcrust pastry
250g tub ricotta cheese
150g pack soft fresh goat's cheese
100g (3½oz) cream cheese
100g (3½oz) soured cream
4 large eggs, separated
225g (8oz) golden caster sugar
zest of 1 lemon, plus 1 tbsp juice
5 tbsp lavender flower heads
25g (1oz) plain flour
icing sugar to dust
1 tbsp rosemary leaves to decorate

1 Preheat the oven to 180°C (160°C fan oven) mark 4. Line a 25.5cm (10in) diameter, 5cm (2in) deep, loose-bottomed fluted flan tin with the pastry, making sure it comes to the top of the rim. Chill for 1 hour.

2 Prick the base all over with a fork, then bake blind (see page 284). Leave to cool. Reduce the oven temperature to 170°C (150°C fan oven) mark 3.

3 Put the ricotta into a large bowl and beat in the goat's cheese, cream cheese and soured cream. Put the

egg yolks into another bowl with 200g (7oz) caster sugar. Beat the mixture with a hand-held electric whisk until creamy, then stir into the cheese mixture along with the lemon zest and juice. Stir the lavender into the remaining 25g (1oz) caster sugar and set aside.

4 Put the egg whites into a clean, grease-free bowl and whisk until soft peaks form. Sift the flour over the cheese mixture and fold it in along with the egg whites. Spoon into the pastry case. Sift the lavender sugar over the mixture and reserve the lavender.

5 Bake for 40–45 minutes until a skewer inserted into the centre comes out clean. Turn off the oven and leave the tart inside with the door ajar until cold. Chill for 3 hours or overnight.

6 To serve, dust with icing sugar and decorate with the reserved lavender and the rosemary leaves.

Treacle Tart

Preparation Time 25 minutes, plus chilling • **Cooking Time** 45–50 minutes, plus cooling • **Cuts into 6 slices** •
Per Slice 486 calories, 15g fat (of which 8g saturates), 88g carbohydrate, 1.1g salt • **Easy**

**Sweet Shortcrust Pastry (see page
284), made with 225g (8oz) plain
flour, 150g (5oz) unsalted butter,
15g (½oz) golden caster sugar
and 1 medium egg yolk**
flour to dust

FOR THE FILLING
700g (1½lb) golden syrup
175g (6oz) fresh white breadcrumbs
grated zest of 3 lemons
2 medium eggs, lightly beaten

1 Preheat the oven to 180°C (160°C
fan oven) mark 4. Roll out the pastry
on a lightly floured worksurface and
use to line a 25.5cm (10in), 4cm
(1½in) deep, loose-based fluted tart
tin. Prick the base all over with a
fork and chill for 30 minutes.

2 To make the filling, heat the
syrup in a pan over a low heat until
thinner in consistency. Remove
from the heat and mix in the
breadcrumbs and lemon zest.
Stir in the beaten eggs.

3 Pour the filling into the pastry case
and bake for 45–50 minutes until
the filling is lightly set and golden.
Allow to cool slightly. Serve warm.

★ TRY SOMETHING
DIFFERENT
*For the pastry, replace half the plain
flour with wholemeal flour. For the filling,
use fresh wholemeal breadcrumbs
instead of white.*

Raspberry and White Chocolate Tarts

Preparation Time 40 minutes, plus chilling • **Cooking Time** 40 minutes, plus cooling, chilling and thawing • **Makes 8** •
Per Tart 648 calories, 49g fat (of which 28g saturates), 52g carbohydrate, 0.6g salt • **For the Confident Cook**

**225g (8oz) plain flour, plus extra
  to dust**
150g (5oz) butter, cut into cubes
**50g (2oz) icing sugar, plus extra
  to dust**
2–3 drops of vanilla extract
1 large egg, lightly beaten
350–450g (12oz–1lb) raspberries
pouring cream to serve

FOR THE FILLING
**275g (10oz) good-quality white
  chocolate, broken into small
  pieces**
300ml (½ pint) double cream
1 vanilla pod, split
2 large eggs, separated
2 tbsp Kirsch

1 Put the flour, butter and icing sugar into a food processor and pulse until the mixture resembles fine crumbs. (Alternatively, rub the butter into the dry ingredients in a large bowl by hand or using a pastry cutter.) Add the vanilla extract and all but 2 tsp of the beaten egg. Pulse, or stir with a fork, until the dough comes together to form a ball. Wrap in clingfilm and chill for at least 30 minutes.

2 Roll out the pastry thinly on a lightly floured worksurface. Cut out rounds and use to line eight 9cm (3½in), 3cm (1¼in) deep, loose-based tart tins. If the pastry cracks as you line the tins, just patch together. Prick the base all over with a fork, then chill for 30 minutes.

3 Preheat the oven to 200°C (180°C fan oven) mark 6. Bake the pastry cases blind (see page 284). Leave in the tin to cool slightly. Reduce the oven temperature to 190°C (170°C fan oven) mark 5.

4 To make the filling, put the chocolate into a bowl. Pour the cream into a small heavy-based pan, add the vanilla and bring just to the boil. Take off the heat and remove the vanilla. Slowly pour the cream on to the chocolate and stir until the chocolate is melted. Cool. Mix the egg yolks and Kirsch into the cooled chocolate mixture. Put the egg whites into a clean, grease-free bowl and whisk until soft peaks form, then fold carefully into the chocolate mixture until evenly incorporated. Pour the filling into the pastry cases.

5 Bake for 10–15 minutes until just set. If the filling appears to be colouring too quickly in the oven, cover with foil. Leave to cool in the tins. Don't worry if the filling seems very soft – it will become firmer on chilling. Chill for at least 5 hours or overnight.

6 Remove from the fridge 30 minutes before serving. Unmould on to plates. Arrange the raspberries on top, dust with icing sugar and serve with cream.

Almond Bakewell Tarts

Preparation Time 25 minutes, plus chilling • **Cooking Time** 50 minutes, plus cooling • **Makes 6** •
Per Tart 931 calories, 52g fat (of which 24g saturates), 104g carbohydrate, 0.8g salt • **Easy**

Sweet Shortcrust Pastry (see page
 284), made with 200g (7oz) plain
 flour, 100g (3½oz) unsalted
 butter, 75g (3oz) caster sugar,
 3 large egg yolks and ½ tsp
 vanilla extract
flour to dust
Plum Sauce (see Cook's Tip) to serve

FOR THE FILLING
125g (4oz) unsalted butter, softened
125g (4oz) caster sugar
3 large eggs
125g (4oz) ground almonds
2–3 drops almond extract
6 tbsp redcurrant jelly

FOR THE CRUMBLE TOPPING
25g (1oz) unsalted butter
75g (3oz) plain flour
25g (1oz) caster sugar

1 Roll out the pastry thinly on a
lightly floured worksurface and line
six 10cm (4in), 3cm (1¼in) deep
tartlet tins. Chill for 30 minutes.
Preheat the oven to 190°C (170°C
fan oven) mark 5.

2 Prick the bases all over with a fork,
then bake blind (see page 284).
Leave to cool.

3 To make the filling, beat the
butter and sugar together until light
and fluffy. Gradually beat in 2 eggs,
then beat in the remaining egg with
one-third of the ground almonds.
Fold in the remaining almonds and
the almond essence.

4 Melt the redcurrant jelly in a small
pan and brush over the inside of
each pastry case. Spoon in the
almond filling. Put the tarts on a
baking sheet and bake for 20–25
minutes until golden and just firm.
Leave in the tins for 10 minutes,
then unmould on to a wire rack and
leave to cool completely.

5 To make the crumble topping,
rub the butter into the flour and
add the sugar. Spread evenly on a
baking sheet and grill until golden.
Cool, then sprinkle over the tarts.
Decorate with plums (see below)
and serve with Plum Sauce.

★ COOK'S TIP
Plum Sauce
*Put 450g (1lb) halved and stoned ripe
plums, 50–75g (2–3oz) soft brown sugar
and 150ml (¼ pint) sweet white wine
into a pan with 150ml (¼ pint) water.
Bring to the boil, then simmer until
tender. Remove 3 plums to decorate; slice
and put to one side. Cook the remaining
plums until very soft (about 15 minutes).
Put into a food processor and process
until smooth. Sieve, if you like, adding
more sugar to taste. Leave to cool.*

Mango Tartes Tatin

★

Preparation Time 30 minutes • **Cooking Time** 30 minutes • **Makes 4** • **Per Tart** 506 calories, 33g fat (of which 5g saturates), 56g carbohydrate, 0.9g salt • **Easy**

2 small ripe mangoes, peeled, the flesh cut away in one piece from each side of the stone
40g (1½oz) golden granulated sugar
40g (1½oz) unsalted butter
375g pack ready-rolled puff pastry

1 Preheat the oven to 220°C (200°C fan oven) mark 7. Slice each piece of mango along most of the length, so that the slices remain joined at the top.

2 Put the sugar into a large heavy-based frying pan. Heat very gently until it starts to dissolve and turn brown. Add 25g (1oz) butter and stir with a wooden spoon to make a caramel. Add the mango and toss gently to coat in caramel. Cook for 2–3 minutes, then remove from the heat.

3 Grease four 8cm (3¼in) tart tins with the remaining butter. Unroll the pastry and put the tins upside down on it. Press a rolling pin over the tins to stamp out four pastry rounds.

4 Put one mango piece, curved side down, into each tin, pressing it gently to fan out, then divide any remaining caramel among them. Top each tin with a pastry round. Bake for 20–25 minutes until the pastry is golden brown. To serve, turn out the tartlets on to plates, with the mango uppermost.

White Chocolate Fruit Tarts

Preparation Time 40 minutes, plus chilling • **Cooking Time** 40 minutes, plus cooling and chilling • **Makes 8** •
Per Tart 688 calories, 48g fat (of which 29g saturates), 58g carbohydrate, 0.5g salt • **Easy**

Sweet Shortcrust Pastry (see page
   284), made with 225g (8oz) plain
   flour, 150g (5oz) unsalted butter,
   50g (2oz) icing sugar, 1 large egg
   and 2–3 drops vanilla extract
450g (1lb) fresh mango, peeled,
   stoned and sliced
flour to dust
fresh mint sprigs to decorate
icing sugar to dust

FOR THE FILLING
275g (10oz) white chocolate,
   chopped
300ml (½ pint) double cream
1 vanilla pod, split

2 large eggs, separated
2 tbsp Kirsch

1 Roll out the pastry thinly on a
lightly floured worksurface and use
to line eight 9cm (3½in), 3cm (1¼in)
deep, loose-based tartlet tins (see
Cook's Tips). Prick the bases all over
with a fork and chill for 30 minutes.

2 Preheat the oven to 200°C (180°C
fan oven) mark 6. Bake the tartlet
cases blind (see page 284). Remove
from the oven. Reduce the oven
temperature to 190°C (170°C fan
oven) mark 5.

3 To make the filling, put the
chocolate into a heatproof bowl.
Pour the cream into a small, heavy-
based pan with the vanilla pod and
bring to the boil. Remove from the
heat, lift out the vanilla pod and add
the hot cream to the chocolate. Stir
until the chocolate is completely
melted. Leave to cool.

4 Mix the egg yolks and the Kirsch
into the cooled chocolate and cream
mixture. Put the egg whites into a
clean, grease-free bowl and whisk
until soft peaks form, then fold
carefully into the chocolate mixture
until well incorporated. Pour the
mixture into the pastry cases and
bake for 10–15 minutes until just set
(see Cook's Tips). Leave to cool in
the tins and chill for 5 hours or
overnight. Don't worry if the filling
seems very soft – it will become
firmer as it chills.

5 Remove the tarts from the fridge
30 minutes before serving. Unmould
the tarts and arrange the mango
slices on top. Decorate with fresh
mint sprigs and dust with icing
sugar just before serving.

★ COOK'S TIPS
● *Don't worry if the pastry cracks when
you're lining the tins – it's easy to patch
together.*
● *If the filling starts to get too dark
during cooking, cover it with foil.*

Apple and Lemon Tartlets

Preparation Time 40 minutes, plus chilling • **Cooking Time** 45–50 minutes • **Makes 8** • **Per Tartlet** 615 calories, 34g fat (of which 20g saturates), 77g carbohydrate, 0.6g salt • **Easy**

3 medium eggs
a pinch of salt
300g (11oz) plain flour, plus extra
    to dust
75g (3oz) icing sugar
175g (6oz) unsalted butter

FOR THE FILLING
700g (1½lb) Bramley or Granny
    Smith's apples
grated zest and juice of 2 lemons
150g (5oz) unsalted butter
225g (8oz) caster sugar, plus extra
    to dust
1 tsp arrowroot

1 Beat 1 egg with a pinch of salt, then set aside 1 tbsp. Put the flour, icing sugar and butter into a food processor and whiz until the mixture resembles fine crumbs. Add the remaining beaten egg with 3 tbsp water and pulse until the pastry comes together. (Alternatively, rub the butter into the dry ingredients in a large bowl by hand or using a pastry cutter. Stir in the egg and water.) Divide into eight balls and chill for 30 minutes. Roll out the pastry on a lightly floured worksurface and line eight 8cm (3¼in) loose-based fluted tartlet tins. Prick the bases all over with a fork and chill for 20 minutes.

2 Preheat the oven to 200°C (180°C fan oven) mark 6. Bake the tartlet cases blind (see page 284). Remove from the oven. Reduce the oven temperature to 180°C (160°C fan oven) mark 4.

3 Peel, core and thinly slice the apples, then toss in 2 tbsp lemon juice. Fry in 25g (1oz) butter for 1–2 minutes. Spoon the apple into the pastry cases.

4 Process, or beat, the remaining butter with the caster sugar for 3 minutes or until pale. Add the arrowroot, lemon zest and the remaining 2 eggs and blend for 2 minutes. With the food processor running, add the remaining lemon juice and blend for 1 minute. Pour the mixture over the apples, then dust with caster sugar.

5 Bake the tartlets for 45–50 minutes until the apples start to caramelise. Serve warm or cold.

Caramelised Apple Tarts

Preparation Time 20 minutes, plus chilling • **Cooking Time** about 30 minutes • **Makes 6** • **Per Tart** 395 calories, 24g fat (of which 4g saturates), 45g carbohydrate, 0.6g salt • **Easy**

1 pastry sheet from a 375g pack
   all-butter puff pastry
125g (4oz) white marzipan, chilled
   and coarsely grated
40g (1½oz) butter
4 crisp dessert apples, quartered,
   cored and sliced
juice of 1 large lemon
25g (1oz) demerara sugar
½ tsp ground mixed spice

1 Preheat the oven to 200°C (180°C fan oven) mark 6. Grease six 7.5cm (3in) tartlet tins. Roll out the pastry a little more thinly. Cut out six 12.5cm (5in) rounds of pastry, using a saucer as a guide. Line the tins and prick the base twice with a fork. Chill for 10 minutes.

2 Bake the tartlet cases blind (see page 284). Sprinkle the marzipan over the pastry and bake for a further 5 minutes or until the marzipan melts and the pastry is cooked.

3 Meanwhile, heat the butter in a large non-stick frying pan. Add the apples, lemon juice, sugar and mixed spice and cook over a high heat for 5 minutes, turning the apples until just tender and most of the lemon juice has evaporated.

4 Pile the apples into the warm pastry cases, then put back in the oven for 2–3 minutes. Serve warm.

Mini Lemon Tarts

⭐

Preparation Time 40 minutes, plus chilling • **Cooking Time** 50–55 minutes, plus cooling • **Makes 4** •
Per Tart 573 calories, 26g fat (of which 13g saturates), 81g carbohydrate, 0.5g salt • **Easy**

FOR THE PASTRY

150g (5oz) plain flour, plus extra
    to dust
a pinch of salt
75g (3oz) unsalted butter, chilled
    and cut into cubes
50g (2oz) icing sugar
2 large egg yolks

FOR THE FILLING

150g (5oz) golden caster sugar, plus
    extra to sprinkle
1 large egg, plus 4 large yolks
grated zest of 3 medium-sized
    lemons and 200ml (7fl oz) of
    freshly squeezed juice
142ml carton double cream

1 Tip the flour, salt and butter into
a food processor and pulse until it
resembles breadcrumbs. Add the
icing sugar and pulse again, then
add the egg yolks and pulse until it
starts to come together. Turn out on
to a lightly floured worksurface and
knead gently. Shape into a ball and
flatten slightly. Wrap in clingfilm and
chill for at least 30 minutes.

2 Divide the pastry into four. Roll
out each piece on a lightly floured
worksurface. Line four 10cm (4in),
2cm (¾in) deep, loose-based fluted
tart tins. Press the pastry into the
edges well and trim off any excess.
Prick each base all over with a fork.
Put on a baking sheet and chill for
30 minutes. Preheat the oven to
190°C (170°C fan oven) mark 5.

3 Bake the tartlet cases blind (see
page 284) until the pastry is dry to
the touch. Remove from the oven
and reduce the oven temperature to
170°C (150°C fan oven) mark 3.

4 To make the filling, put the sugar,
whole egg and yolks into a large jug
and stir together with a wooden
spoon until smooth. Carefully stir in
the zest, lemon juice and cream and
mix together. Leave to stand for
5 minutes.

5 Leave the tarts on the baking
sheet and pour the filling into each
case. Bake for 30 minutes or until
just set. Cool on the baking sheet
for 10 minutes, then remove from
the tins, transfer to a wire rack and
leave to cool for 15 minutes.

6 Sprinkle 1 tbsp caster sugar over
each tart. Preheat the grill to its
highest setting, cover the pastry
edges with foil and grill the tarts
for 2–3 minutes until the sugar
caramelises (or you can use a
blowtorch for this if you have one).
Serve immediately.

Getting Started

Lining tins

When making cakes, you usually need to grease and/or line the tin with greaseproof paper or baking parchment before filling it with cake mixture. Lightly grease the tin first to help keep the paper in place, then, if using greaseproof paper, lightly grease the paper. You will need to use different techniques according to the shape of the tin.

Swiss roll tin
Use this method for a Swiss roll or any other shallow baking tin.

1 Lightly grease the tin with butter, making sure it is completely coated.

2 Cut a piece of baking parchment into a rectangle 7.5cm (3in) wider and longer than the tin. Press it into the tin and cut at the corners, then fold to fit neatly. Grease all over.

Round tin
1 Put the tin on a sheet of greaseproof paper and draw a circle around its circumference. Cut out the circle just inside the drawn line.

2 Cut a strip or strips about 2cm (¾in) wider than the depth of the tin and fold up one long edge of each strip by 1cm (½in). Make cuts, about 2.5cm (1in) apart, through the folded edge of the strip(s) up to the fold line.

3 Lightly grease the tin with butter, making sure it is completely coated.

4 Press the strip(s) on to the sides of the tin so that the snipped edge sits on the base.

5 Lay the circle in the bottom of the tin and grease the paper.

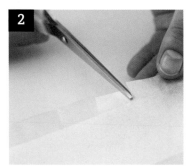

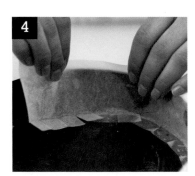

Square tin

1 Cut out a square of greaseproof paper slightly smaller than the base of the tin. Cut four strips about 2cm (¾ in) wider than the depth of the tin and fold up one of the longest edges of each strip by 1cm (½in).

2 Lightly grease the tin with butter, making sure it is coated on all sides and in the corners.

3 Cut one strip to the length of the side of the tin and press into place in one corner, then along the length of the strip, with the narrow folded section sitting on the base. Continue, cutting to fit into the corners, to cover all four sides.

4 Lay the square on the base of the tin, then grease the paper, taking care not to move the side strips.

Loaf tin

1 Lightly grease the tin with butter, making sure it is completely coated.

2 Cut out a sheet of greaseproof paper to the same length as the base and wide enough to cover both the base and the long sides. Press it into position, making sure that it sits snugly in the corners.

3 Now cut another sheet to the same width as the base and long enough to cover both the base and the ends of the tin. Press into place. Grease the paper all over.

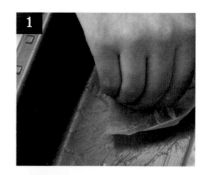

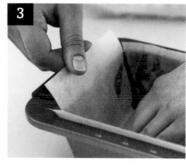

PERFECT LINING

★ Different methods of baking require different types of lining – follow the recipe for best results.
★ Apply the butter with a small piece of greaseproof paper. Don't grease the tin thickly, as this would 'fry' the edges of the cake.

Making cakes

Many of the cakes and bakes in this book use one of these basic techniques: creaming, whisking, or all-in-one.

Creaming

A classic creamed (Victoria) sponge is the basis for many cakes, including chocolate and fruit.

1 Put the butter and sugar into a bowl and beat with an electric whisk or wooden spoon until pale, soft and creamy.

2 Beat the eggs and gradually add to the butter and sugar mixture, beating well until the mixture is thick and of dropping consistency. If you like, put in a spoonful of flour while adding the eggs to prevent curdling.

3 Gently fold in the flour using a large metal spoon or spatula, then spoon the mixture into the prepared tin(s), level the surface and bake.

Whisking

1 Melt the butter in a small pan. Put the eggs and sugar into a large bowl set over a pan of simmering water. Whisk for about 5 minutes with a hand-held electric mixer until creamy and pale and the mixture leaves a trail when you lift the whisk.

2 Gently fold half the flour into the mixture. Pour the butter around the edge of the mixture, then fold in the remaining flour and butter. Pour into the prepared tin(s) and bake.

All-in-one

1 Put the butter, sugar, eggs, flour and baking powder into a large bowl or mixer.

2 Using a hand-held electric mixer, mix slowly to start, then increase the speed slightly until well combined. Fold in any remaining ingredients, such as milk or fruit, then spoon into the prepared tin(s) and bake.

TESTING SPONGES

Gently press the centre of the sponge. It should feel springy. If it's a whisked cake, it should be just shrinking away from the sides of the tin. If you have to put it back into the oven, close the door gently or the vibrations will cause the cake to sink in the centre.

COOLING CAKES

Sponge cakes should be taken out of their tins soon after baking. Invert on to a wire rack covered with sugar-dusted baking parchment.
Leave fruit cakes to cool in the tin for 15 minutes before turning out. Allow rich fruit cakes to cool completely before turning out; there is a risk of breaking otherwise.

TESTING FRUIT CAKES

Insert a skewer into the centre of the cake, leave for a few moments, then pull it out. If it comes away clean, the cake is ready. If any mixture sticks to the skewer, the cake is not quite done, so put the cake back in the oven for a few more minutes, then test again with a clean skewer.

QUANTITIES AND SIZES FOR VICTORIA SPONGE

CAKE TIN SIZE	15cm (6in) round 12.5cm (5in) square	18cm (7in) round 15cm (6in) square	20.5cm (8in) round 18cm (7in) square
Butter, softened	125g (4oz)	175g (6oz)	225g (8oz)
Caster sugar	125g (4oz)	175g (6oz)	225g (8oz)
Medium eggs	2	3	4
Self-raising flour	125g (4oz)	175g (6oz)	225g (8oz)
Baking powder	1 tsp	1½ tsp	2 tsp
Baking time	20 minutes	25 minutes	25–30 minutes

Fruit cakes

QUANTITIES AND SIZES FOR RICH FRUIT CAKES

★ To make a formal cake for Christmas, a birthday, wedding or anniversary, the following size categories will show you the amount of ingredients required to fill the chosen cake tin or tins, whether round or square.

★ Note: When baking large cakes, 25cm (10in) and upwards, it is advisable to reduce the oven heat to 130°C (110°C fan oven) mark ½ after two-thirds of the cooking time.

★ The amounts of almond paste quoted here will give a thin covering. The quantities of royal icing should be enough for two coats. If using ready-to-roll fondant icing, use the quantities suggested for royal icing as a rough guide.

Size 1

Square tin: 12.5cm (5in)
Round tin: 15cm (6in)
Baking time (approx.): 2½–3 hours
Weight when cooked: 1.1kg (2½lb)

225g (8oz) currants, 125g (4oz) each sultanas and raisins, 50g (2oz) glacé cherries, 25g (1oz) each mixed peel and flaked almonds, a little lemon zest, 175g (6oz) plain flour, 4 tsp each mixed spice and cinnamon, 150g (5oz) each softened butter and soft brown sugar, 2½ medium eggs, beaten, 1 tbsp brandy.
Almond paste: 350g (12oz)
Royal icing: 450g (1lb)

Size 2

Square tin: 15cm (6in)
Round tin: 18cm (7in)
Baking time (approx.): 3 hours
Weight when cooked: 1.6kg (3½lb)

350g (12oz) currants, 125g (4oz) each sultanas and raisins, 75g (3oz) glacé cherries, 50g (2oz) each mixed peel and flaked almonds, a little lemon zest, 200g (7oz) plain flour, ½ tsp each mixed spice and cinnamon, 175g (6oz) softened butter and soft brown sugar, 3 medium eggs, beaten, 1 tbsp brandy.
Almond paste: 450g (1lb)
Royal icing: 550g (1¼lb)

Size 3

Square tin: 20.5cm (8in)
Round tin: 23cm (9in)
Baking time (approx.): 4 hours
Weight when cooked: 2.7kg (6lb)

625g (1lb 6oz) currants, 225g (8oz) each sultanas and raisins, 175g (6oz) glacé cherries, 125g (4oz) each mixed peel and flaked almonds, zest of ¼ lemon, 400g (14oz) plain flour, 1 tsp each cinnamon and mixed spice, 350g (12oz) softened butter and soft brown sugar, 6 medium eggs, beaten, 2 tbsp brandy.
Almond paste: 800g (1¾lb)
Royal icing: 900g (2lb)

Size 4

Square tin: 23cm (9in)
Round tin: 25.5cm (10in)
Baking time (approx.): 6 hours
Weight when cooked: 4kg (9lb)

800g (1lb 12oz) currants, 375g (13oz) each sultanas and raisins, 250g (9oz) glacé cherries, 150g (5oz) each mixed peel and flaked almonds, zest of ¼ lemon, 600g (1lb 5oz) plain flour, 1 tsp each mixed spice and cinnamon, 500g (1lb 2oz) each softened butter and soft brown sugar, 9 medium eggs, beaten, 2–3 tbsp brandy.
Almond paste: 900g (2lb)
Royal icing: 1kg (2¼lb)

Size 5

Square tin: 28cm (11in)
Round tin: 30.5cm (12in)
Baking time (approx.): 8 hours
Weight when cooked: 6.7kg (14¾lb)

1.5kg (3lb 2oz) currants, 525g (1lb 3oz) each sultanas and raisins, 350g (12oz) glacé cherries, 250g (9oz) each mixed peel and flaked almonds, zest of ½ lemon, 825g (1lb 13oz) plain flour, 2½ tsp each mixed spice and cinnamon, 800g (1¾lb) each softened butter and soft brown sugar, 14 medium eggs, beaten, 4 tbsp brandy.
Almond paste: 1.1kg (2½lb)
Royal icing: 1.4kg (3lb)

Size 6

Square tin: 30.5cm (12in)
Round tin: 33cm (13in)
Baking time (approx): 8½ hours
Weight when cooked: 7.7kg (17lb)

1.7kg (3¾lb) currants, 625g (1lb 6oz) each sultanas and raisins, 425g (15oz) glacé cherries, 275g (10oz) each mixed peel and flaked almonds, zest of 1 lemon, 1kg (2¼lb) plain flour, 2½ tsp each mixed spice and cinnamon, 950g (2lb 2oz) each softened butter and soft brown sugar, 17 medium eggs, beaten, 6 tbsp brandy.
Almond paste: 1.4kg (3lb)
Royal icing: 1.6kg (3½lb)

Covering cakes

Covering a cake with marzipan

Once you have applied marzipan to the cake, you will need to allow time for it to dry before covering it with icing. Home-made marzipan takes a little longer to dry out than the ready-made variety.

1 Trim the top of the cake level if necessary, then turn the cake over to give you a flat surface to work on. Place on a cake board, which should be at least 5cm (2in) larger than the cake. Brush the cake with apricot glaze (see right).

2 Dust the worksurface with sifted icing sugar, then roll out half the marzipan to fit the top of the cake. Lift the marzipan on top of the cake and smooth over, neatening the edges.

3 Cut a piece of string the same height as the cake with the marzipan topping, and another to fit around the diameter of the cake. Roll out the remaining marzipan and, using the string as a guide, trim the marzipan to size. Roll up the marzipan strip loosely. Place one end against the side of the cake and unroll the marzipan around the cake to cover it. Use a palette knife to smooth over the sides and joins of the marzipan.

4 Leave the cake in a cool, dry place to dry out thoroughly, for at least 24 hours, before covering with ready-to-roll icing. Allow to dry for at least two days before applying royal icing.

APRICOT GLAZE

Brush cakes with apricot glaze before covering with marzipan or with ready-to-roll icing (sugar paste). It can also be used to glaze fruit finishes on cakes and tarts. You will only need 3–4 tbsp at a time, but apricot glaze keeps well in the fridge, so it is worth making a larger quantity than you need. Warm very gently before using.

To make 450g (1lb), you will need:
450g (1lb) apricot jam, 2 tbsp water.
1 Put the jam and water into a saucepan and heat gently, stirring occasionally, until melted.
2 Boil the jam rapidly for 1 minute, then strain through a sieve. Using a wooden spoon, rub through as much fruit as possible. Discard the skins left in the sieve.
3 Pour the glaze into a clean, hot jar, then seal with a clean lid and cool. Store in the fridge. It will keep for up to two months.

MARZIPAN

A versatile and attractive cake topping, marzipan can be used in a number of ways. Home-made marzipan has a good flavour and is easy to make.

To make 450g (1lb) marzipan, you will need:
225g (8oz) ground almonds, 125g (4oz) golden caster sugar, 125g (4oz) sifted golden icing sugar, 1 large egg, 2 tsp lemon juice, 1 tsp sherry, 1–2 drops vanilla extract.
1 Put the ground almonds and sugars in a bowl and stir to combine. In another bowl, whisk together the remaining ingredients, then add to the dry ingredients.
2 Stir well to mix, pounding gently to release some of the oil from the almonds. Knead with your hands until smooth, then cover until ready to use.

Covering a cake with ready-to-roll icing (sugar paste)

Ready-to-roll icing is pliable and can be used to cover cakes or moulded into decorative shapes. You can make your own (see right), but blocks of ready-to-roll icing (sugar paste) are available in a variety of colours from supermarkets and specialist cake decorating shops. A 450g (1lb) pack will cover an 18cm (7in) cake. Wrap any unused icing in clingfilm to stop it drying out and store in a cool, dry place.

1 Dust the worksurface and rolling pin with sifted icing sugar. Knead the icing until pliable, then roll out into a round or square 5 7.5cm (2–3in) larger than the cake all around. Lift the icing on top of the cake and allow it to drape over the edges.

2 Dust your hands with sifted icing sugar and press the icing on to the sides of the cake, easing it down to the board.

3 Using a sharp knife, trim off the excess icing at the base to neaten. Reserve the trimmings to make decorations if required.

4 Using your fingers dusted with a little sifted icing sugar, gently rub the surface in a circular movement to buff the icing and make it smooth.

HOME-MADE SUGAR PASTE

To make about 450g (1lb), enough to cover the top and sides of an 18cm (7in) round cake, you will need:

1 medium egg white, 1 tbsp liquid glucose, 500g (1lb 2oz) icing sugar, sifted, plus extra to dust.

1 Put the egg white and liquid glucose into a clean bowl, blending with a wooden spoon to break up the egg white. Add the icing sugar and mix until the icing begins to bind together. Knead with your fingers until the mixture forms a rough ball. Put the sugar paste on a surface lightly dusted with sifted icing sugar and knead thoroughly until smooth, pliable and free from cracks.

2 If the sugar paste is too soft to handle and is rather sticky, knead in some more sifted icing sugar until firm and pliable. If the sugar paste is dry and too firm, knead in a little boiled water until the paste becomes soft and pliable.

3 Wrap the sugar paste completely in clingfilm, or store in a polythene bag with all the air excluded.

Covering a cake with royal icing or buttercream

If you are using royal icing (see page 282), first cover the cake with apricot glaze (see opposite); buttercream (see page 282) can be spread directly on to the cake.

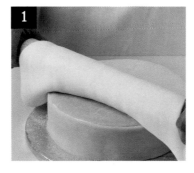

1 Stir royal icing or buttercream just before using, to make sure it is easy to spread.

2 Put the cake on a plate or cake board and use a palette knife to spread the icing evenly over the cake.

Icings and Frostings

ICINGS

Buttercream

To cover the top of a 20.5cm (8in) cake, you will need:

75g (3oz) unsalted butter, 175g (6oz) icing sugar, sifted, a few drops of vanilla extract, 1–2 tbsp milk.

1 Soften the butter in a mixing bowl, then beat until light and fluffy.

2 Gradually stir in the remaining ingredients and beat until smooth.

VARIATIONS

Citrus Replace the vanilla with a little grated orange, lemon or lime zest, and use some of the fruit's juice in place of the milk.

Chocolate Blend 1 tbsp cocoa powder with 2 tbsp boiling water. Cool, then add to the mixture in place of the milk.

Coloured For a strong colour, use food colouring paste; liquid colouring gives a paler effect (see Cook's Tip).

★ COOK'S TIP

Food colourings are available in liquid, paste or powder form. Add minute amounts with the tip of a cocktail stick until the desired colour is achieved.

Royal

Royal icing can be bought in packs from supermarkets. Simply add water or egg white to use.

To make 450g (1lb), enough to cover the top and sides of a 20.5cm (8in) cake, you will need:

2 medium egg whites, ¼ tsp lemon juice, 450g (1lb) icing sugar, sifted, 1 tsp glycerine.

1 Put the egg whites and lemon juice into a clean bowl. Stir to break up the egg whites.

2 Add sufficient icing sugar to mix to the consistency of unwhipped cream. Continue mixing and adding small quantities of icing sugar every few minutes until the desired consistency is reached, mixing well and gently beating after each addition of icing sugar. The icing should be smooth, glossy and light, almost like a cold meringue in texture, but not aerated. Do not add the icing sugar too quickly or it will produce a dull, heavy icing. Stir in the glycerine until well blended.

3 Alternatively, for large quantities of royal icing, use a food mixer on the lowest speed, following the same instructions as before.

4 Allow the icing to settle before using it; cover the surface with a piece of damp clingfilm and seal well, excluding all the air.

5 Stir the icing thoroughly before use to disperse any air bubbles, then adjust the consistency if necessary by adding more sifted icing sugar.

Glacé

To make 225g (8oz), enough to cover 18 fairy cakes, you will need:

225g (8oz) icing sugar, a few drops of vanilla or almond flavouring (optional), 2–3 tbsp boiling water, food colouring (optional).

1 Sift the icing sugar into a bowl. Add a few drops of flavouring, if you like.

2 Using a wooden spoon, gradually stir in water until the mixture is the consistency of thick cream. Beat until white and smooth and the icing is thick enough to coat the back of the spoon. Add colouring, if you like, and use at once.

VARIATIONS

Orange or lemon Replace the water with strained orange or lemon juice.

Chocolate Sift 2 tsp cocoa powder with the icing sugar.

Coloured Add a few drops of liquid food colouring, or use food colouring paste for a stronger colour.

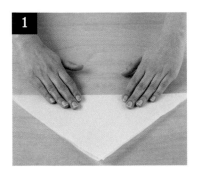

Piping bags

Piping bags can be bought from specialist cake decorating shops, or you can make your own from greaseproof paper. A bag with a very small hole will allow you to make delicate patterns or writing; larger holes are more suitable for textured effects on the cake surface.

1 Cut a piece of greaseproof paper about 20.5cm (8in) square. Fold in half diagonally.

2 Bring the two corners of the long side of the triangle up to meet the top of the triangle, one in front of it and one behind, to make a cone.

3 Holding all three corners of the triangle together firmly, make sure the tip of the cone is closed, then fold over the corners and pinch all around the top of the cone to secure. Snip off the tip. Fill with icing and test the thickness of the line on a piece of baking parchment.

FROSTINGS

Seven-minute frosting

To make about 175g (6oz), enough to cover the top and sides of an 18cm (7in) cake, you will need:

1 medium egg white, 175g (6oz) caster sugar, 2 tbsp water, a pinch of salt, a pinch of cream of tartar.

1 Put all the ingredients into a heatproof bowl and whisk lightly using an electric or hand whisk.

2 Put the bowl over a pan of hot water and heat, whisking continuously, until the mixture thickens sufficiently to stand in peaks. This will take about 7 minutes.

3 Pour the frosting over the top of the cake and spread with a palette knife.

Vanilla frosting

To make about 175g (6oz), enough to cover the top and sides of an 18cm (7in) cake, you will need:

150g (5oz) icing sugar, sifted, 5 tsp vegetable oil, 1 tbsp milk, a few drops of vanilla extract.

1 Put the icing sugar in a bowl and, using a wooden spoon, beat in the oil, milk and vanilla extract until smooth.

To melt chocolate

1 Break the chocolate into pieces and put in a heatproof bowl or in the top of a double boiler. Set over a pan of gently simmering water, making sure the base of the bowl doesn't touch the water.

2 Heat very gently until the chocolate starts to melt, then stir only once or twice until completely melted.

Chocolate curls

1 Melt the chocolate (see left) and spread it out in a thin layer on a clean worksurface or marble slab. Leave to firm up.

2 Using a sharp blade (such as a pastry scraper, a cook's knife or a very stiff spatula), draw it through the chocolate at a 45° angle. The size of the curls will be determined by the width of the blade.

Making pastry

Shortcrust, sweet, puff and flaky pastry are the four most frequently used pastries and are delicious when home-made. Shortcrust is the simplest to prepare. Choux pastry needs more attention, while filo pastry is probably best bought ready-made.

Shortcrust Pastry

To make 125g (4oz) pastry, you will need:

125g (4oz) plain flour, a pinch of salt, 50g (2oz) unsalted butter, cut into small pieces, 1 medium egg yolk.

1 Sift the flour and salt into a bowl and add the butter. Using your fingertips or a pastry cutter, rub or cut the butter into the flour until the mixture resembles fine breadcrumbs.

2 Using a fork, mix in the egg yolk and 1½ tsp water until the mixture holds together; add a little more water if necessary.

3 Gather the dough in your hands and knead lightly. Form into a ball, wrap tightly in clingfilm and chill for at least 30 minutes before using. (This 'relaxes' the pastry and prevents shrinkage when it is baked.)

Sweet Shortcrust Pastry

Make as for shortcrust pastry (above), adding 50g (2oz) caster sugar and 2 medium egg yolks at step 2.

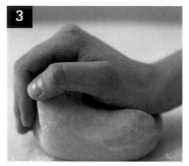

Using a food processor

1 You can make shortcrust or sweet shortcrust using a food processor. Put the dry ingredients into the food processor and pulse quickly to mix. Cut the butter into small pieces and add. Process until the mixture resembles breadcrumbs – do not over-process.

2 Add the egg yolk(s) and a little water if necessary, and pulse until the mixture just comes together. Continue as step 3 for shortcrust (left).

Baking blind

When making a flan or tart, the pastry case is often cooked first without any filling – this is called 'baking blind'. The filling is then added before baking again.

1 Preheat the oven according to the recipe. Prick the pastry base all over with a fork. Cover with foil or greaseproof paper 7.5cm (3in) larger than the tin.

2 Spread ceramic baking beans on top. Bake for 15–20 minutes. Remove the foil or paper and beans and bake for 5–10 minutes until the pastry is light golden.

3 When cooked and while still hot, brush the pastry base with a little beaten egg, to seal the fork pricks or any cracks. This prevents any filling leaking, which can make it difficult to remove the pie or tart from the tin.

DOS AND DON'TS OF BAKING

★ Weigh out all the ingredients carefully before starting the recipe, so that you have everything to hand when you begin to make the cake.

★ Always work in metric or imperial – never mix the two measurements.

★ Check that you have the correct cake tin for the job. The tin sizes quoted in this book refer to the base measurement of the tin.

★ Take care to line the tin properly where necessary. For ease, try baking parchment liners. You just pop them in the tin – there's no need to grease the tin or paper.

★ Allow the oven to preheat to the correct temperature.

★ After it has come out of the oven, leave the cake in the tin to cool for 10 minutes and then turn out on to a wire rack to cool completely.

★ Let the tins cool completely before washing them in warm, soapy water with a non-abrasive sponge.

★ Try not to be heavy-handed – when folding in flour, use light strokes so the air doesn't get knocked out.

★ Don't let a cake mixture sit around once you've made it: pop it straight into the cake tin and into the oven, otherwise the raising agents will start to react.

SUGARS

Unrefined brown sugars really do make a difference to the taste of a dish. They contain the natural molasses of the sugar cane so have a distinctive flavour. To taste the flavours, put a little white caster sugar on your tongue and let it dissolve, then repeat with golden caster sugar. You'll notice that the white sugar tastes of nothing other than sweetness, while the golden caster has a subtle caramel flavour. Here is a guide to the other types.

Golden caster
Use for sponge cakes, meringues, pastry, crumbles and for making sugar syrups when poaching fruit.

Golden icing
This gives a toffee flavour to icing and is good in buttercream fillings or for dusting mince pies.

Light muscovado
Use in sweet sauces such as toffee or butterscotch, savoury barbecue sauce, meringues and mincemeat.

Molasses
The richest sugar of all. Use this in your Christmas pudding or cake for a greater depth of flavour.

Dark muscovado
A soft, crumbly texture and a flavour similar to black treacle. Try it in gingerbread or chocolate cake.

Dark/light soft brown sugar
These have fine granules and a moist texture. Use in biscuits and cakes.

Index